NAPOLEON
AT WORK

Napoleon I and his Staff

NAPOLEON
AT WORK

COLONEL VACHÉE
Translated by G. Frederic Lees

NONSUCH

This translation first published 1914
This edition published 2007

Copyright © in this edition Nonsuch Publishing Limited, 2007

Nonsuch Publishing
Cirencester Road, Chalford, Stroud, Gloucestershire, GL6 8PE, UK
www.nonsuch-publishing.com

Nonsuch Publishing is an imprint of NPI Media Group

British Library Cataloguing in Publication Data
A catalogue record for this book is available from the British Library

ISBN 978-1-84588-374-4

Typesetting and origination by NPI Media Group
Printed in Great Britain

Contents

Introduction to the Modern Edition

NAPOLEON BONAPARTE IS REGARDED BY most historians as being perhaps the greatest military commander ever to have lived. Despite the facts that he introduced relatively few innovations in warfare and was defeated and forced into exile twice, his leadership, strategy and tactics continue to be studied by potential army officers at military academies all over the world to this day. And aside from his extraordinary martial attributes, during a period of the most extreme instability and danger Napoleon would quickly prove his genius as a self-publicist and political manipulator *sans pareil*.

Born on 15 August 1769 in Ajaccio on the island of Corsica, at a time when Corsica was a part of the Republic of Genoa, the parents of Napoleone Buonaparte (he would later change his name so that it sounded more French) were members of the Italian nobility. At the age of nine he was sent to the French military school at Brienne-le-Château before attending the prestigious École Royale Militaire in Paris, where he completed the two-year course in only one year. In 1785 he was commissioned as a second lieutenant into the artillery, posted with the *La Fère* regiment to Valence and Auxonne until the Revolution of 1789, when he returned to Corsica. A supporter of the Jacobin faction there, he became a lieutenant-colonel in a volunteer regiment before falling out with the Corsican nationalist leader Pasquale Paoli in 1793, forcing him to flee with his family back to France.

He was then appointed to command the artillery besieging the town of Toulon, which had been occupied by British forces. By aiming his guns at their ships and thereby threatening their means of supply and avenue of retreat, he forced them to withdraw and earned himself promotion to the rank of brigadier (as well as being wounded in the thigh). His actions at Toulon brought him to the attention of the Committee of Public Safety, and in particular Augustin Robespierre, younger brother of Maximilien, which led to a brief period of imprisonment when the latter fell from power in 1794. The following year Napoleon was in command of a scratch force assembled to defend the National Convention at the Tuileries Palace when it was attacked by Royalists and Counter-Revolutionaries. Assisted by Joachim Murat, a cavalry officer who would later become his brother-in-law, he seized several artillery pieces, which he used to repel the attack; famously, he would later claim that he had cleared the streets of Paris with 'a whiff of grapeshot.'

His defence of the Tuileries earned him the patronage of the Executive Directory, and in 1796 he married Josephine de Beauharnais, the former mistress of Paul Barras, one of the five Directors. In the same year he was given command of the army sent to invade Italy, defeating the Austrians in Lombardy and the army of the Papal States, before marching into Austria; this gave France sufficient leverage to gain control of northern Italy, the Low Countries and the Rhineland under the Treaty of Campo-Formio, before Napoleon went on to conquer Venice. His ability to made good use of both intelligence and artillery is often cited as the reasons for his great success in this campaign, and his army captured 160,000 prisoners, 2,000 cannon and 170 standards.

Following his successes in Italy, Napoleon proposed an expedition to the Ottoman province of Egypt to protect French trade and to threaten British access to India. Outnumbered three to one by Ottoman forces at the Battle of the Pyramids, he achieved an impressive victory by forming his soldiers into hollow squares, to protect his artillery and supplies within; at the end of the battle only 300 French soldiers had died, as opposed to 6,000 Egyptians. Despite the defeat of the French navy by Horatio Nelson in the Battle of the Nile, Napoleon's land forces continued to record victories against the Ottomans, advancing through the Levant as far as Acre, where he was finally stopped as his army was weakened by disease. As his campaign ran out of momentum, he returned to France on the orders of the Directory in 1799, at a time of considerable political instability.

When he arrived in Paris in October of that year Napoleon was approached by one of the Directors, Emmanuel Sieyès, to join him, Roger Ducos, Charles de Talleyrand-Périgord and one of Napoleon's younger brothers, Lucien Bonaparte, in a *coup d'état*. On 18 Brumaire (9 November) they overthrew the government and Sieyès, Ducos and Napoleon were named Consuls, with the latter securing election as First Consul, and shortly afterwards as First Consul for Life. Now the most powerful man in France, he instituted numerous civil reforms, including in local government, higher education, taxation, transport, sanitation and the legal system.

During his absence in the Near East the Austrians had re-taken the territory granted to France under the Treaty of Campo-Formio. Although the campaign began badly, Napoleon routed them at the Battle of Marengo (after which he named his horse) and General Jean Moreau did the same at Hohenlinden, leading to the Treaty of Lunéville in 1801, by which France regained the territory it had previously held in Italy and more besides. In 1802 France signed the Treaty of Amiens with Britain, but it was an uneasy peace; Britain promised to evacuate Malta, but failed to do so, and the two countries went to war again in 1803. In order to secure his rule he had himself crowned Emperor of France in 1804 and King of Italy in 1805. 1805 was also the year in which Britain, Austria and Russia formed the Third Coalition against him. While on 20 October 1805 the newly formed Grande Armée defeated the Austrians at Ulm, the next day, the 21st, Nelson once more gained a great victory against the French navy at the Battle of Trafalgar. On 2 December Napoleon achieved what he regarded as the greatest victory of his military career against the Austrians and the Russians at Austerlitz.

The threat posed by Napoleon to the rest of Europe led to the formation of the Fourth Coalition in 1806, in which Prussia, Saxony and Sweden joined Austria, Britain and Russia. He again defeated the Austrians at Jena-Auerstedt in October of that year and the Russians at Friedland in June 1807, leading to the Treaty of Tilsit, which effectively divided continental Europe between France and Russia. Later in the year the French army invaded Spain; when the initial assault was beaten back Napoleon took command himself, capturing Madrid and pushing the British army, sent to support the Spanish and Portuguese, back to the Atlantic coast. From 1808 until 1814 the armies of Britain, Spain and Portugal under Arthur Wellesley (later the Duke of Wellington) fought to dislodge the French from the Iberian Peninsula, which they finally managed after six years of bloody fighting.

In 1809 the Austrians again went to war with France, forcing Napoleon to leave the Iberian theatre of operations for the Danube. The Austrians were victorious at Aspern-Essling but failed to capitalise on it, and they were defeated once more by the French at Wagram. Shortly thereafter Napoleon divorced the Empress Josephine and married Archduchess Marie Louise of Austria, a member of the House of Habsburg.

In 1812, despite the Treaty of Tilsit, relations between France and Russia had deteriorated, and the Russians deployed troops on the Polish border. Napoleon responded by launching a pre-emptive invasion of Russia. As Adolf Hitler would discover almost a century and a half later, fighting a war on two fronts when one of your enemies is Russia is not a strategy likely to succeed. Although there were some engagements between the two sides, most notably at Smolensk and Borodino, which were both French victories, the Russians preferred to withdraw before the opportunity for a decisive battle arose, laying waste to the land to prevent the French army from foraging. The Russians continued retreating until they were beyond Moscow, and Napoleon assumed that he could capture the city and thus force a capitulation. However, the

Russians burned Moscow to the ground and the French, without food or shelter in the middle of a savage winter, were forced to retreat; of the 650,000 troops who set out only 40,000 returned, mostly victims of the cold rather than enemy action.

Following France's disastrous expedition to Russia, Britain, Spain, Portugal, Prussia and Russia formed the Sixth Coalition, which Napoleon defeated at the Battle of Dresden in 1813. Despite this loss, Sweden and Austria joined the Coalition and together they gained a victory at the Battle of the Nations later in the year (this was the biggest battle of the Napoleonic Wars, with a combined total of 120,000 casualties). Paris was occupied in 1814 and Napoleon surrendered and abdicated; he was exiled to the Mediterranean island of Elba and Louis XVIII restored to the French throne.

Napoleon escaped from Elba in early 1815, returned to France, raised almost quarter of a million regular and volunteer troops, marched on Paris and regained the reigns of powers for the so-called Hundred Days. In response, Britain, Prussia, Austria, Russia, Sweden, the Netherlands, Spain, Portugal and Sardinia formed the Seventh Coalition, and the stage was set for Napoleon's final battle: Waterloo. By 1 June 1815 Napoleon had almost 200,000 troops ready to face the allies; the Duke of Wellington and Gebhard von Blücher, who commanded the two allied armies, had a slight numerical advantage. Wellington later called it 'a damn close-run thing', but Waterloo marked the end of Napoleon's military and political domination of France and Europe. He headed for the port of Rochefort in the hope of fleeing to the U.S.A., but the Royal Navy had blockaded it, and he surrendered to Captain Maitland of H.M.S. *Bellerophon* before being exiled to Saint Helena, a small island and British colony in the South Atlantic. Despite several plots to rescue him, he never escaped, and he died on the island on 5 May 1821, where he was buried. In 1840 his remains were exhumed and transported to Paris, where he is entombed in an enormous sarcophagus in Les Invalides.

Foreword

N O WORK COULD BE MORE appropriate at the present time than this study
of the greatest military genius of all ages. Written by Colonel Vachée, one
of the most distinguished of French tacticians and strategists, with the distinct
object of preparing military students for those "battles of the future" which are
now the wars of the present, it abounds with pages which have a direct application to the mighty struggle which is in progress beneath our eyes.

The author's thesis is that by a careful examination of Napoleon's methods
and those adopted by the German Staff in 1870–71 we can formulate rules of
warfare which will be of the greatest utility when face to face with an enemy. He
takes his hero—the hero of all who have made a study of war, despite his short-
comings and his errors—at the height of his career, and follows him step by step
during the magnificent campaign of 1806. The Battle of Jena, and the events
which led up to it, are subjected to the minutest analysis, and conclusions are
drawn which lead one to believe that, in spite of the new factors which have
entered into warfare during the last hundred years, everything is by no means
antiquated in the methods inaugurated by Bonaparte. However inadvisable his
excessive but unavoidable centralization may have been, it is evident that many
lessons are still to be learnt from "the greatest captain of modern times."

How interesting to learn these lessons whilst following the momentous
events which are taking place at the present time on the old battle-fields of
the Continent! We must not seek in Napoleon's tactics for any system or
narrow formula. But by observing his methods and reading the invaluable
advice given in his "Commentaires" we can undoubtedly arrive at fundamen-
tal principles which are as true to-day as they ever were. "The most difficult
thing," said Napoleon, "is to discover the enemy's plans, and to detect the
truth in all the reports one receives; the remainder only requires common
sense; it is a bout at fisticuffs, and the more blows you get in, the better it is
for you … The reason why I have won so many battles is this, that, on the eve
of the fight, instead of giving an order to diverge, I converged all my forces on
the point I wished to force, and massed them there. I overthrew that which
was before me, for naturally it was *a weak point.*" There we have a fundamen-

tal principle which is as valuable in our present struggle for liberty and the overthrowing of militarist ideals as it was when applied by the man who, notwithstanding his many admirable qualities, certainly did much to build up those ideals. A second principle of this master of war was "to begin the fight, and get in as many blows as possible;—the offensive in dead earnest along the whole line." Finally, "at the weak point, and at the moment chosen by him, the General-in-Chief *himself* should give that formidable and decisive blow which overthrows his adversary."

The necessity for a great military personality, in whom his men place implicit faith, and who, on the eve of the fight, are filled with that "sacred fire" which Napoleon knew so well how to instil into their veins by words and material encouragements, should be carefully noted. The subject forms one of the most important sections of Colonel Vachée's book, in which an attempt is made to answer that puzzling question—What is the role of the modern commander-in-chief, and where should he be stationed when the decisive struggle is taking place? "If we consider the battles for which we are preparing," he says, with admirable foresight—"battles which will be fought with a front of one hundred kilometres—we have a right to ask ourselves if the art of a commander will consist in being personally present during the whole day on that corner of the battlefield where he presumes the decisive blow will be given." However that may be, and it is as well, perhaps, to reserve our opinion on that point until the conclusion of the present war, in which for the first time millions of men are engaged on an enormous front, there can be no doubt as to the modern military ideal regarding the role of a commander-in-chief. His decision is the result of a conference between a number of experts—the lesson learnt from Von Moltke and the German Staff in 1870-71. But Colonel Vachée does well to emphasize the necessity of carefully selecting the advantages and avoiding the dangers of this Staff conference. By rigorously following the methods of Von Moltke and his eight advisers, "the resultant of a number of opinions is substituted for the will of a chief, which generally ends in an intermediate solution of a given problem. The orders are indeed given in the name of a leader who assumes responsibility for them, but the soldiers know that he is not their author, and that he has adopted—without enthusiasm—*a collective creation*. From the point of view of *moral*, this effacement of the leader has a tremendously debilitating influence on troops." Therefore, "whilst favouring the application of the principle of the division of work, of the development of initiative, of a wide diffusion in the army of intellectual life," Colonel Vachée believes that "nothing can replace the personal work of a leader. By the very fact that he exists, and that his action is felt, he increases the 'sacred fire' which was in Napoleon's army, he gives a characteristic turn to the execution of his orders."

Our author follows up this striking passage with the illuminating words: "A command thus exercised, if addressed to an army exalted by ideas of duty, patriotism, and sacrifice, will obtain from it that intense effort which is an almost certain pledge of victory"; and he concludes by quoting that ever true maxim of Machiavelli, "Let only one command in war: several minds weaken an army."

The reader, whilst observing how Napoleon succeeded in warfare, thanks to the manner in which he concentrated his forces, his marvellous activity, and his firm determination to perish with glory, must be left to judge for himself as to the manner in which these "great but very simple directing principles" of the art of war are being observed by ourselves and our glorious Allies. Let us beware, however, of drawing too hasty conclusions at the beginning of a struggle which leading military men contemplate will be a long one, and, if it is to be brought to a satisfactory conclusion, will necessitate all their science, fortitude, and patriotic ardour. It is better to play the part, not of critics, but of observers, who, convinced that they are on the side of justice, place all their confidence in Lord Kitchener, General Joffre, and the Grand Duke Nicholas of Russia.

It will not be out of place, perhaps, to conclude these brief remarks with a personal note. The greater part of this translation of Colonel Vachée's study, the masterly qualities of which have been said to give it a prominent place among the most noteworthy contributions to modern military literature, was prepared in that land of many friends which is now, alas! the land of "the enemy." By a curious and interesting series of circumstances that do not call for detailed explanation, I was stationed this summer at Frankfurt-on-Main, at no great distance from the historic battle-fields mentioned in *Napoleon at Work*. As my translation progressed in the upper room of a house in the Grosse Eschenheimerstrasse, within a stone's throw of the *Frankfurter Zeitung* Office, the political situation became more and more strained, and on reaching the chapters treating of the Battle of Jena the storm broke. I can still hear the wild outburst of applause from the crowd beneath my windows when the declaration of war on Russia was announced. Soon the atmosphere of war in which we lived at the end of July and the beginning of August became intolerable. I had reason to believe that one of the chapters of this book, sent to London in a closed registered envelope, had been confiscated by the police, and that my movements were being watched by a spy, whose sudden appearance at the pension where I was staying coincided with the mysterious disappearance of one of my note-books. Foreseeing that England would soon be called upon to take her part against the military party of Germany, I seized the opportunity, on August 2, in the midst of the mobilization, of taking a train to Brussels—the last train, as it turned out, for many a day. Friends had predicted that I should never be allowed to cross the frontier at Herbesthal, and it was indeed a trying moment when we English fugitives arrived there and saw the search made in passengers' luggage for compromising documents and photographs. But my passport, backed up by assurance, saved me from a fate which can easily be imagined. A German officer, over-excited by the report that a French airman had been killed at Coblenz, passed my luggage without asking for any but a single package to be opened. It was indeed fortunate for both the reader and myself that he did not choose the one containing the final pages of "Napoléon en Campagne."

G. Frederic Lees
London, *August* 17, 1914.

Introduction

DURING THE SUMMER OF 1807, General Kosciusko, the hero of the independence of Poland, then exiled at Fontainebleau, was visited by one of his young compatriots, Chlapowski, an orderly officer of the Emperor Napoleon. Thinking of the future of Poland, Kosciusko spoke to the young officer in the following terms:

"You do right to serve and study. Work hard, and on the outbreak of war pay attention to everything. Side by side with the Emperor, you can gain much information and experience. Increase your knowledge as much as possible, in order, later, to be useful to our unhappy country. You are at a good school. But do not imagine that he (the Emperor) is going to reconstruct Poland. He thinks only of himself … He is a despot, whose only object is his personal satisfaction and ambition. He will never create anything durable—of that I am certain. However, do not let all this discourage you. You can learn much from him—experience and above all strategy. He is an excellent leader. Although he does not intend to reconstruct our fatherland, he can prepare for us many good officers, without whom we can do no good, if God allows us to find ourselves in better circumstances. Once more I repeat to you: study and work, but remember he will do nothing for us."

Let us apply Kosciusko's advice to ourselves. To instruct ourselves in the art of war, let us go—in thought—to Napoleon's headquarters.

What a splendid training for an officer, to live in Napoleon's immediate surroundings during his campaigns and to see him work, draw up his plans, give orders, watch over their execution, and rouse his generals and soldiers to action!

Napoleon's campaigns have been made the subject of many didactic studies; the plans for his campaigns and battles have been submitted to learned analysis, which forms the basis of the higher military instruction of all armies. There is very little to be added, it would seem, to the numerous works of that class. However, it is not in that direction that our ambition lies. It is the man himself, in thought and action, that we would depict from life; we would recall the impressions felt by the attentive and prudent observer whom Kosciusko, in the interests of his native country, wished to see near the Emperor.

Without doubt, that which, before everything else, would have struck this witness of the life of Napoleon in his campaigns would have been the power of his personality. He was a giant who towered over all who surrounded him. Collaborators he had none; he had only agents, who carried out his orders. Napoleon centralized everything—a centralization, however, which was quite excessive and by no means to be imitated, for it was that which, by suppressing all initiative, contributed to bring about the ruin of the system. But, apart from this exaggerated power of absorption, what lessons are to be learnt from the method of the master of war in action and in command! His method was characterized by prodigious labour and an indomitable determination to attain the object in view. The problem was solved—unexpectedly and decisively—by the shortest and simplest means. There was incessant meditation until the luminous idea took shape in his brain, a clear and rapid decision, and immediate execution, without any loss of time. Such appear to us to be the sources of Napoleon's genius.

In conjunction with the psychological side of his work as a commander there was the professional part. "Napoleon's study was a laboratory which had a quite mechanical side."[1] "The Emperor," adds Fain, "spent his life in his study ... one may say that all the other circumstances of his life were merely digressions." This was true whether he was on campaign or at the Tuileries, whether his study was in the palaces of kings or in the most wretched cottage in Poland. How interesting to a soldier to see the door of this sanctuary open before him! It is the dead of night and, behold! The Emperor is before us, bent over his maps, illuminated by twenty candles. Whilst the enemy sleeps or holds councils of war, he, alone, meditates, decides, dictates his orders, utilizes every moment of time.

We then see him outside, superintending the execution of the work prepared amidst the silence of his sanctum, and filling his army with the spirit of his faith and genius.

Our object will be attained—far beyond our hopes—if, at the close of this study, we begin to see, as Taine demands of the historian, Napoleon living, thinking, and acting in his imperial quarters, with his passions and his habits, his voice and his physiognomy, his gestures, and his clothes, distinct and complete, somewhat as though, being an officer of his staff, we had just finished a campaign under his orders.

NOTE

1   *Mémoires du baron Fain*, p. 75.

I

Thought and Decision

The role of a general-in-chief—Power of Napoleon's individuality—
Essentially personal ideas—Incessant meditation—Power of
Napoleon's work—Night work—Quality of Napoleon's work—His
unremitting attention and concentration—Audacity in decision—
Moral courage—Four principles of war.

To keep incessantly in mind the material and moral situation of his
army, to discover from information which is often vague and contradictory the condition and plans of the enemy, with these uncertain data to arrive
at a decision and carry it out without loss of time, to guard against the unexpected, to husband and accumulate his forces, so as to use them unsparingly
at the decisive hour—such, in the main, is the role of a general-in-chief. No
one in history knew how to fill this role with greater ability than he who was
successively General Bonaparte and the Emperor Napoleon I.

Good fortune doubtless played its part in this man's prodigious career, but
one cannot attribute to luck alone the continuity and grandeur of his victories, which can only be explained by a strict adaptation of his faculties to
the art of war. What were the natural or acquired faculties which made the
little Corsican cadet into a Caesar who triumphed in eighty pitched battles?
What were his methods of work and command? These are the questions we
would succeed in elucidating—more or less completely—by studying the life
of Napoleon during his campaigns and the society in which he lived.

First of all, the work of a commander-in-chief calls for thought, preliminary to any decision. An idea is born, evolves, becomes well defined, and
by an act of the will is transformed into a decision. But the role of a leader
does not end here; he must also participate in the carrying of the decision
into execution, by superintending, directing and controlling his agents.
This participation is indispensable to the union and consequence of their
efforts, the rectification of errors, and the vigour of the action. Finally, the
duty of a chief is also to distribute to the executants the rewards or penalties which correspond to their merit or their incapacity.

Every command, if exercised completely, is subject to these various obligations: intellectual work, the arrival at a decision, the superintendence of
its execution, and the distribution of rewards and penalties. The manner in
which these obligations are carried out gives the command its characteristic
physiognomy. None of them can be evaded without bringing about a weak-
ening of the action and of the authority of the command.

We will examine successively under these different aspects, and by trans-
porting ourselves to his headquarters, Napoleon's method of command. But
before entering on this analysis a general glance at his campaigns and life
shows us immediately the dominant character of his influence. That which,
above all, characterized Napoleon was the power of his individuality. This
individuality, animated by an ardent and passionate soul, impatient for
movement and eager for success, overwhelmed all who surrounded him, and
invaded every employment. His egoistic ambition impelled him to direct
everything in order to conduct all things to his own profit. It is related that,
when about to leave for his first Italian campaign, he said to a journalist
friend: "Bear in mind, when writing the narratives of our victories, to speak
only of *me*,—always of *me*, do you understand?" This *moi* was the eternal cry
of his wholly selfish ambition. "Refer to no one but myself—celebrate, praise,
and paint no one but me," he said to orators, musicians, poets, and paint-
ers. "I will buy you what you like, but you must all sell yourselves."[1] Place at
the service of this formidable egoism, from which, however, all narrow ideas
must be excluded, the most powerful and embracing mind, the strongest and
most tenacious will, and an audacious soul, and you will understand the reason why, in his command, Napoleon reduced to the role of blind instruments
of execution all those men who, by the nature of their duties, ought to have
been conscious collaborators in his work.

We shall see, later, how he quickened the execution of his orders, how he
gave his generals and soldiers that principle of life which he called "the sacred
fire." Let us linger, for a moment, over the birth of the governing idea which
was, as it were, the conducting wire of a campaign or a manoeuvre. This idea
was absolutely his own; it belonged to him entirely. His only rule was his own
opinion, and, as he himself said, that good instrument, his head, was more
useful to him than the advice of men who were accounted to possess both
knowledge and experience.[2] "In war," he wrote on August 30, 1808, "men are
nothing; it is one man who counts ... When, at the dead of night, a good
idea flashes through my brain, the order is given in a quarter of an hour, and
in half an hour it is being carried out by the outposts."[3] This was not an idle
boast. Acts conform to words—on that point we have the evidence of a man
who, from 1802 to 1813, followed the Emperor in all his campaigns, living

and sleeping under his roof. Notwithstanding his habitual admiration for his master, Méneval, his private secretary, indulged, as regards this matter, in a discrete criticism: he tells us that Napoleon's indefatigable activity of mind and body led him to practise in too absolute a manner the principle "that one must not leave to others what one can do oneself."[4] Having pointed out this tendency once, Méneval returns to it again and expresses himself in the following significant and peremptory words:

"Berthier, Talleyrand, and many others did no give an order or write a despatch which had not been dictated by Napoleon. He took not only the initiative in thought, but also attended personally to the details of every piece of business. I do not content that he was quite justified in thus wishing to do everything himself, but his genius, superhuman in it activity, carried him away: he felt he possessed the *means* and the *time* to manage everything ... in reality it was he who did everything."[5]

But the very originality of Napoleon's work precluded all collaboration. His orders and instructions bear the master's signature. Manoeuvres such as those of Ulm, Austerlitz, Jena, and Echmühl, to mention only these particularly great and striking masterpieces, could only have been conceived by one mind, that of the Emperor. As a contrast, notice how, at the same moment, among his adversaries, controversy in councils of war was killing originality of thought, retarding a decision, leading to intermediate and slow solutions which let the opportunity for success slip by.

An example will enable us to see more clearly Napoleon's method in the elaboration and birth of an idea. We take it from Ségur, who was at once his historian and aide-de-camp.[6]

The scene took place at the imperial quarters at Pont-de-Brique[7] in September 1805. The Emperor had just learnt that, after the battle of Cape Finisterre, Admiral Villeneuve, instead of following the English fleet, had entered Ferrol and thus shattered the hope of crossing the Channel by surprise. He sent for Daru, commissary-general of the army. Daru appeared at four in the morning and found the Emperor in his room, with a grim look on his face, a fulminating expression in his eyes, over which his hat was pulled down, and breaking forth into bitter invectives and reproaches against Villeneuve. Then, suddenly changing his tone, Napoleon, pointing to a desk loaded with papers, said to Daru: "Sit down there and write." Immediately, without transition and apparently without meditation, he dictated, unhesitatingly and in his concise and imperious manner, the plan of the 1805 campaign, as far as Vienna. For four or five hours did he thus dictate. Having made certain that his instructions were well understood, he dismissed Daru with the words: "Leave immediately for Paris, but feign to set out for Ostend. Arrive at your destination alone and at night;

and let no one know you are there. Go to the house of General Dejean[8]; closet yourself with him, and prepare, but with him only, the orders for the marches, stores, etc., etc. I do not want a single clerk to know of this; you will sleep in General Dejean's study, and no one must know you are there ..."

The absolute exactitude of this narrative, which is contained in a note communicated to the Archives (January 14, 1836) by Daru's son, matters little. Certain details are open to discussion. But it depicts the man from whose brain there seemed to spring, by a flash of genius, a host of plans and projects. However, we must not be deceived; the improvisation was only apparent. For a certain time past Napoleon had been pondering over his business, but had said nothing about it to any one. "If I appear to be always ready to reply to everything," he said to Rœderer,[9] "it is because, before undertaking anything, I have meditated for a long time—I have foreseen what might happen. It is not a spirit which suddenly reveals to me what I have to say or do in a circumstance unexpected by others—it is reflexion, meditation."

Thus practised by a mind so extensive and so powerful—a mind at once analytical and imaginative—meditation gave birth to the plans of fourteen campaigns of the greatest captain of modern times. He meditated constantly; his brain was ever at work, whether at table or at the theatre. Even at night he awoke from his sleep to work. When at work he was like a woman in travail. "No man is more pusillanimous than I am when I draw up a military plan. I exaggerate every danger and every evil possible under the circumstances. I am in quite a painful state of agitation. That does not prevent me appearing very calm before those who surround me. I am like a woman in travail. But when I have come to a resolution everything is forgotten, except that which may lead to its attainment."[10]

We here see in Napoleon one of his masterly qualities, one of those which most contributed to raise him up—his power of work. The nineteen years of what we may call his public life were filled with almost superhuman labour. One of his principles of war was that time is everything, and he knew that lost time could never be regained. Through natural disposition, as well as by temperament, his capacity for work was extraordinary. He himself said to Las-Cases[11] that "work was his element, that he was born and made for work. He had known the limit of his eyes and the limit of his legs, but he had never known that of his capacity for work." "Working as many as twenty hours a day, one never perceived the slightest trace of either mental or bodily fatigue, and I often thought,"says Chaptal, "that such a man, face to face with the enemy, must possess through that alone an incalculable advantage."[12] Without being a man of war, Chaptal foresaw that, owing to his method and power of work, Napoleon, getting the better of the enemy through speed, was ever in a position to impose his will upon it.

Napoleon possessed, in addition, a precious and rare faculty: he worked as easily at night as during the day. He said that he had worked more at night than in the daytime. This was not because his affairs caused sleeplessness, but because he could sleep during spare hours, and little sleep sufficed. When on campaign, often awakened at dead of night, he would rise immediately and give his orders or dictate his replies with the same clearness and freshness of mind as he would have done during the day. This was what he called "after-midnight presence of mind"; it was complete and extraordinary in his case. "Such was the special organization of this man, extraordinary in every respect, that he could sleep for an hour, wake up to give an order, go to sleep again, and reawaken without either his rest or his health suffering. Six hours' sleep was sufficient, whether he took them uninterruptedly or at various intervals during the twenty-four hours."[13] On campaign, on the eve of battle, night was specially devoted to his intellectual work. Having generally retired to rest about eight o'clock, after dinner, he rose at the moment the reports on the reconnaissances reached imperial headquarters, that is, about one or two in the morning. Bacler d'Albe had spread out for him on a large table in the room which served as a study the best map of the seat of the war. On this map, set very accurately to the compass and surrounded by twenty to thirty candles, were marked with pins with coloured heads the various positions of the army corps and, as far as they were known, those of the enemy. It was on this that he worked, moving his compasses, open to the scale of six to seven leagues—a march—here and there. Before the night was over he had made up his mind, and dictated and despatched his orders, which the troops carried out at break of day.[14] In a later chapter we shall see him thus at work in a concrete case, but already we can judge of "the incalculable advantage," as Chaptal said, that such a method of work gave him over an enemy which devoted the hours of night to sleep or wasted them in endless deliberations.

However, it must be pointed out that this period of intense work was only of limited duration; such an expenditure of energy necessitated the sacred fire and the vigour of youth. That was the opinion of Napoleon himself. He thus expressed himself in 1805: "There is only one time in your life for war. I shall be good for it six years longer (until the age of forty), after which I must pull myself up." As he foresaw, he began to decline after 1809. His thought lost its clearness and precision, his will was less strong, his character less determined. Already in 1806 his marshals noticed that he took less cheerfully to life on campaign; he began to like to take things easy, and had, as it were, a "negligent manner" of making war.

If few men have done as much intellectual work as Napoleon, fewer still have been able to show so great a result from it. This was owing as much to the extent of his intelligence, which was singularly remarkable, as to the strength of his will. To a vivid imagination, which from a single idea produced a thousand others, he united "that supereminent faculty of geometry which he applied to war with the same ease and breadth as Monge when applying it to other objects."[15] "The geometrical habits of his mind ever prompted him to analyse even his own feelings. Napoleon was the man," we can say with Mme. de Rémusat, "who meditated the most on the *causes* which govern human action. Incessantly concerned with the smallest actions of his life, and always discovering a secret motive for each of his movements, he was never able either to explain or understand that natural indifference which causes us sometimes to act without design and object."[16] No man possessed a clearer or more positive mind; no one was further removed from that defect from which, according to Frederic II, men suffer the most: "Lack of application in forming a clear idea of the subjects on which they are employed."

A characteristic of Napoleon's genius was the strength and constancy of his attention. His effort of the moment was entirely concentrated on the object before him, and without allowing his imagination to wander from it for a single instant he prolonged this effort until he had arrived at a solution. He himself compared his brain to a devonport in which the various questions under examination were arranged in order. During his work he opened a drawer and took into consideration the subject found there. The question having been considered, he passed in the same way to the next, until the time when, wishing to rest, he closed all the drawers of his brain. Intellectual work so methodical and precise as this could only be arrived at through the effort of a persevering and inflexible will which obstinately led back the naturally wandering mind into the path traced for it. Always master of his subject, Napoleon "thought quicker than others." He attributed his rapidity of thought to a greater mobility of the fibres of his brain. Cannot this economy of time be also attributed, in great part, to the intensity of his attention?

Audacity in coming to a decision, another distinctive mark of Napoleon's military genius, is connected, like rapidity of thought, as much with the vigour of the will as with the nature of the mind. He was an unrestrained gambler. Time after time he boldly staked his whole fortune in a decisive game, but, being the most skilful of gamblers, he employed all the resources of his intelligence and experience in winning. "The skilful man must profit by everything, neglect nothing which may give him an additional chance. Sometimes, through despising only a single point, the less skilful man loses everything." That is what he wrote to Talleyrand, whose nonchalant and cautious diplomacy augured ill, however, for this continual challenge to fortune. "I will succeed!—such was his motto, the basis of his calculations; and often the earnestness with which he uttered it helped him to attain his ends."[17] Confidence in his star was without doubt one of the reasons for his prodigious elevation to power, but, by a natural consequence, that which was excessive in Napoleon's genius was also the cause of his ruin.

This audacity was supported by a tremendous ambition to attain glory,[18] by a keen desire for his name and work to be transmitted to posterity, and by a fixed resolution to do great things or perish with honour. This audacity, which seems rash in our more prudent age, when people are more ambitious to attain comfort than glory, is revealed in Napoleon's plans of campaign and in his manoeuvres, inasmuch as he was constantly endeavouring to make them result in a decisive act, a conclusive battle. Everything was done, it is true, to limit the part of chance, but this "sacred majesty" ever retained an influence. Napoleon knew it and said: "All great events depend upon a single hair."[19] Doubtless, as he declared, if his wars were audacious, they were also methodical. "He constantly kept in view the relation between cause and effect and that of force over matter." But, in spite of his mathematical mind, he often exaggerated, through pride or diplomacy, and whilst under the influence of an unconscious or premeditated illusion, the value of his resources and his power of action. Expeditions such as those of Egypt and Russia, far from any line of support and revictualling base, may be considered as rash adventures. What would have happened if he had been conquered at Arcola, Marengo, Austerlitz, Jena? ... Especially at Marengo did he veritably stake his whole future on a throw of the dice. Sometimes this bold game may succeed, but, repeated indefinitely, it is bound to bring ruin to the player, despite all his skill.

Notwithstanding the failure of this mortal game, how much ought we not to admire the moral courage of a man who consciously engages his whole fortune, with the future of his country, in such formidable struggles? Returning in imagination to the hours when he was called upon to come to great decisions, Napoleon, at St. Helena, declared "that people formed a very incorrect idea of the strength necessary to wage, with a full knowledge of its consequences, one of those great battles on which depended the fate of an army and a country, and the possession of a throne."[20] Consequently he declared more than once that the primary quality of a man of war is firmness of character. This is an opinion over which we cannot meditate too long in these days of democracy and prolonged peace, when often, through circumstances which in no way permit of our judging firmness of character, a man is put in supreme command of armies.

Napoleon's moral courage was never manifested with more strength than in 1796 before Arcola. His army was then weighed down with fatigue, was discontented, and less than half the number of the enemy. Moreover, the Directory obstinately refused any assistance. "At that critical time (November 11 to 15, 1796) Bonaparte himself became alarmed, and did not dare to answer for anything. Collot himself told me," writes Ségur,[21] "that he sent him back to Milan with instructions to be ready for every eventuality. Moreover, however unpleasant might be the effect of this precaution, he entrusted him with a letter for Josephine, whom he authorized to retire from Milan to Genoa. Only a few years later, at St. Cloud, she herself told me that in this letter Bonaparte confessed 'that he had no more hope, that everything was lost, that everywhere the enemy showed three times his own strength, that he had only *his courage* left, that probably he would lose the Adige, that then he would fight for the Mincio, and that when this last position was lost, if he was still in existence, he would join her at Genoa, to which he advised her to retire.'" But Bonaparte retained his moral courage, his determination to perish with honour whilst playing a last game, and also his audacious and meditative thought. That was enough to save a despaired-of situation. We are acquainted with the Arcola manoeuvre, the desperate struggles in the swamps of the Alpon (November 15, 16, and 17, 1796), and the triumphal entry into Verona by the eastern gate. If we had only possessed, in 1870, at Metz, a similar determination to conquer!

In brief, an essentially personal conception, incessant meditation, an active and audacious mind, remarkable for its breadth but essentially practical, and a strong, stubborn, energetic will—such were the vigilant and laborious workers who wove the woof of the decisions and plans of Napoleon. A few great but very simple directing principles were the axes of the activity of his ever-wakeful brain. Napoleon points out the essential ones in a letter to Lauriston, at that time in charge of the Antilles expedition.

> "Always remember these three things:
>   Concentration of forces;
>   Activity;
>   A firm determination to perish with glory."

We are tempted to add this fourth maxim, which is also quite Napoleonic:

> "Surprise the enemy by strategy and secrecy, by the unexpectedness and rapidity of your operations."

Such was his theory, which is quite simple, but only of value when put into execution. We will now see how he understood this part of his work.

NOTES

1 *Mémoires de Mme. de Rémusat*, vol. ii. p. 324.
2 Chaptal's *Souvenirs sur Napoléon*, p. 227.
3 Conversation with the Russian general, Batachof, quoted by Vandal in *Alexandre et Napoléon*, p. 600.
4 *Mémoires du baron de Méneval*, vol. iii. p. 8.
5 *Ibid*, vol. iii. p. 50.
6 Ségur's *Mémoires d'un aide de camp*, p. 158.
7 Pont-de-Brique is a small château a league from Boulogne, where Napoleon stayed when he went to inspect the Ocean camps.
8 The Minister of War.
9 Rœderer's *Mémoires*, vol. iii. p. 380.
10 *Ibid.*
11 Las-Cases, *Mémorial de Sainte-Hélène*, vol. vi. p. 359.
12 Chaptal's *Souvenirs sur Napoléon*, p. 318.
13 *Mémoires du baron de Méneval*, vol. iii. p. 42
14 According to Jomini's *Précis de l'art de la guerre*, p. 289.
15 Sainte-Beuve's *Causeries du lundi*, vol. iii. p. 150.
16 *Mémoires de Mme. de Rémusat*, vol. i. p. 103.
17 *Ibid*, p. 385.
18 *Mémoires de Marmont*, vol. ii. p. 41.
19 Napoleon to Talleyrand, September 26, 1797.
20 *Mémoirial de Sainte-Hélène*, vol. ii. p. 18.
21 Ségur's *Histoire et Mémoires*, vol. i. p. 308.

II

Execution

Impulsion given by Napoleon to execution—Suppression of all loss of time between the decision and the execution—Value of time—Napoleon's intervention in the work of the staff—Drawing up of orders for movements—Berthier's situation as regards Napoleon—Napoleon his own director of marches.

I N WAR THE FINEST CONCEPTION is vain unless materialized into acts—the best plan is of value only when put into execution. This opinion never had a more zealous supporter than Napoleon, who by temperament was hostile to purely speculative reverie, to the turn of mind of those whom he disdainfully called "dreamers." This ardently imaginative man of the Midi was at the same time the most practical of realists. With him vigour and rapidity in execution were in no way inferior to conception. In the finest imperial manoeuvres one does not know which to admire the most: the initial idea or the manner in which it was carried out. The splendid combinations which threatened the existence of the armies of Wurmser, Mélas, Mack, and Brunswick were in themselves skilful manoeuvres and would alone have brought about the defeat of the enemy, but they would only have jeopardized the fate of these armies, they would not have destroyed them without that brilliant execution, vigour, and rapidity which have astonished the world.[1]

We have seen that, with Napoleon, the idea of a manoeuvre was essentially personal; it could not be quite the same in the case of its execution, which necessarily brought into action, in various ways, a large number of men. What was the degree of Napoleon's influence in execution? In what measure did he intervene therein? There, as elsewhere, his individuality was strongly marked by the execution being singularly firm and rapid.

First of all the Emperor intervened by insisting on the suppression of all loss of time between the conception of the idea and the act which was its consequence. Volition and execution were thus as it were united ... "Napoleon's art consisted above all in this, that in executing a plan which he had carefully studied from every point of view he chose with a strong, inflexible will the means which were calculated to lead him in the shortest time and in the most vigorous manner to his object. His redoubtable authority dispelled like an idle fancy every objection, every proof of impossibility."[2]

No one more than he took heed of the value of time. "Loss of time is irreparable in war," he wrote to his brother Joseph on March 20, 1806. "The excuses made are always bad, for operations come to nothing only through delays."[3] Consequently, how many recommendations do we find in his orders to accelerate execution! On October 17, 1805, he wrote to Murat from the Abbey of Elchingen as follows: "I congratulate you on your successes. But no rest! Pursue the enemy closely and cut all their communications." From Augsburg, on October 12, 1805, he wrote to Soult: "If the enemy is not at Memmingen, descend to us like lightning." In 1809 he addressed to Masséna, at the time of Landshut, this animating appeal: "You see at a glance that never did circumstances demand a more active and rapid movement than this ... Activity, activity, swiftness, I commend myself to you!"

After the battle of Coutras (1587), Henry of Navarre lost the fruits of his victory through leaving his army to go to Béarn and present to the Comtesse de Guiche, with whom he was then in love, the banners, standards, and other spoil of the enemy, and which he had formed into a gallant offering.[4] This is very different from the manner of Napoleon, who, without being insensible to feminine charms, would never have wasted a minute of the time set aside for his operations for the sake of a beautiful lady. Before as well as after the battle it was one of his rules to impose both upon himself and the whole army an almost superhuman effort. There was then no obstacle in his way; he would not hear of anything being impossible; in no case would he accept excuses of that kind. It was a sort of sublime "bluff" to which he had recourse to stimulate the energy of his men, to keep alive what he called the "sacred fire" in those whom he was driving towards a goal which could only be attained by boldness.[5]

It was whilst in this state of mind that he wrote, on February 26, 1814, to the aged and fatigued Augereau the following letter, in which the brief, sonorous, and abrupt phrases follow one on the other like bugle blasts sounding the attack:

"Cousin, what! Six hours after receiving the first troops from Spain you are not already in campaign! Six hours' rest were sufficient for them. I won the battle of Nangis with a brigade of dragoons which had come from Bayonne at a stretch ... I order you to leave twelve hours after the receipt of the present letter and enter on the campaign. If you are still the Augereau of Castiglione, retain your command; but if you are feeling the weight of your sixty years, resign and hand it over to the eldest of your general officers. The country is threatened and in danger; it can only be saved by boldness and willing-ness—not by vain delays. Be the first in the field. We must no longer act as we have done recently, but set to work with the determination of '93."

It was thanks to this rapidity in execution, combined with secrecy in his operations, that Napoleon created surprise and disconcerted his adversary.

Rapidity and secrecy in operation are two great factors of victory which, for many reasons, tend to escape modern armies. But everything is relative in human combinations, and the one of two adversaries who, in the next war, excels in this respect will have many chances of success on his side.

As regards execution, Napoleon also intervened in many other ways, par-ticularly by incessant control and the enthusiasm which he instilled into his army. I shall return to this shortly; but for the moment I would confine myself to watching him live and act at his headquarters; I would contemplate him as it were through an open window of his study, in the solitude of which so many fertile ideas sprang to his mind. It is there that we have already seen him come to a decision and that we will continue to follow him.

A decision having been reached, execution necessitates first of all, on the part of a commander-in-chief, an essential act—that of giving orders. It is here that we see the immediate auxiliaries of the commander—his staff—enter into play.

Thiebault defined the staff of the head of an army as "the central point of the great military and administrative operations of an army, the centre where, in accordance with the orders of the general-in-chief, everything is settled and directed, and whence all activity and superintendence springs."[6] It is beyond human strength, he adds, to give oneself up to the meditations necessitated by an extensive command and at the same time to attend to details concerning the execution of plans which must be con-stantly modified and changed.

Meditation, the preparatory work in coming to a decision, and the setting in motion of that decision are the exclusive business of the general-in-chief. From him comes the general direction of the movement by means of instruc-tions or orders to his staff, which takes charge of the details concerned with the execution of the movement and the maintenance of the armies. If one does not conform to this rational division of work, one fails either through an excessive centralization exceeding the limits of human strength, or by so neglecting the command as to cause the action to lose the desired firm-ness and vigour. Falling into the former of these excesses, Napoleon left to Berthier's staff only what he could not do himself.

The staff in no way participated in the Emperor's intellectual work; it was never taken into his confidence; it had but to obey scrupulously. "Keep strictly to the orders which I give you; I alone know what I must do."[7] Such were Berthier's orders. He kept strictly to them, to a blind faith in the Emperor, and refrained from all ideas of his own. He despatched the orders. Chief of the Staff, despatching the Emperor's orders, such was his title and his duty. Let us see how these orders were established.

The decision having been come to, the Emperor, in his study, dictated a general order, which was addressed to Berthier and which gave the whole of the movements to be executed, and the positions to be occupied by the various corps. After making himself acquainted with this order, Berthier handed it, not to the officers of the general staff, but to the military or civil employees of his own department.[8] Each of them cut out from it, as it were, the portion concerning his speciality and formed it into a special order, which was nothing but an almost *textual* extract of the Emperor's order. Only copyists were to be found there. In brief, in orders concerning operations both the form and substance were Napoleon's.

Were it merely a matter of receiving a report, settling a question or giving a reply, Berthier would never have taken the responsibility of acting on his own initiative. Such an act of initiative would have been considered by Napoleon as a veritable breach of confidence. When an officer, the bearer of despatches, arrived at night, he was introduced to the Chief of the Staff, who always lived near the Emperor. "Berthier, followed by the officer, then went to the Emperor, so that Napoleon, if need be, could question the latter. If the Emperor were in bed, he rose immediately, slipped on either his *molleton* or white *piqué* dressing-gown, and dictated the reply to the Chief of the Staff. Berthier transmitted it textually to the generals or marshals, and at the same time had it transcribed into his order book, with the name of the officer charged to carry it to its destination, and an indication of the hour at which this officer was sent forth. Before giving a subsequent order, the Emperor had the order book brought to him and re-read therein the preceding order."[9]

The Emperor dictated, Berthier copied—such was the rule. "The only exception was when, whilst on the march, the Emperor gave verbal orders to the Chief of the Staff. Under these circumstances Berthier dictated them to some one around him. But, on reaching headquarters, these verbal orders were always confirmed by written ones, more explicit than the first."[10]

If then, with Jomini, we consider the chief of the staff as being, and rightly so, the confidential assistant of the general-in-chief—his intellectual collaborator "who seconds him, is even in a position to direct everything himself, and who prevents errors by supplying him with sound information"—we must recognize that Berthier did not fill with

Napoleon such a role, for which, moreover, he had no aptitude. But this was not what Napoleon required of him. As Chief of the Staff, Berthier's duties were to copy the Emperor's instructions, give movement orders[11] and those concerning the administration, superintend the muster-rolls, the organization, the staff, and, finally, carry out the active duties of war near the Emperor.[12] In this more restricted, though still very important role, Napoleon appreciated Berthier's punctual exactitude, his passive obedience, exempt from the slightest comment, his discretion, modesty, vigilance, and scrupulous foresight in the copying and transmission of orders—all qualities which, on more that one occasion, assured the success of operations. In his commentaries, Napoleon, relating his 1796 campaign, has left us his appreciation of Berthier. "He showed (in 1796) great activity; he followed his general in all his reconnaissances and journeys, without in any way slackening in his office work. *His character was irresolute, not very suitable for a commander-in-chief*, but possessing all the qualities of a good chief of the staff. He was well acquainted with the country, knew thoroughly the business of reconnaissances, attended personally to the copying of orders, was accustomed to present with simplicity the most complicated movements of an army."[13] Here we once more see Napoleon's idea of the duties of the chief of the staff, the restricted role assigned to him as regards thought, and which differs so profoundly from Jomini's definition.

But when we judge a man it is well to denote periods. Man modifies with circumstances and time. Like Napoleon, Berthier did not escape this general rule. "From 1805 his activity began to decline, and he contributed to the spoiling of the army by substituting egoism in the hearts of its officers for the enthusiasm of glory."[14] On the other hand, the effective forces increased, the Emperor's prodigious activity also slackened, and there then clearly appeared, even to Napoleon himself, the insufficiency of the system which made all the movements of the armies depend on a single brain. On July 2, 1812, the Emperor wrote to the Chief of the Staff: "The staff is organized in such a manner that nothing is foreseen." During this Russian campaign Berthier was on several occasions reproached. "Berthier, I would give an arm to have you at Grosbois. You're not only worth nothing to me, but you hinder me." All this proves that the machine was working badly, and it could not be otherwise, because activity of mind was incapable of animating the work of the assistants in so extensive a command.

In consequence of these cruel remonstrances, Berthier sulked and did not come to dinner. Napoleon sent for him and waited until he came before sitting down to table. He put his arms round his neck, told him that they were inseparable, joked with him on the subject of Mme. Visconti, and finally placed him opposite to him at table.[15]

Napoleon was not without having some attachment for the man whom he called his brother-in-arms, his faithful companion in war, sometimes even "his wife."[16]

Whilst considering him to be "a very mediocre man," he took pleasure in recognizing that, when nothing diverted him, he was not without a certain leaning towards him.[17] With his perpetual need of analysing everything, even his own feelings, he came to ask himself why he, who hardly ever wasted his time over useless feelings, amused himself by loving so mediocre a man. "It is because he believes in you," replied Talleyrand. To have inspired this fondness was one of Berthier's qualities. He was Napoleon's man; he was the chief of the staff who adapted himself to the genius and personality of the leader whom he served. This harmonious juxtaposition of two men, in so many ways so different, was, without doubt, one of the elements of the military masterpieces of the imperial epoch.

With our modern ideas, we are apt to consider Berthier as a chief of the staff of very limited competence, but it would be unjust not to recognize that, in this restricted sphere of action, he rendered Napoleon very precious services, although without brilliance, and gave proof of estimable qualities. To render him the homage which new generations have sometimes refused him, we cannot do better than terminate this outline of his military character than by quoting the eulogistic appreciation of Mathieu Dumas, who was well qualified to judge him, since he was his assistant chief of the staff in 1805, and in 1812 worked by his side as general commissary of stores of the army. "During nineteen years, occupied by sixteen campaigns, almost all double, summer and winter, the history of the life of Marshal Berthier is no other than that of the wars of Bonaparte and of his operations, the carrying out of all the details of which he directed in the study and on the field of battle.

"His indefatigable activity seemed to challenge the ardent genius into the sphere of whose influence he had been drawn; he worked with admirable order, seized with promptitude and sagacity general views, barely indicated arrangements of troops, and afterwards gave all the execution orders with foresight, perspicuity, and conciseness. Discreet, impenetrable, and modest, he never pushed himself forward; he was exact, just, and even severe, but he ever set an example of zeal and vigilance; he maintained discipline with rigour, and knew how to make those who were his subordinates, whatever might be their rank, respect the authority entrusted to him." Such were the words of a friend who at the same time was a subordinate; they refer to the finest period in Berthier's career, and it is appropriate to quote them in order to preserve for the Chief of the Staff of the Grand Army the rank which is his due in the glorious company of Napoleon's companions.

We shall again return to Berthier's personality, but in examining the part taken by Napoleon in the work of the staff it was indispensable to establish clearly the situation of the Chief of the Staff as regards the Emperor.

The administrative measures which the maintenance of an army necessitate form a part of the art of war no less important and often more difficult than arrangements concerning operations at the front. They were also the object of Napoleon's constant meditations. Not only, as is advisable, did he himself draw up the main lines which must be closely connected with strategical combinations, but in orders dictated either to the Chief of the Staff or the General Commissary of Stores of the army, he fixed the details of them. He depended upon no one for the choice of the sites for the big depots, arsenals, hospitals, storehouses, and military bakehouses. He was his own director of marches, and encroached, even often, on the departments of inferior authorities by issuing orders dealing with the smallest details.

This excessive concentration of command was a consequence of his authoritative system. "His authority was the principle and the sole end of all the acts of his government ... In his palace, or under his tent, in whatever place he might be, all the wires were ever stretched by this iron hand, his jealous distrust would not allow him to let a single one go."[18] This manner of commanding cannot be given as a model. How many men, even chosen from the flower of an army and in the greatest vigour of manhood, would be capable of successfully copying Napoleon's career? In the case of Napoleon himself we can say, with Clausewitz, that the setting at naught and the exaggerated tension of all natural conditions resulted in he himself destroying the edifice which he alone had raised. Nevertheless, from a military point of view, this concentration in command enabled Napoleon to reduce to a minimum the blank time between the arrival at a decision and the setting in movement of the troops. This economy of time, of great importance in all branches of human industry, is an essential condition of success in war. To seek to attain it by Napoleon's methods would be rash; we must aim at it, whilst respecting the essential principles of division of labour and economy of strength, by a methodical organization of the working of stalls.

NOTES

1   Jomini's *Traité des grandes opérations militaires*, vol. iii. p. 215.

2   Odeleben's *Relation circonstanciée de la campagne de Saxe en 1813*.

3   *Lettres inédites de Napoléon I*, published by Léon Lecestre, vol. 1. p. 62.

4   Sainte-Beuve's *Causieres du lundi*, vol. viii. p. 157.

5   *Mémoires du baron de Méneval*, vol. iii. p. 251.

6   Thiébault's *Manuel général des états-majors*, p. 17.

7   Napoleon to Berthier, February 1806. Berthier looked upon this effacement of his own personality as perfectly natural. "I am nothing in the army. I receive, in the Emperor's name, the reports of the marshals, and I sign these orders for him, but I am personally null" (Berthier to Soult, Osterode, March 1, 1807). "The Emperor, Monsieur le Maréchal, needs neither advice nor plans of campaign. No one knows his thought, and our duty is to obey" (Berthier to Ney, Warsaw, January 18, 1807).

8   We shall see, in another chapter, the composition of the Privy Cabinet of the Emperor, that of Berthier and that of the staff, with the detailed working of these parts of the administrative machine.

9   *Mémoires du baron de Méneval*, vol. iii. p. 48.

10 According to the Commissary of Stores, Denniée, attached to Berthier's staff.

11 By "movement orders" is meant orders for the movement of detachments from the interior to the army, movements between the depots and the troops at the front, etc. Orders concerning operations are in no way in question.

12 Report of the Chief of the Staff to the Emperor, Mayence, April 19, 1813.

13 *Commentaires de Napoléon, campagne de 1796*, vol. i. p. 178.

14 Standhal's *Vie de Napoléon*, p. 229 *et seq.*

15 Mémoires du baron de Méneval, vol. iii. p. 46, 47.

16 Méneval. "Everybody knows," writes Mlle. Avrillon (*Mémoires*, vol. ii. p. 15), "how much the Emperor was attached to Marshal Berthier. I had proofs of this during our sojourn at the Château de Marrac (1808). As the Marshal was then suffering from gout, of which he had frequent attacks, the Emperor went very often to see him in the little house he inhabited a quarter of a league from the Château ... "

17 *Mémoires de Mme. de Rémusat*, vol. i. p. 231.

18 Mathieu Dumas' *Précis des événements militaires*.

III[1]
Execution (continued)

The Emperor during the opening of the campaign of 1806—
Preparatory measures—Secrecy, pacific attitude, confidence—The
gathering of the army—Departure of the Emperor from Saint
Cloud—Sojourn at Mayence—Feverish activity—Sojourn at
Würzburg: taking over of the command of the Grand Army—Plan
of operations—Crossing of the forest of Franconia—Entry into
Saxony—Means of acquiring superiority of moral strength—Political
action—Effect on the soldier—The historic night of October 11-
12 at Auma—Fresh information—The decision—Calculations
concerning marches—The general order for operations of October
12—The Emperor's instructions—The special orders of the Chief
of the Staff—Rapidity of the setting in movement of the Army
Corps—Execution of the movement of the 3rd Corps—Conclusions.

IN THE CONCRETE CASE WE are going to examine, our desire is to show
Napoleon at his headquarters, following on a given day a military situation, coming to one of those great decisions on which the fate of a campaign
depends, and then expressing it by means of orders which set the troops in
movement with a promptitude which modern staffs may envy but which they
are still far from attaining. We have chosen the historic night of October 11-
12, 1806, during which the Emperor ordered that change of front to the left
which was to lead his army to the fields of Jena and Auerstädt.

But before coming to this, let us cast a rapid glance at the opening of this
Prussian campaign by which, as in the previous year at Ulm, he surprised
the enemy in the very act of manoeuvring, thanks to the secrecy of his plans,
promptness of decision, and rapidity of execution.

Although not desiring war, and feigning up to the last moment not to believe
it was coming, the Emperor had already prepared his plan of campaign in the
month of August[2]: to use his own expression he had "laid on the map" ("il a
pondu sur la carte").[3] By aid of the box with compartments which Berthier had
had made for him the preceding year, he was able to judge at a glance of the

movements of the Prussian troops, regiment by regiment and battalion by battalion.[4] Amidst the fluctuations of his thought, which was centred on various
hypotheses, his correspondence after September 5 clearly showed that "his main
idea was to march from Bamberg to Berlin across the Frankenwald."[5] The period
from September 5 to 18 was a preparatory one, during which the Emperor, without wishing to appear to give up hope of peace, prepared to enter his army, if
need be, on campaign—it was the period of political tension, during which an
arrangement still being hoped for, preparations for war were to be made with the
greatest discretion. "We must talk peace, but act as though for war."[6] "Secrecy
and mystery" was the watchword. Whilst precautions were taken to avert a possible coalition between Prussia, Russia, and Austria, the defence of the coasts of
France was organized, and the Grand Army, which since the beginning of 1806
had been recuperating in the south of Germany, received orders to provide itself
with everything necessary for war: equipments, ambulances, pioneers' tools,
saucepans, and buckets. Levies of men and horses were also ordered. In case
of war the army had to be assembled, a week after the Emperor had given the
order, in the district of Bamberg, ready to march straight on Berlin. Officers
were sent on reconnaissances "at all hazards" to the ends of the roads crossing
the forest of Franconia; others went to Berlin and Dresden; and emissaries were
sent to the Russian frontier to find out what was happening there. From the
strategic point of view, the Emperor took steps to cover his flanks: in the north,
the King of Holland, Louis, was to assemble his army at Utrecht and be ready
to march on Wesel, in order to create a diversion; whilst Eugène, in Italy, was to
command an army whose role was to watch Austria.

On September 30, events pointing more and more to war, preparatory
measures increased. The Emperor ordered Caulaincourt, the Chief Equerry,
to arrange all his field telescopes in order, and on the 11th to despatch his
horses, mules, etc., but to do everything as secretly as possible, and endeavour to lead people to believe that he was going hunting at Compiegne. This
would at least, on their arrival there, mean a gain of two days. Marshal
Bessières, Duroc, the Grand Marshal of the palace, General Lemarois,
Prince Borghèse, and Ségur, the Deputy Marshal of the palace, were also to
send forward their horses, but Caulaincourt was to tell them that they were
intended to accompany the Emperor to the Diet of Frankfort.[7]

Notwithstanding this, he still declined to believe in war, and wrote to
Berthier: "In conversing with the King of Bavaria, tell him secretly that, if I
fall out with Prussia, which I do not think will happen, but if ever she does
commit that folly, he will gain Baireuth."[8]

In reality, he did not desire war; he would have considered himself criminal in provoking a "guerre de fantaisie," which was not justified by the

policy of his states ... for his policy was directed to the south and not to the north. That was what he wrote to the King of Prussia and to M. de Laforest, the French Minister in Berlin.[9] These pacific declarations, perhaps sincere, were to have an unexpected influence on the progress of the war, for, until the eve of Jena, they strengthened at Prussian headquarters the opinion of the temporizers, at whose head was even the commander of the army, Brunswick, and put an end to all idea of acting on the offensive.

However, the Emperor had set a limit to his patience: the entry of Prussian troops into Saxony. The French Ministers at Berlin and Dresden were then to demand their passports, at the same time instructing Marshal Berthier, who was at Munich, by special messenger; and the troops were to move immediately in order to assemble, a week later, in the neighbourhood of Bamberg. Napoleon had the greatest confidence in success if obliged to make war. On September 12 he wrote to Murat: "Have no fear whatever on political grounds: march as though nothing had happened. If really I must strike again, my measures are so well taken and so sure that Europe will only hear of my departure from Paris through the entire ruin of my enemies. It is well for your journals to describe me as occupied in Paris with pleasures, hunting, negotiations ..."

The Prussians entered Dresden on September 13. The news undoubtedly reached Napoleon on the evening of the 18th. At 11 p.m., without losing a minute, the Emperor gave orders for his guard to set off post-haste, and thus make the journey from Paris to Mayence in six days. On the morning of the 19th and during two hours he dictated to Clarke, Secretary to the Cabinet, the order for the whole army to move and assemble in the district of Bamberg.

On the morning of the 20th Napoleon wrote to the Chief of the Staff: "I send you the army movement order. It is now September 20, 6 a.m. I hope that you will receive my letter in the daytime of the 24th, and that before October 3 or 4 all my wishes will be carried out. I count on being at Mayence on September 30, and probably at Wurzburg on the 2nd or the 3rd. I shall there decide on my ulterior operations."

Although war had been decided upon, the Emperor remained at Saint Cloud until September 25, continuing to give orders for the organization of the army and the victualling of the frontier towns. During this period of the 20th to the 24th his attention was specially directed to the Electorate of Hesse-Cassel, whose doubtful attitude was all the more disquieting because the most dangerous offensive warfare on the part of Prussia might happen in that quarter.

The execution of the plan of operations was made subordinate to the crossing by one or the other army of the forests of Thuringia or Franconia. If the Prussian army preceded the French army, the first battles would be fought in the valley of the Main; the Emperor would have to submit to the initiative of his adversary.

A first letter from Berthier, written on the 19th, announcing that the Prussians were gathering at Hof, Magdeburg, and Hanover, a second letter from him, relating the activity of the Prussian troops and expressing a fear that the French army would be retarded, filled Napoleon's mind with uneasiness. This disquietude is visibly betrayed in the letter written by the Emperor on the 24th to hasten the movement of his troops and make them gain, if possible, two days.

It was doubtless under this impression of uncertainty that the Emperor made his journey from Saint Cloud to Mayence. He left Saint Cloud on the 25th, at 4.30 a.m., with the Empress, who during the campaign was to hold her court at Mayence. He stopped on the 26th at Metz for a few hours and reached Mayence on the 28th, with the intention of proceeding on October 1 to the vanguard, if circumstances demanded it.[10]

Information received at Mayence showed that the fears expressed by Berthier were very exaggerated, and on September 29 the Emperor was able to write to Fouché: "We are here in time."

During his sojourn at Mayence Napoleon displayed prodigious activity. Arriving in this town at noon on September 28, after travelling post for four days and three nights, he set to work on the morning of the 29th and dictated, almost without interruption, until nine o'clock in the evening of October 1, up to the very moment, in fact, when he stepped into his carriage to go to Würzburg. Questions relating to the organization of the army, supplies of flour and provisions, the organization of the general defence of the empire, correspondence with his allies and the German princes were the object of numerous notes, letters, and instructions, dated from Mayence.

Most of the work preparatory to entering on a campaign, thus improvized by the Emperor at the last moment, and which called for so formidable an effort on his part, is prepared in our days in time of peace with the assistance of numerous officers of the staff, and a simple telegram suffices to put the huge machine in motion. This scientific method, which was bequeathed to us by Marshal von Moltke, presents without denial great advantages over the Napoleonic improvization.[11] It is related that in July 1870, after the declaration of war, an American reporter, received at Berlin by Marshal von Moltke, found him reading, in the Latin text, a book of Tacitus. Everything had been foreseen and organized in time of peace; the order for mobilization having been sent out, all the army corps were transported without further intervention of the head of the army.

In 1806 the anterior military situation rendered a similar preparation impossible. But, notwithstanding that, what a contrast between Marshal von Moltke's placidity and the feverish activity of Napoleon, who appears to us at this time amidst the manifold duties of the head of the Government, the head of the army, the head of the staff, and the commissary of stores! All authority was concentrated in him, and he alone set all departments in movement. Could he do otherwise? Without a doubt, no; for the decentralization of work necessitated a preliminary education which not one of Napoleon's assistants had received. He was condemned by the nature of things to foresee and direct everything, consequently we can easily believe what he wrote from Mayence, on September 30, 1806, to the King of Wurttemberg: "that he was the greatest slave of all mankind, obliged to obey a master who was heartless: the calculation of events, and the nature of things."

Napoleon, parting not without emotion, it appears, from the Empress Josephine, left Mayence on October 1, about nine o'clock in the evening. After travelling all night in his berlin, he arrived about six o'clock on the morning of the 2nd at Aschaffenburg, stopped there two or three hours to breakfast and converse with the Prince Primate, and then, continuing his journey, reached his Würzburg headquarters at ten o'clock at night. Berthier was awaiting him.

He first of all brought his attention to bear on the question of provisions, and saw if his orders on that subject had been executed. He undoubtedly expressed to Berthier his very great dissatisfaction at the "shameful slowness" with which the prescribed measures were being carried out. In the correspondence of the Chief of the Staff we can detect at this time the master's lash.[12]

On October 3 the Emperor, by an order of the day announcing his arrival, took command of his army and ordered his marshals to pass their corps in review, preparatory to entering on campaign.

It was not until October 5 that he gave Berthier the general order for subsequent operations. Without a declaration of war the frontier was to be crossed on the 7th. The plan of operations, kept secret until then, was not revealed until the last minute. It was set forth in a masterly manner by the following letter from the Emperor to Soult:

The Emperor to Marshal Soult

WÜRZBURG, October 5th, 1806, 11 a.m.

The Chief of the Staff is at this moment writing out your orders, which you will receive during the day ...

I think fit to make you acquainted with my plans, in order that this knowledge may guide you in important circumstances.

I have had occupied, armed and victualled the citadels of Würzburg, Forchheim and Kronach, and I may debouch with my whole army into Saxony by three outlets. You are at the head of my right, having at half a day's journey behind you the corps of Marshal Ney, and at a day's journey in the rear 10,000 Bavarians, which makes more than 50,000 men. Marshal Bernadotte is at the head of my centre. Behind him is the corps of Marshal Davout, the greater part of the cavalry reserve, and my Guard, which makes more than 70,000 men. He will debouch by Kronach, Lobenstein, and Schleiz. The 5th corps is at the head of my left. Behind it is the corps of Marshal Augereau. He will debouch by Coburg, Grafenthal and Saalfeld. That forms more than 40,000 men. The very day you arrive at Hof, all these will be occupying positions on the same level.

I shall keep myself with the greatest constancy on a level with the centre.

With this tremendous superiority of force assembled on so narrow a space, you will understand that my wish is to run no risks and attack the enemy, wherever it may choose to take its stand, with double forces ...

... On arriving at Hof your first thought must be to establish communications between Lobenstein, Ebersdorf and Schleiz ...

According to information I have received to-day, it appears that if the enemy is in movement, it is on my left, since the greater part of its forces appears to be at Erfurt.

The first operation to be carried out was the crossing of the forest of Franconia and the marching out of the Grand Army into Saxony. It was a critical period,—"the most important moment of the campaign." One of the columns might be attacked before the main portion of the army had debouched, and thus be placed in a dangerous situation. Consequently, in addition to the question of victuals, that of the communications to be established between the columns was, during the days preceding the march, one of the Emperor's great anxieties. According to information, Napoleon knew that the greater part of the enemy's forces was in the Naumburg, Weimar, Erfurt, and Gotha district; he had, therefore, especially to watch over his left column, at the head of which was Marshal Lannes, who, if unable to resist, would retreat and cover the great Bamberg causeway until the central column came to its assistance. Every precaution, therefore, had been taken to avert possible attacks on the part of the enemy, and to assure the junction of the three columns. Once this junction was accomplished, the Emperor intended to push on to Neustadt and Triptis in order to free the outlets of the defiles. After this, whatever the enemy might do to attack him, he would be delighted; if they allowed themselves to be attacked, Napoleon would not miss the opportunity; if they withdrew by Magdeburg, Soult, with the 4th corps, would be before them at Dresden. "I greatly desire a battle ... After this battle, I shall be at Dresden or Berlin before them."[13] Such was Napoleon's state of mind on the morning of October 10.

On the 10th the central column entered into connection with that of the right; there was only wanting the left column, positive news of which had not yet reached the Imperial quarters. A fairly loud cannonade had been heard at Schleiz, coming from the direction of Saalfeld, and as it had ceased before the end of the day, it had been decided that the French were victorious. At seven o'clock in the evening the Chief of the Staff wrote to Lannes: "The Emperor *impatiently* awaits your coming to Neustadt *at all speed*; you are to form the left of the army which will march on Gera. The Emperor counts on your usual activity in making this movement rapidly."

At Gera "matters would be made clear"; that is to say, they would see whether the enemy intended to attack, whether it would allow itself to be attacked, or whether it would retreat. A decision would follow. On October 11 the head of the central column found Gera evacuated. Notwithstanding this discovery the Emperor decided, during the day of the 11th, that he was not sufficiently informed to be able to conclude that the enemy had given up the idea of attacking between Saale and Slater. However, he had thought out a manceuvre responding to the probable hypothesis that the enemy intended to concentrate on the left bank of the Saale, and in the course of the day he informed Murat of it,[14] but postponed his decision until the last news of the day had come in. The following letter, written to Ney at midnight, October 11, by the Chief of the Staff, clearly shows that the decision was reserved for the second part of the night:

> Auma, October 11th, 1806, midnight.
>
> The Emperor, *Monsieur le Maréchal*, orders you to march immediately with your army corps to Neustadt, where you will await fresh orders. It is probable that on arriving there you will receive orders to continue your march.
>
> Marshal Davout is beyond Auma. Marshal Bernadotte is at Gera. Marshal Lannes, who was at Saalfeld, has received orders to march on Possneck, but we have no news of him. If you should hear anything, communicate it to head-quarters, as well as any information you may learn concerning the enemy.

It is evident from this letter that, whilst aware of the concentration of the Prussians on Erfurt, the Emperor considered that it was not impossible that he might still come into collision with part of their forces on the right bank of the Saale, near Roda. Ney, marching from Schleiz to Neustadt (15 kilometres south of Roda), ought, in this hypothesis, to connect the main body of the army with Marshals Lannes and Augereau, who were also directing their steps from Saalfeld to Neustadt. Such was the point of view of the Emperor at Auma, on the evening of October 11, 1806.

From what precedes, we see with what attention and prudence he matured his plans and prepared his decisions. There was neither effervescence nor precipitation in the thought of his exceedingly active brain which, even then, understood very exactly the hesitations, wavering, and contradictory velleities of his adversary. For now we know that, until October 10, the Prussian superior command had not renounced the idea of assuming the offensive on the right bank of the Saale, and that, in spite of the order given on the 10th to concentrate on the left bank, between Jena and Weimar, Prince von Hohenlohe did not withdraw the Saxons from the right bank until the night of October 10-11.[15]

We will now endeavour to follow as closely as possible the working of the Emperor's mind on that historic night of October 11-12, to be present at the evolution of his decision, the giving of orders, and the setting in movement of the troops.

One more remark, however, before coming to those decisive hours. During the week from October 5, 1806, the day on which the Emperor gave his first order for operations, to Sunday, October 12, we would note a few other manifestations of his activity, which was far from being absorbed by the regulation of the strategic and material part of the war. The Emperor sought to dominate the enemy as much by the superiority of moral forces as by the setting in action of more powerful material means. He had already in his favour the prestige of his anterior victories, but this was not enough; by his repeated pacific declarations he sought to cause division in the enemy's camp and strengthen his alliances; despite the absolutism of his power, he pleaded the justice of his cause before the tribunal of public opinion. To Austria he made offers of alliance;[16] he addressed to the Saxons a proclamation in which he presented himself as their liberator;[17] and with a refined Machiavelism, at the very moment when, full of confidence in victory, he was directing his army corps by forced marches on Jena and Naumburg, he addressed to the King of Prussia, in order completely to paralyse his hesitating will, a letter in which he put him on his guard against "the sort of infatuation which animated his councils and made him commit political errors at which Europe is still quite astonished, and military errors of the enormity of which Europe would not be long in hearing."[18] To the Kings of Bavaria and Wurttemberg, and to the Princes of the Germanic Confederation he solemnly declared the justice of his position;[19] to the opinion of France and Europe he spoke by the message to the senate and the first bulletin of the Grand Army.[20] Fouché was instructed to create the same impression among the general public.[21] All this was drawn up by the Emperor himself; and we cannot help admiring the suppleness of his marvellous mind when we note to what an extent the arguments and even the style are, in their variety, suited to the intelligence and state of mind of the recipients of these various documents.

In the case of his soldiers he issued a rousing proclamation destined to excite their anger against foolish and provocative enemies, who had had the presumption to disparage the honour of the soldiers of Austerlitz, and at the very moment they were about to be received in France with triumphal fêtes .

On the approach of a battle he had still another means of action on his soldiers: he hastened into their midst, made his appearance everywhere, doubled their courage and confidence in success by his presence. If he had remained in the rear until the heads of his columns were ready to attack, deferring his departure under various pretexts, announcing himself, and keeping his escorts waiting in various directions, keeping minds in suspense in order to counteract curiosity and conjectures, immediately his corps were in line, he crossed them rapidly, generally at night, in order not to hinder the progress of the columns, and pushed on to the vanguard. There he received reports, questioned prisoners, spies, travellers, and inhabitants—entered into the minutest details, and, by the rapidity of his journeys and reconnaissances, appeared in so many places that his soldiers had all seen him, or thought and wished they had seen him.[22] It was thus that, having left Würzburg on October 6, 1806, he came to Auma. He arrived on the morning of October 11, had his headquarters established, but went in person as far as Gera to make inquiries at the vanguard. He was back again at night to sleep at Auma, the central point, where news would reach him without delay.

It is from this time that we will begin to follow the course of his thought still more closely.

After having spent the whole day at Gera, Napoleon, who was back at Alma about ten o'clock at night, installed himself in the local schoolrooms. Between midnight and 2.30 in the morning fresh information came in. First of all there was a letter from Soult, dated Weyda, October 11, 10 p.m.[23]

The Saxon troops which were at Weyda (two regiments) left three days ago (the 9th) for Jena, and those which were at Gera went at the same time in that direction. According to the reports which I received on arriving here, there are no forces of the enemy between here and Jena, but at the latter place there must be a strong body of troops. Those whom I sent reconnoitring have not yet been able to hand in their reports, but everything leads me to believe that between the Saale and the Elster there is nothing of importance ...[24]

A report from Lasalle and a letter from Murat confirmed this information, which was exact. From Wachholder-Baum, a village eight kilometres north of Gera, Lasalle wrote:

> Prisoners say that the King is at Erfurt with 200,000 men; they circulate the rumour that a column of Russians have reached Dresden, but the Prussian officer who gave me this news does not himself believe a word of it.[25]

Murat, who transmitted this report, added the following letter to it:[26]

> I have the honour to address to Your Majesty the report which I have just received from General Lasalle. I have sent you, with M. Montjoie, two merchants who have traversed the whole of the enemy's forces. They may be able to give you very positive information if they can be forced to be sincere, for, truth to tell, I believe they are spies. The route they took seems to prove it, for why, in travelling to Leipzig via Saalfeld, go from Gotha to Erfurt and thence to Jena?
>
> The fresh information which I have been able to procure seems to confirm that which Your Majesty has already received anent the gathering of the army at Erfurt[27] The Austrian sergeant whom you questioned[28] has left for Naumburg. He has promised to be back during the morning, and immediately on his arrival I will send him to Your Majesty. As soon as my aide-de-camp, who has left for Zeitz, is back, I will hasten to send you his report.
>
> Two roads lead from Gera to Naumburg: one via Zeitz, the other via Crossen. The former is much the better, and is only a league and a half longer than the latter; thus Your Majesty can always carry out his *plan* by moving as far as Zeitz.

From all these concordant reports the Emperor decided that, positively, the enemy had gathered in the neighbourhood of Erfurt in a defensive attitude. But what could it do? Remain at Erfurt or retreat to the Elbe. In either case the concentration of the French army on Roda was useless. Ney should be directed to the central point of Auma, where he would replace, in the central column, Bernadotte and Davout, who would be despatched to the north and would constitute, with Souk's corps and the Guard, the main manoeuvring force. Consequently, at three o'clock in the morning the Chief of the Staff sent Marshal Ney the following counter-order:

> AUMA, October 12th, 1806, 3 a.m.
>
> Monsieur le Maréchal, I send you an officer of my staff with a fresh order from the Emperor. In consequence of *new* information which we have just received

of the enemy, His Majesty orders you to proceed immediately to Auma and to regard the order, dated midnight and instructing you to go to Neustadt, as null and void. (Order carried by M. Thomas, officer of the staff, who left at 3.15 a.m.)

Having thus guarded against the most pressing difficulty, Napoleon, who, as we have seen, had decided at least since the morning on his plan of action (we know that he always based his scheme on two hypotheses), determined to proceed against the enemy by manoeuvring on its left, so as to surround it in the region of Erfurt, if it had remained there, or to cut it off from Dresden and Berlin, if it had retreated towards the Elbe.[29] He studied the movements in detail and calculated the length of the marches; and in order the better to rivet his thought, as he had done at other times, he set the latter down on paper and with his own hand wrote the following note:

Guard 10 in the evening at Bamberg, 11 at Lichtenfels, 12 beyond Kronach, 13 at Lobenstein;

From Hautpoul, the 11 to two leagues beyond Kronach, 14, at Auma, 15, at Jena;

Klein, the 11 to two leagues from Kronach, the 15 at Jena, the 14 at Jena, the 13 at Auma;

Klein, the 12 at Lobenstein;

Jena to Weimar, 4 leagues, reserve cavalry, the 14 at Jena;

Naumburg to Weimar, 7 leagues, Guard, the 15 at Jena; Kahla to Weimar, 5 leagues, park, the 15 at Auma;

Neustadt to Jena, 5 leagues, Davout, the 14 at Apolda;

Gera to Jena, 7 leagues, Lannes, the 15 at Weimar;

From Zeitz to Jena, 7 leagues, Augereau, the 14 at Mellingen

Bernadotte, the 14 at Dornburg;

Soult, the 14 at Jena;

Ney, the 14 at Kahla.

This preparatory work ended, Napoleon dictated his general order for operations:

The Emperor to the Chief of the Staff

AUMA, October 12th, 1806, 4 a.m.

Give orders to Marshal Davout to leave his position for Naumburg, where he must arrive as quickly as possible, but always holding his troops ready to fight. He will be preceded by all his light cavalry, which will send out skirmishers as far as possible, as much for the purpose of obtaining news of the enemy as to make prisoners, stop baggage, and get accurate information.

General Sahuc's division of dragoons[30] will be under his orders. It will proceed to Mittel-Pöllnitz, where it will receive Marshal Davout's orders. Prince Murat and Marshal Bernadotte are also ordered to Naumburg, but are to follow the Zeitz road.

Marshal Lannes proceeds from Neustadt to Jena. Marshal Augereau proceeds to Kahla. Marshal Ney will be at MittelPollnitz. Headquarters will be at Gera, noon.

Give orders for the sending off of the divisions of heavy cavalry and the divisions of dragoons which have remained in the rear, as well as the park of artillery, to Gera.

Such was the clear and concise expression of the Emperor's decision.

Nowadays it is an acknowledged principle that the leader of an army, in order to allow the commander of his corps to show a just and salutary initiative, should, in his instructions, inform them of the general idea of the manoeuvre and define the roles assigned to them in the movement as a whole. But there is no such thing in Napoleon's order. Berthier had simply to transmit without explanation, to each commander of a corps the instructions which concerned him alone. Shortly we shall see Berthier at work. But before coming to that let us complete our analysis of the work of the Emperor.

In the above order to Berthier there is no question of Soult's corps. To Soult the Emperor sent direct the following private order:

The Emperor to Marshal Soult

AUMA, October 12th, 1806, 4 a.m.

Muster at Gera and Ronneburg. It is possible that you will not make any other movement to-day. I shall, moreover, be at noon at Gera, where headquarters are.

Since the beginning of the campaign the Emperor had shown particular confidence in Soult. "He informed him of his plans, in order that this knowledge might guide him in important circumstances," and in case he had to operate as a detachment. This special situation, which resulted since the opening of the campaign in a continuous correspondence between the Emperor and Soult, is the only explanation we can find of this special order addressed directly by the Emperor to Soult.[31]

The Emperor's general order contains, as we have just seen, no information regarding the enemy, no indication of the nature of the manoeuvre, or of the role of the various corps. In the case of commanders of corps likely to come into contact with the enemy, Napoleon completed the order relating to movements which they received from the Chief of the Staff by a private letter in which, more or less completely, he acquainted them with his ideas and defined their mission. In the present case, he wrote the following "instructions" to Lannes, Murat, and Davout:

The Emperor to Marshal Lannes

IMPERIAL HEADQUARTERS, AUMA,
October 12th, 1806, 4 a.m.

I have received with great pleasure the news of your affair of the 10th inst ... [32] I was yesterday evening at Gera. We have routed the enemy's baggage escort and taken 500 carriages. The cavalry is loaded with gold.

You will receive the order concerning movements from the Chief of the Staff.

All the letters intercepted prove that the enemy has lost its head. They hold councils day and night, and do not know what measure to take. As you see, my army is united, and I bar their way to Dresden and Berlin.

Our art at present consists in attacking everything we encounter, in order to beat the enemy in detail and whilst it is uniting its forces. When I say we must attack everything we encounter, I mean we must attack everything that is on the move and not in a position which makes it too strong.

The Prussians had already despatched a column to Frankfort, but they soon retreated. Up to the present they indeed show their ignorance of the art of war.

Do not fail to send many skirmishers ahead of you, in order to intercept travellers and collect as much information as possible.

Should the enemy make a movement from Erfurt to Saalfeld (which would be absurd, but, considering its position, we must expect all sorts of events), you will join Marshal Augereau and fall on the Prussians in flank.

The Emperor to the Grand Duke of Berg

AUMA, October 12th, 1806, 4 a.m.

I shall be at Gera to-day before noon. You will see from the position of the army that I am completely surrounding the enemy. But I need information as to what it intends doing. I hope that you will find out at Zeitz.

You saw what I did at Gera. Do the same. Attack boldly everything which is on the march. These forces on the move are columns which endeavour to reach a meeting place, and the rapidity of my movements prevents them receiving counter-orders in time. Two or three successes of this kind will crush the Prussian army and perhaps make a general encounter unnecessary.

Marshal Davout sends all his cavalry direct to Naumberg. Cover the whole plain of Leipzig with yours.

These were the only two instructions sent by the Emperor at four o'clock in the morning.

However, at 8.30 a.m., doubtless on receiving the news that the enemy had evacuated Jena, the Emperor wrote thus to Davout:

The Emperor to Marshal Davout

AUMA, October 12th, 1806, 8.30 a.m.

I mount into the saddle to go to Gera. Inform me of the road you are taking for naumberg. It is possible that the enemy will carry out its retreat behind Ilm and the Saale; for it seems to me that it is evacuating Jena. It will be easy for you, on arriving at Naumberg, to make certain of this.

Scour the plain with the whole of your light cavalry and send news as rapidly as you can to Prince Murat, who will be near Zeitz, and to me near Gera. Marshal Ney will be at Gera[33] early. You can inform him of what comes to your knowledge.

The other marshals were to receive only the order relating to movements sent by the Chief of the Staff. Strictly speaking, this might be sufficient for Ney, Soult, and the Guard, who were in the second line and in proximity to the Emperor. As to Bernadotte, Murat was in a position to set him in the right direction, since they were working together. But, owing to the transmutation of the army, Augereau at Kahla was, every bit as much as Lannes at Jena, exposed to an encounter with the enemy, and, as he himself wrote to Lannes on October 13: "The Emperor had given him no other orders than to move to Kahla." We can detect in this phrase Augereau's regret that he had not received instructions as to his role. However, like a good comrade, he subordinated his movements to those of Lannes, with whom he was materially and morally in harmony. One cannot say the same of Bernadotte and Davout on the night of October 13-14. The conflict which arose between these two marshals and which resulted in Bernadotte's regrettable inaction in the battles of the 14th, would doubtless have been avoided had Bernadotte been more completely informed of the idea of the Emperor's manoeuvre.

As regards the department specially concerned with movements, the Emperor's work stopped there, on the morning of the 12th, for the letters to Talleyrand and the drawing up of the second bulletin of the Grand Army had no direct reference to movements.

Let us now pass to an examination of the work of the Chief of the Staff.

The first two orders relative to movements, sent by Berthier, were those of Murat and Bernadotte, who were both at Gera, twenty-nine kilometres from Imperial Headquarters of Auma. The portion of the Emperor's order concerning this was as follows:

Prince Murat and Marshal Bernadotte are also ordered to Naumberg (like Marshal Davout), but are to follow the Zeitz road.

This phrase, which was doubtless completed by verbal indications given by the Emperor, resulted in these orders:

The Chief of the Staff to the Grand Duke of Berg

AUMA, October 12th, 1806, 4 a.m.

The Emperor orders, Mon Prince, that you leave Gera immediately for Zeitz, and send out skirmishers in the direction of Leipzig.

It is the Emperor's wish that from Zeitz, if the information you receive shows that the enemy is still near Erfurt, you should proceed to Naumburg, where Marshal Davout will be.

Headquarters will to-day be at Gera.

The position of the army to-day, the 12th, is as follows:

Marshal Soult at Gera, Marshal Ney at Mittel, Marshal Lannes at Jena, Marshal Augereau at Kahla, and Marshal Davout *en route* from Mittel to Naumburg.

The Chief of the Staff to Marshal Bernadotte

AUMA, October 12th, 1806, 4 a.m.

I beg to inform you, Monsieur le Maréchal, that I am sending an order to the Grand Duke of Berg to proceed to Zeitz and thence to Naumburg, if the information which he gathers concerning the enemy still leads him to believe that its principal forces are near Erfurt.

The Emperor's intention is that you should support the Grand Duke's movement. Arrange with him regarding your march.

Headquarters will be transferred to-day, at noon, to Gera.

The drawing up and the contexture of these two orders of the Chief of the Staff call for a few remarks on the details of this part of the work of the staff of the Grand Army.

In the first order to Murat the mission of the cavalry is well defined, but there is no question of the support it is to receive from the 1st army corps. Doubtless Bernadotte was expected to concert with Murat and make known the import of his order; but, if a delay interfered with their understanding, there would no longer be concordance in the movements of the two corps.

Moreover, Bernadotte was in no way instructed as to the general movement of the army; he was not even told that Davout was at Naumburg, and could learn this only through Murat. The two orders, incomplete in themselves, complete each other. They were doubtless written by one and the same officer who, knowing that the two marshals had to act in concert,[34] decided that it was superfluous to repeat in one of the orders what the other contained. We can here perceive the haste with which this work was done. It was essential to act quickly, even at the cost of a few gaps in the wording of a document.

If we now compare the order of the Chief of the Staff to the Grand Duke of Berg with the instructions which, at the same time, were sent to the latter by the Emperor, we shall note a want of concordance as regards the mission of the cavalry—a fact which did not escape Murat, who considered it necessary to write on the subject to the Emperor:

ZEITZ, October 12th, 1806.

Sire, I have received Your Majesty's letter, written to-day at 4 a.m., and that of the Prince of Neufchâtel, written at the same hour. The Minister directs me to confine myself to sending out a few skirmishers in the direction of Leipzig if I learn that the enemy has retreated towards Erfurt, and to march with my whole army corps on Naumburg, whilst Your Majesty orders me to cover the plain of Leipzig, not with a few skirmishers, but with the whole of my cavalry. To carry out this double object, here is the arrangement which I have thought fit to decide on. (The arrangement of troops which he then set forth constituted a middle course[35])

In this way we shall be, so to speak, in a body, and in a position to carry out the movements which it may please Your Majesty to make on Weissenfels or on Naumburg ...

I shall remain at Zeitz until it has pleased Your Majesty to inform me if you approve of my plan, and if I am to proceed to-morrow on Weissenfels or Naumburg.

The picturesque but indefinite phrase, "cover the whole plain of Leipzig with your cavalry," had the regrettable consequence of transferring the Beaumont division of dragoons and the Lasalle and Milhaud brigades east of the Zeitz-Naumburg road, with the result that these bodies of cavalry arrived late on October 14 on the battlefield of Jena.

Letters written by the Emperor direct to the marshals were sent off by
Berthier's department. It should therefore have been within the province of
the Chief of the Staff to take note of their contents and point out to the
Emperor the contradictions between the orders contained in this direct correspondence and the orders relating to special movements. But this would have
involved an intellectual collaboration between the head of the army and the
Chief of the Staff, which in no way existed between Napoleon and Berthier.
The Emperor was at that time regarded by all who surrounded him as an
infallible being, and no one would have taken the responsibility of drawing
his attention to even an evident error.

Marshal Davout, with the 3rd corps, was directed, like Murat and
Bernadotte, to Naumburg, but, instead of making a bend, via Zeitz, he was to
reach Naumburg by the direct road, so as "to arrive there as quickly as possible, but always holding his troops ready to fight." These, as we remember, are
the very words of the Emperor's general order to the Chief of the Staff. Here
is the special order which, as a consequence, was sent by Berthier to Marshal
Davout:

AUMA, October 12th, 1806, 5 a.m.
Marshal Davout is ordered, with the whole of his army corps, to leave the
position he occupies[36] and proceed direct to Naumburg, but always holding his troops ready to fight. He will be preceded by all his light cavalry,
which will send out skirmishers as far as possible, as much for the purpose
of obtaining news of the enemy as to make prisoners, stop baggage, and get
accurate information.

General Sahuc's division of dragoons will be under Marshal Davout's orders.
I beg to inform Marshal Davout that I am instructing General Sahuc to proceed to Mittel, where he will receive the Marshal's orders.

The Grand Duke of Berg and Marshal Bernadotte are also ordered to proceed to Naumburg, but to follow the Zeitz road. Marshal Lannes proceeds
towards Jena from Neustadt. Marshal Augereau proceeds to Kahla; Marshal
Soult to Gera; and Marshal Ney to Mittel. Imperial headquarters will be to-
day, at noon, at Gera.

This special order is almost a word for word copy of the Emperor's general
order given to Berthier at four in the morning.

In the eyes of the Emperor, Davout's movement had an extremely important bearing on the success of his combination. The very contexture of the
general order to Berthier shows the interest which the Emperor attached to
the carrying out of this movement. The general order opens, in fact, with

indications relative to Davout's movement, and these take up more than half the entire text of the order.

To go from Mittel to Naumburg the 3rd corps had to cover from forty-five to fifty kilometres, a much longer march than that of any other army corps. The Emperor had ordered that this distance should be covered as rapidly as possible. For these reasons the order to Davout ought, one would think, to have been sent off without a moment's delay. On the contrary, it was sent off the last, at five in the morning. Owing to this error on the part of the staff, the movement of the 3rd corps was delayed about an hour.

Prince von Hohenlohe, in his *Letters on Strategy*,[37] expresses astonishment that Napoleon directed Bernadotte to Zeitz and Davout to Naumburg, and thus imposed on the latter a march of more than forty-five kilometres. By directing Bernadotte to Naumburg and Davout to Zeitz, each of the marshals would have had only thirty-four kilometres to travel. He adds: "Napoleon usually directed his corps in so masterly a manner that these measures astonish us and force us to seek for the reasons." He discovers an explanation in Napoleon's intention to entrust Davout with the mission calling for the most initiative. This explanation is very admissible.[39] In any case, from the point of view of results the measure was most fortunate, for one may question whether Bernadotte, whose disposition led him in but a small degree to take the offensive, would have won or even fought the battle of Auerstädt.

General Sahuc, who was placed at Davout's disposal, received the following awkwardly drawn up special order:

AUMA, October 12th, 1806, 5 a.m.

General, the Emperor orders that you place yourself under the orders of Marshal Davout, who is in advance of you at Mittel. General Sahuc will send for his orders, his division having to march with the marshal's army corps. I inform the Grand Duke of Berg of this. Meeting at once with your division to Mittel.

The orders to Lannes and Augereau concluded the series of special orders.

In his general order the Emperor contented himself by indicating the movements of these two marshals by the laconic phrases: "Marshal Lannes proceeds from Neustadt to Jena; Marshal Augereau proceeds to Kahla," rather summary indications in the case of two corps of the vanguard which were to come into contact with the enemy. The special orders contained no further information, either as regards the enemy or on the attitude to be adopted. They were as follows:

The Chief of the Staff to Marshal Lannes

AUMA, October 12th, 1806, 4.30 a.m.

Marshal Lannes is ordered to proceed to-day, with the whole of his army corps, to Jena.

I am ordering Marshal Augereau to proceed towards Kahla. Marshal Ney will this evening be at Mittel, and Marshal Soult at Gera; Marshal Davout will be on the road from Mittel to Naumburg, and Marshal Bernadotte on the road from Gera to Naumburg, via Zeitz. Headquarters will be at Gera, at noon.

The Emperor's wish, Marshal, is that immediately on your arrival at Jena you obtain all possible information as to the enemy's doings during the past three days. Open the letters at the post; question the postillions and keepers of posting-houses in order to learn what the enemy is doing; and send messengers to Weimar.

I beg to inform you that we captured yesterday, on our right, between Gera and Zeitz, more than 300 baggage vehicles, some artillery, precious objects, and 200 prisoners.

There can be no doubt that the Emperor told Berthier to instruct Lannes, on reaching Jena, to send messengers in the direction of Weimar to obtain all information on what the enemy had been doing during the past three days.

The Emperor again lays stress on this point in the letter which he sent direct to Lannes at four in the morning. "Do not fail," he wrote, "to send many skirmishers ahead of you, in order to intercept travellers and collect as much information as possible."

It was also certainly in accordance with a verbal order from the Emperor that Berthier informed Lannes of the capture by Lasalle's hussars, on the 11th, of one of the enemy's escorts. This little success on the part of the French cavalry was doubtless very pleasing to the Emperor. He took a delight in spreading the news; he did not fail to communicate it himself in his private letter to Lannes; and on the same day he inserted it in the second bulletin of the Grand Army, as follows: "General Lasalle, of the cavalry reserve, has routed the enemy's baggage escort. Five hundred ammunition waggons and baggage vehicles have been taken by the French hussars. Our light cavalry is covered with gold." It was not a bad idea, when face to face with the Prussian cavalry, reputed to be so redoubtable, to praise and at the same time magnify the exploits of the French horse-soldiers.

In the statement of the position of the army given to Lannes there is no mention of Murat's cavalry. This was evidently an omission. On the other hand, this information appears, as we shall see, in the order to Augereau, to whom it was certainly less useful.

The Chief of the Staff to Marshal Augereau

AUMA, October 12th, 1806, 4.30 a.m.

The Emperor, Monsieur le Maréchal, orders you to proceed with your army corps to Kahla.

Marshal Lannes is ordered to Jena. Send skirmishers ahead to obtain news of the enemy. Send me all the news you can to headquarters at Gera.[39]

Put yourself in correspondence with Marshal Lannes at Jena.

The position of the army on the 12th will be as follows:

The Grand Duke marches on Zeitz and thence to Naumburg if the enemy is still near Erfurt.

Marshal Bernadotte follows this movement.

Marshal Soult at Gera, Marshal Ney at Mittel, and Marshal Davout *en route* from Mittel to Naumburg.

The movements of the various corps were thus completely arranged by these brief orders, dictated and sent off between four and five in the morning. Their tone, the incorrectness of the style, the numerous omissions, the evident rapidity with which they were drawn up—everything leads us to believe that these orders were written by officers or secretaries, writing to the dictation of Berthier himself, who had before him the Emperor's general order, which he occasionally completed by drawing upon information received verbally and perhaps set down in his green notebook.

In short, these orders, although verbose, contained little: the object of the march, the position of the army, and, in the case of the corps in the front line, instructions to obtain information concerning the enemy. But as to what the general-in-chief himself knew about the enemy, as to the ensemble of the projected manoeuvre and the mission of each corps in that manoeuvre, there is no mention. This, as we know, was the system adopted, and in as much as it favoured the preservation of the secret of the manoeuvre it was an advantage. On the other hand, the commanders of the army corps were marching in the dark, and could with difficulty show initiative. There was no indication either as to the zones covered whilst on the march or the routes to be followed by each of the army corps. The commanders of the corps themselves chose the roads leading to the destinations fixed for them and sent in the information to imperial headquarters. "Inform me of the road you will take when going to Naumburg," wrote the Emperor to Davout on October 12, 1806. This method of procedure, which was probably due to an insufficiency of maps,[40] was none the less embarrassing, as proved by the letter written by Davout on September 26, 1805, from Oggersheim, to the Chief of the Staff. "... I have the honour to beg Your Excellency," he said, "kindly to fix the roads we ought to take, in order to avoid the very serious difficulties arising from passing such large army corps through defiles of this nature, and those which may arise as regards provisions."

Moreover, as we have seen, this system of special orders, taken from the Emperor's general order, lent itself to the multiplication of omissions or fairly numerous errors.

The orders thus drawn up by Berthier were carried to those to whom they were addressed by officers. On reaching their destination, the instructions were carried out with a rapidity which calls for our closest attention, for without a doubt this was one of the chief reasons for Napoleon's successes. Two hours on an average[41] after the receipt of the army order by the commander of a corps, the troops were in movement. Even less time than this was taken when, as in the case under examination, the troops had been warned to hold themselves in readiness. The table on the facing page gives precise indications as to the conditions of transmission and execution of the orders on the night of October 11-12, 1806.

Let us follow, in the execution of the order of the 12th, one of the corps of the Grand Army—the 3rd, the one which had, the longest march before it.

The order from the Chief of the Staff was handed to Davout about six in the morning. The 1st division (Morand) was at Mittel with headquarters, the 2nd division (Friand) was bivouacked half a league to the rear, and the 3rd (Gudin) a little farther in the rear, on the heights between Mittel and Auma.

Davout immediately gave the assembled troops:

First, the route to be followed—Rauchwitz, Molau, and Naumburg;

Second, the order in which they should march, 1st, 2nd, and 3rd division;

Third, the formation of the troops—in a mass.[42]

Before the departure he had read in front of the companies a proclamation calculated to excite their ardour. "Thanks to his skilful manoeuvres, the Emperor has just placed the Prussians in the same position in which the Austrian army was at Ulm." Immediately afterwards the corps, amidst cries of "Long live the Emperor," set off: the light cavalry and the infantry regiment of the vanguard at 6.30, the 1st division (Morand) at 7, the 2nd division (Friand), followed by Sahuc's division of dragoons, at 8, and the 3rd division (Gudin) at 9.30.

At 9.30, at the moment General Gudin's division set of on the march, it rendered honours to the Emperor, who was passing before its front *en route* for Gera.

The march—very difficult—"occasioned many stragglers." The vanguard covered 45 kilometres and reached its destination in the case of the cavalry at

Army Corps.	Situation of Headquarters on the night of October 11-12.	Distance to Imperial Headquarters at Auma.	Hour of sending off the Army Order.	Hour of its Receipt by the Commanders of the Corps.	Hour of Departure of the Heads of the Columns.	Places reached on the evening of the 12th by the Heads of the Columns.	Distances covered.	Observations.
		Kilom.	A.M.	A.M.	A.M.		Kilom.	
Murat	Gera	29	4	7.15	9	{ Mölsen / Teuchern }	40-45	
1st Corps (Bernadotte)	Gera	29	4	7.15	9	Meineweh	27	
3rd Corps (Davout) .	Mittel	7,500	5	6	7	Naumburg	45	
4th Corps (Soult) .	Weyda	17	4	6	7	Gera and Naulitz	24	
5th Corps (Lannes) .	Neustadt	13,500	4.30	6	10	Winzerla (6 kilom. from Jena)	24	Combat
6th Corps (Ney) . .	Schleiz	18	3	5.30	6	Mittel and Auma	16	{ The 6th Corps was under arms from 2 A.M.
7th Corps (Augereau)	{ Marching from Saalfeld to Neustadt }	30	4.30	8.15	{ 10 (Change of direction) }	Kahla	37	{ The 7th Corps set off for Neustadt at break of day

3.30 a.m., and in the case of the infantry at 8 p.m. The 1st, 2nd, and 3rd divisions covered respectively 40, 37, and 28 kilometres.

The arrival of the 3rd corps at Naumburg on October 12 was so little expected at the Prussian headquarters that, when the news was announced at Weimar to the Prince of Brunswick, he refused to believe it and exclaimed: "But they cannot fly!"[43]

To what was this rapidity of execution, which thus created surprises and disconcerted the enemy, due? Without a doubt to the ardour of the 3rd corps, which its leader justly compared to Caesar's tenth legion, but also to Napoleon's method of work, and to the organization of his system. The secret of the system lay in the centralization in a single person of the duties of Commander-in-Chief and Head of the Staff. Napoleon not only decided on movements, but he had also, so to say, need of no one either in preparing or expressing his decision. The position of his corps, what could be foreseen, according to information received, of the enemy's positions—all this was ever present in his brain, making it hardly necessary for him to cast his eyes on the figurative map which was drawn up day and night in his room. He alone was what we now call the second office of the Staff. He was also the third office, for he himself elaborated his orders relating to movements. All he wanted was a secretary to whom he could say: "Sit down and write," then "Send off." Finally, owing to working at night, he reduced to a minimum the time between the decision and its execution. At daybreak the troops carried out the movements ordered by the Emperor during the last hours of night.

The superhuman work of Napoleon, who in reality was his own Chief of the Staff, cannot be taken as the basis of an organization, for it exceeds the physical and intellectual strength of almost all men. But, whilst respecting the initiative of each, and the prolific principle of the division of work, and maintaining the duties of the staff-office, such as we now understand them, as an aid to the Commander-in-Chief, we ought to aim at attaining that rapidity of execution which characterized the Emperor's command. "Night is the work time for a General-in-Chief," said Napoleon. It is also the work time for the staff. One ought to organize in a methodical manner, as is done in certain industries, the night work of army staffs, with squads of workers who relieve each other. That would necessitate numerous staff-officers, picked men in the confidence of the General-in-Chief—a state of things which did not exist at the Imperial staff. Such a staff, with rapid means of transport at its disposal, might, despite the great extension of the front of armies, by means of brief orders, reduced to the strictly indispensable,[44] set troops in motion under the conditions of rapidity realised on October 12, 1806. It would thus largely contribute to the victory of our arms.

NOTES

1 See the sketch for the entry into campaign of the Grand Army in 1806 and Petri's map used by Napoleon in that year.
2 "Things are happening here exactly as I calculated two months ago in Paris, march after march, almost event after event. I was right about everything" (the Emperor to Talleyrand, Auma, October 12, 1806, 7 p.m.).
3 Mathieu Dumas' *Precis des evinemens militaires*, vol. xix. p. 403.
4 On August 28, 1805, the Emperor ordered Berthier to have made for him two portable boxes with compartments: one for himself and the other for Berthier. They were to be so arranged that, by means of playing-cards, bearing written indications, the movements of the whole of the enemy's troops, regiment by regiment, battalion by battalion, and even those of inconsiderable detachments, could be seen at a glance. Every fortnight the changes that had taken place during the preceding fortnight were to be sent in, utilizing not only the information in the journals but also the various pieces of intelligence which had come to the knowledge of Berthier, the Minister of War, and the Minister of Foreign Affairs. The same person was to arrange the cards in the box and draw up the fortnightly statement of the position of the enemy's army (*Correspondence militaire*, No. 552: the Emperor to Berthier, Boulogne camp, August 28, 1805).
5 General Bonnal's *La Manoeuvre d'Jéna*, p. 29.
6 The Emperor to Talleyrand.
7 The Emperor to Caulaincourt, Saint Cloud, September 10, 1806.
8 The Emperor to the Chief of the Staff, September 10, 1806.
9 The Emperor to the King of Prussia, Saint Cloud, September 12, 1806. Note for a despatch to M. de Laforest, Saint Cloud, September 12, 1806.
10 The Emperor to the Chief of the Staff, Saint Cloud, September 24, 1806.
11 Bonnal's *La Manoeuvre d'Jéna*.
12 Letters of the Chief of the Staff written on October 2, 11 p.m., to Marshals Davout and Bernadotte; and various letters written by him on the following day.

13 The Emperor to Soult, Ebersdorf, October 10, 1806, 8 a.m.

14 Letter from Murat to the Emperor, October 11, 1806, 11 p.m.

15 Hohenlohe's *Letters on Strategy*, vol. i. p. 79.

16 Letter from the Emperor to M. de la Rochefoucauld, Ambassador at Vienna, Würzburg, October 3, 1806.

17 Proclamation to the people of Saxony, Ebersdorf, October 10, 1806.

18 The Emperor to the King of Prussia, Imperial Camp, Gera, October 12, 1806.

19 Letters of October 7, 1806.

20 Message to the Senate, Bamberg, October 7; first bulletin of the Grand Army, Kronach, October 8.

21 The Emperor to Fouché, Bamberg, October 7, 1806

22 Mathieu Dumas' *Précis des événements militaires*, vol. iii. p. 285.

23 Weyda is about 16 kilometres from Auma. This letter must have arrived at Imperial headquarters about midnight.

24 Marshal Soult to the Chief of the Staff, Weyda, October 11, 1806, 10 p.m.

25 General Lasalle to General Belliard, Wachholder-Baum, October 11, 1806, 8 p.m.

26 The Grand Duke of Berg to the Emperor, Gera, October 11, 1806, 11 p.m. Gera is about 29 kilometres from Auma.

27 In reality, on October 11, the King and his army were not at Erfurt, but at Weimar.

28 Napoleon had passed the afternoon of the 11th at Gera, had conferred there with Murat, had, as it were, been present at the capture by Lasalle's hussars of a convoy bound for Camburg, and had questioned the prisoners, spies, etc. We see from Murat's letter that Napoleon had spoken to him, during the day, of his plan of moving part of his troops to Naumburg.

29 "Things are happening here exactly as I calculated two months ago in Paris, march after march, almost event after event. I was right about everything ... Interesting things will happen in two or three days, but everything appears to confirm my opinion that the Prussians have hardly any chance. Their generals are great imbeciles ... Dresden is completely unguarded" (the Emperor to Talleyrand, Auma, October 12, 1806).

30 The 4th division of dragoons (General Sahuc) formed part of the cavalry reserve. A part of this reserve was in the rear of the central column. At the head of the central column there was only, with Prince Murat, the brigade of hussars (Lasalle), the brigade of chasseurs (General Milhaud), having at this time only one regiment, the Beaumont division of dragoons (the 3rd) and the Sahue division of dragoons (the 4th).

31 It must, however, be added that on October 10 Marshal Soult had received from the Chief of the Staff an order to proceed to Gera.

On the other hand, on October 11, at 10 p.m., Soult wrote two letters: one to the Emperor and the other to the Chief of the Staff, stating the position occupied by his army corps and saying that, unless he received an order to the contrary, he would be at Gera on the 12th. Therefore he need only have been left to do so. The Emperor's short letter of October 12, 4 a.m., is but a confirmation of the order of the 10th.

32 Reference is made to the Saalfeld encounter. Until his instructions came Lannes was astonished that he had not yet received the Emperor's congratulations, and feared that his report on the fight had gone astray.

33 The Emperor's general order to Berthier, October 12, 4 a.m., said: "Marshal Ney will be at Mittel-Pöllnitz" (18 kilometres south-west of Gera.)

34 In this first part of the campaign, the 1st corp was to a certain extent placed under the orders of Murat, the Emperor's lieutenant-general.

35 Lasalle brigade at Mölsen, 3rd division of dragoons at Teuchern, headquarters of the cavalry at Teuchern, 13th chasseurs of the Milhaud brigade in the direction of Weissenfels and Naumburg, and the 1st corps at Meineweh. In brief, the whole of the

cavalry reserve was to the right of the Zeitz-Naumburg road, and bore against. Leipzig. As a result, on the evening of the 13th and the morning of the 14th, it was bottled up behind the 1st corps in the defile of the Basle, between Naumburg and Camburg, and consequently did not reach the battlefield of Jena in time. (See diagram below)

36   Mittel-Pöllnitz.

37   Vol. i. p. 54.

38   "In the profession of war, as in literature, each has his own style" (Napoleon to the King of Naples, Joseph, Saint-Cloud, January 6, 1806).

39   Here, as in the special order sent to Murat, the hour at which headquarters would be at Gera is not given.

40   See Petri's map of Saxony, with the aid of which the Emperor gave his orders.

41   Time given by Lannes to Berthier, in a letter of October 11, 1806.

42   In column and by companies, either spaced or in serried ranks, with the infantry apart from the road reserved for the artillery (Bonsal's *Manoeuvre d'Iena*, p. 291).

43   Hohenlohe's *Letters on Strategy*, vol. i. p. 76.

44   Preparatory order (instructions relating to the working of staffs).

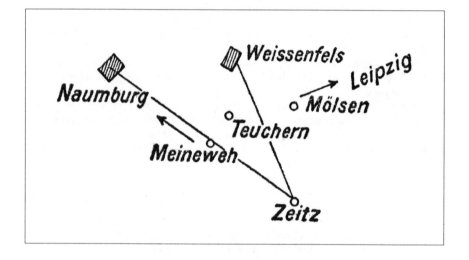

IV
Imperial Headquarters: The Emperor's Household

The Emperor's household—Berthier, Duroc, Caulaincourt—General
officers in the service of the Emperor—Aides-de-camp—Orderly
officers—Marshal of the Palace—Prefect of the Palace—
Chamberlain—Doctors and surgeons—Pages—Servants—The
Emperor's study and private secretaries: Bourrienne, Méneval, and
Fain—Secretaries of the Cabinet—Topographical office—Bacler
d'Albe and his duties as an officer of the staff—The information
department of the Emperor's Cabinet—Lelorgne d'Ideville, auditor
to the Council of State—Dictation of orders—Duties of the aides-
de-camp and orderly officers—The "Salon de Service"—Life at
Imperial headquarters—Cantonment arrangements—Service at
table—The Emperor *en route*—The carriages—Equitation—Order
of march of the Emperor's suite—The Emperor doubling the
columns—Women during the campaign.

B EFORE CONTINUING OUR EXAMINATION OF the action which the Emperor
exercised over his army by the superintendence of the execution of his orders
and the rewards which were the consecration of his control, we would reconsti-
tute the society in which he lived whilst on campaign and obtain as clear an idea
as possible of the life he led. What kind of existence did people lead at the great
Imperial quarters in the years of glory—in 1805, 1806, 1807, and 1809? Who were
the men who had the honour to live side by side with the Emperor?

Imperial quarters comprised two quite distinct departments: the Emperor's
military household and headquarters.[1]

The military household was composed of those whom Napoleon had
immediately about him, and of the staff in attendance on him: grand officers,
generals, aides-de-camp and orderly officers, secretaries, dignitaries, and Court
employees. This large staff entailed numerous other attendants and servants.
On December 21, 1806, the Emperor's household consisted of 800 persons.

In that gold-braided Court which followed the Emperor there were three
great dignitaries of the Crown who were on intimate terms with him: Berthier,

at one and the same time Vice-Constable, Master of the Hounds, Minister of War, and Chief of the Staff of the Grand Army; Duroc, Grand Marshal of the Palace; and Caulaincourt, the Master of the Horse. O that we possessed, in order to picture Napoleon on his campaigns, the memoirs or private correspondence of these three personages!

Having already spoken of Berthier, we know his defects and his qualities as Chief of the Staff. We will now complete the physical and moral portrait of this faithful companion-in-arms of Napoleon, who ever lived under the same roof as the Emperor, sitting at his table and in his carriage, following him everywhere on horseback whilst on his rounds and on the field of battle, sticking to him as close as his shadow from the first Italian campaign until the abdication at Fontainebleau, and finally killing himself in despair for having, in a moment of aberration, abandoned him.

"Berthier, small, stout, ever laughing, very full of business, and in love with Mme. Visconti,"[2]—such was Desaix's impression of the Berthier of the Italian days, and which he has left us in his account of a journey in Switzerland and Italy in 1797.

The very feminine and less succinct appreciation of the Duchesse d'Abrantes is no more flattering. "Berthier was small and, without however being deformed, was awkwardly built. His head was a little too big for his body, and his hair, of a colour which was neither dark nor light, was rather frizzy than curly ... His hands were naturally ugly, and he made them look still more frightful by continually biting his nails, so much so as to have almost always bleeding fingers. Add to this that he stammered a good deal and made not grimaces, but movements so singular in their vivacity that he provided great amusement for those who were not directly concerned with his dignity."

"He spoke with a strong nasal accent, and had almost always his hands in his pockets or a finger in his nose. His coat and trousers fitted badly and hung about his body."[3]

Generally speaking, he placed great importance in having everything around him done as at the Emperor's, and he carried this even to the point of affectation.[4] He seemed to wish to imitate his master in the choice of a small and simple hat which he wore after Napoleon's manner, consequently he was often mistaken for the Emperor, whom he resembled as regards figure when he was in his carriage. Always lively, he went at full speed on horseback and was always well mounted, which accorded perfectly with his duties as Master of the Hounds. He was passionately fond of sport, so much so that when an old crow passed above his head he let fall his reins, even whilst galloping, and pretended to fire a shot at it.

Despite Berthier's zeal for the service, and the severe tone in which he spoke to his subordinates, he was always polite.

His tone towards the Emperor somewhat resembled familiarity, but when Napoleon summoned him to his presence he assumed a very respectful air, and when he received orders, he walked for some time with his hat in his hand.[5]

Duroc, Duc de Frioul, was, like Berthier, a faithful companion of Napoleon. As Grand Marshal of the Palace, his functions included the authorization of payments (food, lighting, heating, servants, etc.) and the management and superintendence of the Emperor's household, which he kept in a remarkable order, "but," according to Mme. de Rémusat, "with inflexible rules, all of which were inspired by the Master's severity." When the Emperor grumbled, a succession of severe measures followed at the Palace, and the lowest footman felt the consequences. The attendance was carried out with military exactitude, punishments were severe and discipline was unrelaxed; consequently everything passed silently and regularly. Every error was repressed; the profits of the servants were calculated and regulated in advance. In the kitchens and dependencies the smallest thing, a mere plate of soup or a glass of sugared water, could not be distributed without the authorization or ticket of the Grand Marshal. Nothing happened in the Palace of which he was not informed. Duroc was discretion itself, and repeated everything, but only to the Emperor, who inquired about even the least important matters.[6] He also rendered to Napoleon services of a special nature—with Murat, Talleyrand, and others he attended, in the short intervals between business or battles, to Napoleon's feminine fancies.[7] The Duc de Frioul did not possess a brilliant mind, but one that was wise and just; he had few passions, but a deep power of reasoning and a naturally restricted ambition. With his careless and indifferent air, he appeared to care for nothing, unless it was Mlle. Bigotini, a *danseuse* at the Opera.

Although employing his influence with discretion,[8] he rendered a multitude of services to persons who did not know him. Simple, true, modest, upright, and disinterested, very attentive and exempt from small passions, he was very useful to the Emperor, whose entire confidence he possessed, and for whom he often made friends. Although already very busily occupied, he was often entrusted by the Emperor with foreign missions, and although he sometimes grumbled about the obligations of lofty positions, he always carried them out to Napoleon's satisfaction. Consequently, on June 7, 1813, the Emperor wrote to Mme. de Montesquiou: "The death of the Duc de Frioul has grieved me. For the first time for twenty years he has not divined what would please me."[9]

The duties of the Chief Equerry Caulaincourt, Duc de Vicence, included the superintendence of the stables, pages, messengers, and couriers. For the departures he received orders at sunrise and sunset. He had to accompany the Emperor everywhere. He walked before him when he left his apartments to mount on horseback, gave him his whip, held the left stirrup for him, and handed him the ends of the reins. He made certain of the solidity of the carriages, of the skill of grooms, drivers, and postillions, of the safety and training of the horses. On the road he was in a vehicle which preceded the Imperial carriage;[10] on horseback he had to hand to the Emperor the map of the district, ready to be consulted; if the Emperor's horse fell, the Chief Equerry's duty was to assist him to his feet and offer him his own mount.

Castellane, who, in his campaign diary, is rather severe on Duroc, has only praise for Caulaincourt, whom he depicts as follows:

"The Duke of Vicence, a man of five feet eight inches, has a severe and noble air; frank and loyal, is loved and esteemed by all. The Emperor prizes him, but as he tells him the truth, His Majesty prefers the Grand Marshal, who has a more flexible disposition. He is an excellent general officer, very military in character."[11] Although recognizing his good qualities, the Emperor was much more familiar with Duroc than Caulaincourt, whose manners, more ruled by etiquette, were colder. According to Odeleben,[12] Caulaincourt "thought with inexpressible zeal of all Napoleon's needs." He carried out his duties with "unparalleled exactitude and attention." "His chief quality was boundless activity. He possessed the talent of saying everything in a few words. After having spent the night working with Napoleon, he was at daybreak the first on duty ... He was almost always on horseback, and was constantly at the Emperor's door. After Puree's death he combined the duties of Grand Marshal with those of Chief Equerry, and the attendance of the household was carried out equally well. Like his predecessor, and with still more inflexibility as regards rules, he imposed in every department the most rigid economy." It was one of Napoleon's gifts to inspire such zeal in his servants, taking care, nevertheless, never to recognize their merit to the fullest extent. "Caulaincourt was mindless," said the Emperor to Gourgaud one day at St. Helena; "he did not know how to write and was merely an excellent Chief of the Stables."[13]

By the side, and under these officials, a few generals, without definite duties, but ready to be trusted with eventual missions, were near the Emperor. These, in October 1806, were Brigadier-General Corbinau, the Empress's equerry, and Brigadier-General Gardanne, governor of the pages. During the whole campaign the Emperor employed them as general aides-de-camp. At the opening of this same campaign, Major-General Clarke was also with the Emperor as *secrétaire du cabinet*, a post created by a decree of the 30th of

Vendemiaire, year XIII. In this capacity "Clarke was in charge of His Majesty's topographical office, and had to write, either from the Emperor's dictation or from his own notes, everything which referred to the administrations of war and the navy, plans of campaign, and all other objects relative to these departments which His Majesty might entrust to him. He was not permitted to have a clerk. He was authorized to employ a private secretary, but this private secretary under no pretext whatever could be acquainted with the above specified work or take any part in it."[14] Major-General Clarke, ex-chief of Carnot's topographical bureau, as much a scribe as a soldier, and a skilful, trustworthy administrator, certainly possessed all the necessary ability to make an excellent *chef de cabinet*, but these subordinate duties ill-accorded with his high rank and his personal importance;[15] consequently, in 1806, he was in his office but a short time, and was soon appointed, first of all Governor of Erfurt, and then of Berlin.

The military household consisted of the Emperor's aides-de-camp and orderly officers.

The aides-de-camp, almost always general officers selected from the faithful ones of early days, and all known for their conspicuous bravery, were entrusted with important missions, distant reconnoissances, and verbal communications to commanders of army corps. Napoleon liked to give them on the field of battle a momentary and perilous command, which would enable them to be classed in the front rank of the brave.

In 1806 we find the following as the Emperor's aides-de-camp: Brigadier-General Lemarois, "handsome Lemarois," who, known to the Emperor since the Toulon days, had been the First Consul's aide-decamp, and had signed as a witness Josephine's marriage contract; Brigadier-General Bertrand, whose bravery in Egypt had attracted Bonaparte's attention; Rapp and Savary, Desaix's two former aides-de-camp whom the First Consul had picked up on the battlefield of Marengo; and finally Mouton, a brigadier-general and an Alsatian like Rapp, with the same frank speech and the same bravery. Rapp, save on a day of battle,[16] was a weak and very insignificant man, but he pleased the Emperor, despite his "quite Germanic frankness," by his heroic horsemanship. Savary, in command of the picked gendarmery, was an all-round man, either diplomat, soldier, or detective, and one of whose duties was to watch over the Emperor's personal safety.

The orderly officers, aides-de-camp of the second class with the rank of major, captain, or lieutenant, were also employed on missions and in the transmission of orders, concurrently with the staff assistants. By a decree of September 19, 1806, their number was fixed at twelve. Recommendations and favour generally presided over the nomination of young officers to these choice posts. The

Emperor and Berthier often chose them from noble families that had joined the party of the Empire. In 1806 the Emperor's orderly officers were MM. Deponthon, captain in the engineers; de Lamarche, captain in the 4th Hussars; Scherb, in the 10th Cuirassiers; Castille, captain in the infantry; Eugène de Montesquiou, aide-de-camp to Marshal Davout; and Amédée de Turenne, captain. The last named, whom we find later in the position of Chamberlain and Grand Master of the Wardrobe, was one of the Emperor's favourites; witty and well-informed, he amused him by relating the news of the day. Napoleon nicknamed him, because of his Anglo-mania, "Milord Kinsester."[17]

In 1806 and 1807 the uniform of the Emperor's orderly officers was dark green, without embroidery, but with a gold shoulder-knot hanging from the left side, and attached to a buttonhole on the breast. Later, in 1810 and 1811, the uniform became more elegant, and was sky-blue with silver embroideries.[18] At the end of the Empire the expenses of a newly promoted orderly officer amounted for dress, equipment, and horses to at least 6000 francs.[19]

Each of the Emperor's general aides-de-camp had themselves as aides-de-camp two or three under officers whom Napoleon employed as his own orderly officers.

Joined to this military suite were a few Court personages.

During the 1813 campaign there was first of all, as Marshal of the Palace, Comte de Beausset, who for several years past had been in charge of His Majesty's kitchen staff. A good liver and gouty, Castellane depicts him in Spain, in 1808, as following the Imperial staff on his mule with meritorious zeal, and breaking drawing-room chairs into a thousand pieces under his enormous weight. He had under his orders, as Prefect of the Palace, Baron de Canouville, the brother of "handsome Canouville," one of the favourite lovers of Princess Pauline.

In 1813 Comte de Turenne d'Aynac, the orderly officer of 1806, was Chamberlain. The equerries were Baron de Mesgrigny and Baron Lenneps.[20]

Four Court physicians and four or five surgeons, including Ywan, who had gone through all campaigns and was invariably seen on horseback behind the Emperor,[21] formed part of the Imperial household.

A paymaster of the Crown was also attached to the household.

Four pages, who in case of need could be sent on messages, followed the Emperor to war. These, destined later to become cavalry officers, were recruited among the children of generals, high functionaries, and noble families who had rallied to the Empire. Between 1805 and 1814 a hundred and thirty young men entered the Imperial household as pages.[22] Among these pages we find the sons of Marshals Moncey and Oudinot, of General Gudin, young de Barral, nephew of the Archbishop of Tours, and Ferdinand de Lariboisiere, who, when sub-lieutenant in the 1st regiment of Carabineers, was killed at Moskowa. Their duties in the army were to lead the Emperor's horse, to carry the field telescope, to prepare the relays, etc.[23] Their undress included a three-cornered hat ornamented with a twisted knot and a silver cocade, a green coat with silver galloon, green velvet breeches, and riding boots.[24]

The quarter-masters of the Palace attended to the cleaning, furnishing, and victualling of the Imperial household. They wore a green uniform and had the rank of lieutenant. In 1806 two quarter-masters of the Palace, MM. Bayou and Deschamps, were under the orders of M. Philippe de Ségur, who then wore the epaulettes of a captain, was assistant to the Grand Marshal, and carried out the duties of Chamberlain.

An understaff of butlers, *valets-de-chambre*, cooks, outriders, and grooms was employed in domestic labours.

The Emperor's personal domestic staff consisted of four *valets-de-chambre*, who for a long time were Constant, Senechal, Pelard, and Hubert. Constant, the head *valet-de-chambre*[25] from 1800 to 1814, was veritably Napoleon's valet-de-ehambre; he habitually assisted in the toilette, and his help was indispensable to the Emperor, who, to use Constant's own words, was "helpless without a valet—*homme à valet-de-chambre*." Senechal was Constant's assistant.

After Constant, the most intimate of Napoleon's servants was the Mameluke Roustan. Within his Imperial master's bedroom, he helped him on with his boots, held the mirror when he shaved, and guarded him at night. Outside he carried out the duties of an outrider, following him on all his journeys with His Majesty's field-flask, greatcoat, cloak, and portmanteau. He was to be seen galloping at every parade, dressed in a gorgeous oriental costume.

Stable duties were entrusted to the head outrider Jardin *père*, who employed all his skill in preparing for the Emperor the best broken-in and reliable horses.

A commissary was specially responsible for the table, which he "farmed out."

To complete the description of the Emperor's household, we hasten to speak of his Cabinet. To Napoleon's mind, this was certainly the most important department in his immediate surroundings—it was the instrument with which he worked. It was from this sanctuary of genius that sprang those victories, the names of which will be for ever resplendent in military history.

The very restricted staff of Napoleon's Cabinet consisted of private secretaries, ministerial secretaries, and those of the topographical office. There were also in his Cabinet, as we have already seen, the *secrétaires du cabinet*, appointed by a decree of October 22, 1804, but their institution did not come up to the Emperor's expectations, and as they worked but intermittently we may regard them as a secondary part of the ministerial machinery.

What strikes us the most in this organization is the small number of employees who sufficed for the tremendous work incumbent on them. Two or three masters of requests or auditors to the Council of State—civilians who had no knowledge of military matters—"lived constantly within the sphere of this extraordinary man, whose volcanic mind gave birth to a thousand divers ideas,"[26] and were the only channels for transmitting to the staff, ministers, and all the authorities of France the orders which the Emperor addressed to them directly. Their instructions were, to be present day and night, ever ready to respond to the master's call; their duties, to take down rapidly and accurately from the Emperor's dictation, and to send his orders forth. They lived a sort of cloistered existence. "Méneval and Fain," wrote the Emperor at St. Helena, "lived so retired a life that there were chamberlains, who, after having served four years in the Palace, had never seen them."[27]

Napoleon did not like new faces, consequently he had the same private secretaries during the whole of the Empire. There were only three: Bourrienne, Méneval, and Fain.

Bourrienne held the post of private secretary until 1802. A former fellow-student of Napoleon at the Ecole Militaire, he possessed abilities, spoke German well, and was an intriguer, but also a thief. Such was Napoleon's judgment.[28]

"He was a thief to the extent of taking a casket of diamonds from a mantelpiece ..."added the Emperor. "When dictating orders in which I spoke of millions, his face changed and was lit up with satisfaction. It was a pity, because he was useful to me. He wrote a good hand, was active and indefatigable, was a patriot, and had no liking for the Bourbons. But he was too much of a thief." He became too important, gave *soirées*, and aped the manners of a prime minister. On October 20, 1802, Napoleon dismissed him under the pretext that Bourrienne had clandestinely participated in a contract for military supplies. He was replaced by Méneval, former secretary of Joseph Bonapart. Méneval—"little Méneval"as the Emperor called him when in a good humour—was in all the campaigns from 1802 to 1813. A learned and laborious student, he was a precious auxiliary to Napoleon, owing to the regularity of his work and attendance and his perfect discretion. Yet at St. Helena the fallen Emperor, sometimes so hard on his good servants, said of Méneval that he was but a clerk knowing hardly how to spell. From 1806 Fain, who "possessed more ability," was added to Méneval as secretary and archivist ; he replaced him as private secretary after the Russian campaign, whence Méneval returned fatigued and ill. During the splendid period of the campaigns of the Empire, "Méneval and Fain, to whom we must doubtless add an assistant archivist, Bary, constituted almost the whole of the staff of the Cabinet."[29]

As we have said, there were intermittently in the Cabinet officials of a higher order than the private secretaries, whose duties hardly exceeded those of a confidential clerk: these were the *secrétaires du cabinet* appointed by the decree of the 30th Vendemiaire, year XIII. We consider it interesting to give the full text of this decree, an extract from which we have already quoted above, because it clearly shows Napoleon's intentions regarding the organization and the working of the Cabinet, his intention to admit only a restricted and trustworthy staff in order to avoid indiscretions, leakages. "Mystery and secrecy," such was ever the watchword, and to Napoleon's thinking secrecy and bureaucracy were two incompatible things.

Decree appointing two Secrétaires du Cabinet of the Emperor and determining their Functions

SAINT CLOUD, 30th Vendémiaire, year XIII (October 22, 1804). There shall be appointed to the Emperor two councillors of state as *secrétaires du cabinet*. One of them will be in charge of His Majesty's topographical office, and will himself write, either from the Emperor's dictation or from his own notes, everything which concerns the War Office and the Navy, plans of campaign, and all other objects relative to these departments which His Majesty may entrust to him.

The other will compile the statistics of the various powers of Europe, and himself write, either from the Emperor's dictation or his own notes, everything which concerns Home Affairs and Finance, political plans, and all other objects relative to these departments which His Majesty may entrust to him.

Neither one nor the other may have a clerk.

If they have a private secretary, under no pretext whatever shall he become acquainted with the above specified work, nor shall he be employed in it in any manner whatever.

They will be on weekly duty for the analysis and work connected with petitions addressed to the Emperor.

This work they will also do without the aid of any clerk.

Necessary maps and plans will be drawn up either in the Navy Department, in the War Office, or in the Road-Surveying Department, in order that *no draughtsman or any other employee for this object* shall be in the Emperor's palace.

NAPOLEON

As already stated, General Clarke was for a certain time the holder of the head position as *secrétaire du cabinet,* and in this capacity he accompanied the Emperor at the opening of the 1805 campaign until the time he was appointed

Governor of Vienna. During the 1806 campaign, Clarke again appeared in the Cabinet, but he soon assumed the duties of Governor of Erfurt and then of Berlin, and his post as secretary remained unoccupied, like that of his colleague, until the month of February 1809. At this time one was given to M. Edouard Mounier, an auditor of the Council of State since 1806. The original duties were singularly restricted. Mounier, who knew most European languages, became the head of the office of translators attached to the Cabinet. He accompanied the staff on the campaigns of 1809, 1812, and 1813.

The second position as *secrétaire du cabinet* was held in 1810 by M. Deponthon, a most distinguished officer of engineers who had made his debut with the army of Italy, had gone through all the campaigns, and whom the Emperor, in 1806, had appointed as one of his orderly officers.

We have seen that the only duties of the *secrétaires du portefeuille*, destitute of all knowledge of military matters, were to write from Napoleon's dictation and send out his orders and notes, after having clearly transcribed them. Only in this mechanical way did they contribute to the Emperor's work; we must come to the topographical office to find the work relating to the preparation of military operations.

There was the same unchangeableness of the staff in the topographical office as in that of the *secrétaires du portefeuille*. The geographical engineer, Bacler d'Albe, who had already been employed as a geographical draughtsman to the staff of the army of Italy, was chief of the topographical office until 1813. In 1806, when major, he alone attended to this department. He became a colonel in 1807 and a general in 1813, at which time he had two assistants, MM. Duvivier and Lameau. Desaix introduces us to Bacler d'Albe in 1796 as "a little dark man, handsome, pleasant, well educated, talented, and a good draughtsman." In 1813 he had become, according to Castellane, who doubtless had a poor opinion of topographical science, "fat d'Albe, that pre-eminent topographer who is not over quick-witted." However that may be, he carried out his duties to the Emperor's satisfaction for seventeen years, which gives us a very good idea of his professional value. Castellane adds, however: "His perseverance and study had rendered him almost *indispensable* to the Emperor." Napoleon expressed himself in a few words; d'Albe understood him and carried out in his own manner and with independence (a very rare quality in the Imperial staff) the task imposed upon him ... He was in the particular confidence of the Emperor, who did not hesitate, however, "to rate him sometimes." Napoleon summoned him more often and more suddenly than any of his aides-de-camp. D'Albe had not a moment to himself. He was on duty day and night. He was always the last with whom Napoleon consulted at the hour of departure, the first whom he called to him at the moment of arrival. "Call d'Albe" were Napoleon's first words when, in the course of operations, an interesting despatch arrived in the middle of the night.[30]

What were the duties which thus made d'Albe indispensable to the Emperor? "He was principally charged with the rectification of maps, the combination and preparation of materials, the determining of marches and of all very extended lines of operation."[31]

On arriving at the cantonment, d'Albe saw to the installation of the Emperor's study. The portfolios containing papers, the maps, the two or three mahogany boxes with compartments in which was a travelling library, were spread out on tables when there were any, or on planks or doors supported by trestles.[32] In the middle of the room was a large table on which the best map of the seat of war was spread out. By means of colours, d'Albe had made clear on this map the position of rivers, mountains, or frontiers. This map was very accurately oriented before Napoleon entered, and with pins with heads of various colours there was marked, first of all the position of the different corps of the French army, and then the positions of the enemy as far as they were known. This was Bader d'Albe's business. In the four corners of the room were the secretaries.

At night time the map was surrounded by twenty candles, in the midst of which was a compass for measuring distances.[33] On the arrival of a despatch d'Albe made a summary report, the Emperor following with his finger on the map, and moving amidst the pins the compass, the extent of which corresponded to the distance of a march. Often the large scale of the maps forced the Emperor to stretch his whole length on the table and d'Albe immediately to do the same, in order to remain master of his ground. "I have seen them more than once," adds Fain, "stretched out on this large table, and interrupting each other by a sudden exclamation, right in the midst of their work, when their heads had too rudely come into collision."[34]

That is what made d'Albe indispensable, for all this preparatory work is the veritable work of a staff, singularly facilitating the arrival at a decision of the commander, resulting also in a great economy of time, and contributing more than one thinks to the success of operations. No other officer—not even Berthier—seems to us to have been associated in so close a manner with Napoleon's intellectual work. In this respect, Bader d'Albe held a unique position on the Imperial Staff; he alone carried out in Napoleon's presence those staff duties which we ought to consider as the most important, and which consisted in preparing the Emperor's decision. This is a point which up to the present has not, in our opinion, been sufficiently brought to light. It is regrettable that d'Albe left no memoirs, which we may imagine would have enabled us to follow step by step the evolution of Napoleon's thought during the decisive periods of his campaigns.

Crossing in this manner the frontiers of topography, Bacler d'Albe constantly placed under Napoleon's eyes the strategic chessboard; in a tangible form he kept him accurately informed of the situation of the army in relation to the enemy's positions. Nowadays this is the most important duty of every chief of the staff. Where did he find the information on which to base this work of centralization, which was the result of the sorting and re-arrangement of numerous documents, movement orders, reports relating to cantonments and the position of the corps, and information from various sources concerning the enemy?

The detailed report on the position of the Grand Army, drawn up in the *offices of the general staff,* was supplied daily to the Emperor[35] by Berthier.

Information about the enemy was presented to the Emperor "under the form of a résumé with a detailed report" by the head of the statistical office, which was one of the most important departments of the cabinet.[36]

In time of peace the Emperor possessed, thanks to his *book on foreign armies,* detailed information about the armies of Europe. "All the legations had secret instructions to keep a continuous record of all the movements of troops which passed under their eyes, or which came to their knowledge … This intelligence was the object of a special bulletin, and the Ministry (of Foreign Affairs) at Paris had an office set apart for its classification."[37] The head of this office, under the Ministry of the Due de Cadore, was the auditor to the Council of State, Lelorgne d'Ideville.

We find Lelorgne d'Ideville in the Emperor's cabinet, during the majority of the campaigns, in the position of secretary-interpreter for Northern languages, but under this title he was in reality the head of a veritable statistical office. "He was entrusted in the cabinet,"writes Méneval,[38] "with important work, which consisted in extracting from the despatches of our diplomatic agents and foreign publications, particulars about the composition as well as about the *movements* of foreign armies, and to present a résumé of them with a detailed report. The muster-rolls which M. d'Ideville succeeded in supplying were drawn up with so much sagacity and accuracy that the Emperor knew the composition of foreign armies quite as well as that of the French. During the Russian and German campaigns, the Emperor was constantly followed on horseback by the secretary-interpreter, whom he employed to question prisoners or country people, and to inform him of the contents of letters and reports which the chances of war threw in his way. He thus obtained, through the zeal and insight of M. d'Ideville, information which was often of great interest to him."

Espionage was another source of information. This department at Imperial headquarters was for several years under the direction of General Savary.

In 1805 all Mack's spies were bought very easily, and almost all the Austrian staffs were morally "done for." Fouché had handed to Savary all his secret notes concerning Germany, and the latter, with hands full of gold, quickly and successfully employed them through the assistance of the famous Schulmeister, a veritable turncoat.[39] This Schulmeister, indicated in Savary's letters under the name of "the emissary Charles," occupied the position of spy from 1805 to the end of 1809. He directed a veritable information office, and often went himself in search of facts, but he also sent out emissaries who, like himself, knew how to obtain entrance everywhere, and was acquainted with officers in each army.[40]

Each commander of an army corps had also an information office supplied with agents who went about and sent in news. Napoleon, in his letters, incessantly ordered his marshals to supply him with information concerning the enemy, and urged them to obtain it by all the means in their power. He often indicated to them on what points their investigations ought to be directed. All this information, coming from sources so various, enabled the statistical office "to seize the impress of truth,"[41] and to establish accurately that résumé with detailed report which was supplied to the Emperor, and which without doubt, when communicated to Bader d'Albe, enabled him to indicate on his map the probable positions of the enemy in juxtaposition to those of the Grand Army.

The Emperor, with the power of his personality and the activity of his mind, took a great part in the preparation of his decisions; he certainly did not wait for d'Ideville's reports and Bacler d'Albe's map to comprehend the *ensemble* and details of a military situation. But, in aiding him to co-ordinate and see at a glance the elements on which he formed his decision, d'Albe, and in a less degree d'Ideville, who is hardly known in history, were precious auxiliaries for Napoleon.

Before leaving the Imperial Cabinet we would complete our picture of the Emperor and the various phases of his work. We have just seen him working on the map with Bacler d'Albe before coming to a decision. The decision taken, he dictated his orders.

"When his idea had reached maturity," Méneval tells us, "he began to walk slowly about the room and traverse its entire length. He then began to dictate in a serious and emphatic voice, without resting for a moment. As inspiration came to him, his voice assumed a more animated tone, and was accompanied by a sort of habit, which consisted in a movement of the right arm, which he twisted, at the same time pulling the cuff of the sleeve of his coat with his hand. In rendering his thought, expressions came without effort. They were sometimes incorrect, but their very incorrectness added to the energy of his language, and ever marvellously described what he wished to say."[42]

"Whilst on campaign the Emperor dictated to General Clarke, *secrétaire du cabinet*, to M. Méneval , *secrétaire du portefeuille*, and to M. Fain, archivist. General Duroc, chief of the staff, M. Daru, general commissary of stores, the aides-de-camp, and, later, the first orderly officer, also wrote from the Emperor's dictation. In the absence of the *secrétaire du portefeuille* the Emperor dictated preferably to the one whom the order concerned, if he happened to be present. The one who wrote, himself wrote out clearly what the Emperor had dictated to him, whether an order or a note, and immediately handed it to him. Owing to the rapidity with which the Emperor dictated, it would have been impossible for any one other than he who had written to put the orders dictated by the Emperor in a clear form."

The dictations and minutes, which replaced the rough draughts, were written down the right-hand side of a piece of double elephant paper divided into two.[43] They were headed by the address: "To the Chief of the Staff, Marshal Soult." Within the margin, the secretary indicated the place, date, hour, and often a summary of the subjects contained in the despatch. He added the name of the officer or courier who carried the despatch and the hour of his departure.

Despatches, which were copied the first, in order to be sent off without delay, were on vellum-post, with gilt edge, little elephant size,[44] written without a margin and presented to the Emperor for his signature.

The archivist kept daily a numbered work-sheet, containing a summary of the despatches sent out during the day by the Emperor. These work-sheets bore, at the top, for example, "Feuille de travail number 13," and the date below, "Auma, October 12th, 1806," was written on one half of the paper, and constituted, a repertory of the Emperor's work. The archivist inscribed on the sheet the names of the officers or couriers entrusted with the despatches, and the hour of their departure. And when the Emperor changed his residence and worked twice on the same day, the same sheet of paper, with an indication of the new residence and hour, served the whole of the day.

What is truly surprising is that with so small a staff Napoleon was able to attend to all the matters he treated whilst on campaign. A few men sufficed, thanks to the simple and laconic method to which those around him were accustomed.[45]

Las-Cases gives us an interesting account of this method.

"The Emperor worked very rapidly. Letters and business matters were set in order in advance and placed on the Emperor's table before his arrival in his study. The Emperor quickly acquainted himself with everything. He settled many things in silence and threw aside everything which he considered useless. He read all letters himself, replying to some by a few words in the margin, and in the case of others dictating the reply. Those of great importance were always put on one side, *read twice, and never replied to until an interval had elapsed.* He believed in the principle that it was necessary to sleep over things calculated to put one out of temper. On leaving his study it was his custom to recall essential matters and to say they must be ready at the hour fixed; and they always were. Sometimes he said 'until tomorrow, night brings counsel,' a customary phrase with him."[46]

According to Méneval, Napoleon showed extraordinary facility and penetration in his work. Those who surrounded him were astonished at the systematic progress and abundance of his ideas in everything which he dictated to his secretaries or aides-decamp.

Ordinarily, he treated his secretaries with affectionate familiarity; sometimes he was even jovial and, laughing noisily, jested with them. On ordinary occasions his face bore a calm, meditative, and pleasantly serious expression. It was lit up with a most gracious smile, and his whole physiognomy was sweet and caressing when he was filled with good humour or the desire to please.

When excited by some violent passion his face assumed a severe and even terrible expression. It was translated into a series of movements on his forehead and eyebrows, his eyes flashed, and his nostrils dilated. But these passing movements did not disturb his mind. He appeared to be able to regulate these explosions, which moreover, with time, became more and more rare. His head remained cool ...

Thus, thanks to an excellent method, and also to great power of work, and by reducing his leisure hours to a strict minimum, Napoleon, with his masterly organization, alone gave impulsion not only to his army but to all the departments of the Empire. Confining ourselves to his military role, we can almost say that the whole of the intellectual activity of his staff was concentrated in himself. We cannot help admiring this prodigious effort of an exceptional man, but he must not be taken as an example, for, since man fails sooner or later, the edifice which he alone supports cannot but fall immediately into ruins, as happened to the Imperial throne.

Whilst the Emperor was working thus, what were his numerous aides-decamp and orderly officers doing? They were out on missions and journeys, outside work for which the Emperor utilized them a great deal. But this was almost the only useful thing they did. At headquarters they remained quite unconnected with any work of the staff; they had only to remain in the *salon de service*, ready to set off. "They read, played, conversed, or slept there," says Castellane, "as in every other *salon de service* in the world."[47] In Berthier's *salon de service* it was even forbidden to write.

A decree of April 29, 1809, settled the dirties of the Emperor's aides-de-camp as follows:

> The aide-de-camp on duty shall place every morning on the Emperor's desk the *liste de service* for which he is responsible.
>
> Those on duty shall be relieved every morning at seven o'clock by the following:
>
> Two general aides-de-camp during the day and one at night;
>
> An equerry;
>
> Half of the orderly officers;
>
> Half of the aides-de-camp of the general aides-de-camp; Half of the pages.
>
> At night the whole of this staff, with the exception of the general aide-de-camp and the equerry on duty, who have a room apart, shall sleep in the salon de service on mattresses, or carriage cushions, or even on straw.
>
> There shall always be a brigade[48] of the Emperor's horses, saddled and bridled, held in readiness by grooms, whilst a detachment of light cavalry-men shall also hold their horses by the bridle, in readiness. The horses of the aides-de-camp and general officers on duty shall also be saddled and bridled and held ready by grooms.

In what sort of an atmosphere did they live at headquarters? In one that was very agitated. Everybody was always on the alert. In the course of operations, according to Odeleben, everything at headquarters[49] was done on the spur of the moment. No one had any idea of regular work; there was no fixed hour for anything; everything happened unexpectedly and every one had to be ready to fulfil his task immediately. Unexpected moments of rest, unforeseen departures, changes in the hours fixed upon, and often also of the routes and stopping-places, followed one another continuously. People cudgelled their brains to know what was going to happen. The news, reports, and estafettes that came in constituted the pendulum which guided Napoleon in the distribution of his time.

Often in the middle of the night, about one or two in the morning, the Emperor would call one or several of those who were attached to his cabinet. "Call d'Albe and wake everybody," he would cry. He would then dictate for part of the night, retiring to his room again towards dawn and resting for at least an hour.

When, whilst working in his study, the time for setting off had come, the last word of his dictation had hardly fallen from his lips than he uttered the sharp order, "The carriage—to horse," and everybody who was to follow him rushed away as though set in motion by an electric current. Nobody was forewarned; only at that moment did they learn whither they were going.[50]

This kind of agitated existence was part of the Emperor's favourite system, which consisted in keeping people's minds in a state of anxiety, or, as he used to say, "on the alert."

Although admirably served and ever obeyed to the minute, says Mme. de Rémusat, he used to complain and spread a petty fear anent detail within the most private part of his palace. If the ardour of his conversation momentarily established moderate ease, one could immediately see that he feared advantage would be taken of it, and by a hard, imperious word he put in his place, that is to say in a state of fear, the person whom he had received and encouraged. He gave the impression of incessantly detesting repose both for himself and others ... To be in his employment was the hardest thing in the world. "The truly happy man," he himself said one day in an open-hearted moment, "is he who hides himself from me in the depths of a province, and when I die the world will utter a great exclamation of relief."[51]

Mme. de Rémusat, unappreciated at her true value, was, as we know, sometimes severe, in her *Mémoires*, on Napoleon; her testimony must not be accepted without being checked. But in this case we have many confirmations. Méneval, whose admiration is ceaseless, whilst describing the affectionate familiarity with which the Emperor generally treated his secretaries, tells us that he took care to "place sometimes in quarantine" his confidence in his best servants. Berthier himself, despite his zeal and devotion, had fits of despair. Sent one day by Napoleon to the Chief of the Staff, Méneval found him alone in his bedroom, with his head buried in his hands and his elbows on the table. Berthier looked at him with eyes full of tears. On being asked the reason for his distress, Berthier burst forth vehemently on the subject of his wretched position. "What is the good," he said, "of having given me an income of one million five hundred thousand francs, a fine house in Paris and a magnificent estate, to inflict upon me the tortures of Tantalus? I am being killed here with hard work. A mere soldier is happier than I am!" Then, passing his hand over his eyes, he exclaimed: "Well, what is the business? We must summon Salamon and Le Duo." These were his secretaries.[52]

However, apart from periods of active operations, there were periods of calm, as at Schoenbrunn, after Wagram. Let us listen to Castellane, then aide-decamp to General Mouton, who was aide-de-camp to the Emperor.

"Those on duty were relieved at seven o'clock ... We lunched at ten. At our table were orderly officers, the aides-de-camps of the general aides-decamp, officers of the guard who were on duty, quarter masters of the palace, pages, doctors, and the ordinary staff surgeons.

"Review at eleven o'clock (before the Emperor).

"We dined at five.

"The Emperor lunched after the review and dined at six or seven o'clock with the Prince of Neuchâtel and Prince Eugène. When the marshals were at Imperial headquarters, he also invited them to his table. His Majesty often walked after dinner in the gardens of Schoenbrunn, we following him. He went to bed at nine or ten o'clock and got up at night to work."

More or less agitated, according to events, but always full of contrasts and the unexpected, this exciting existence passed amidst the most varied surroundings—magnificent palaces, homely residences, simple cottages, or bivouacs in the open.

When Napoleon was going to spend the night in a town, the Prefect of the Palace, or a quartermaster of the court, went on ahead to make the necessary arrangements. Before the Emperor's arrival there was posted up in the *salon de service* a list indicating the quarters of everybody attached to the court. "When three rooms could be placed at the Emperor's disposal that was sufficient. The apartment was then composed of a *salon de service*, a study, and a bedroom. The Emperor being provided for, any other rooms in the house were for the Prince of Neuchâtel, the Grand Marshal, and the Grand Equerry. Corners could always be found for the secretaries and the staff surgeon Ywan. According to the size of the building you were either comfortable or crowded one on the top of another.

"When there was no study, the secretary worked in the bedroom.

"The room preceding the study or bedroom formed the *salon de service*.

"When this room was lacking, when, as the Emperor used to say, they were lodged à la Pologne,' the officers on duty established themselves on the staircase or in the vestibule, the livery servants were pushed back in the same manner and were crowded together in the outhouses of the courtyard.

"Independently of the room or apartment which the Prince of Neuchâtel occupied in the Emperor's house, he needed a neighbouring house for his staff, which formed *a company apart*."[53]

In the absence of a house, the soldiers of the guard constructed, as they did on the eve of Austerlitz or Jena, a shed or a straw shelter for the Emperor, or else they pitched in the midst of the encampment of the guard the five Imperial tents of blue and white striped canvas. Two of these tents communicated and served, one as Napoleon's bedroom and the other as his study. The chief officers ate and slept in the third; the fourth was used by officers of inferior rank, those who could find no place there remaining around the bivouac fire. Finally, the fifth was reserved for Berthier, who, after Napoleon, enjoyed the greatest prerogatives.[54]

Whatever his installation might be, the Emperor's first care was for his study. When he had only one room, there were placed by the side of his instruments of work—the portfolio containing papers, the travelling library, and Bader d'Albe's large map—his little iron bedstead, with curtains of green silk fringed with gold, and his dressing-case. It is within this narrow compass that we can now picture him, passing almost his entire days conceiving plans and manoeuvres.

Whilst on campaign, meals in the Emperor's household were served at four tables. First of all there was the Emperor's table, at which only Napoleon and Berthier ate, unless some important personage was at Imperial headquarters. In Berthier's absence, the Grand Marshal and the Grand Equerry took his place. The meal was served on a silver service bearing the Imperial arms, the golden eagle on an azure ground, and consisted of twelve to sixteen dishes. But Napoleon ate sparingly and drank little. His only indulgence was his chambertin wine, with which one may say he was never without on his campaigns, not even when in the Egyptian desert. Berthier, who took little part in the conversation, filled the Emperor's glass. Roustan or another valet-de-chambre waited at table. The repast generally lasted not more than twenty minutes. After dinner, Napoleon was fond of playing at whist and sometimes at vingt-et-un, a game which he preferred because every one present could take part in it. He often cheated whilst playing it and laughed over his trickery.

Of the three other tables, one was reserved for the members of the Emperor's Cabinet and the officers of the topographical bureau (Colonel d'Albe and his assistants), and another for the head officers, marshals, generals, and colonels, including the equerries, who, as barons, held the rank of colonel. The third table was that of the "petty officers"—orderly officers, pages, surgeons, doctors, and paymaster.[55]

In the course of operations this laborious existence was only interrupted by obligatory journeys, reconnaissances, visits to the troops, and changes of cantonment. Out of the twenty-four hours, nine at the most were devoted to sleep and rest, fifteen being productive of activity—an activity which was wholly directed towards the goal in view. This life, which, in the case of ordinary men, would have rapidly produced physical breakdown, was supported by Napoleon during his best years without apparent fatigue. Thus it was that, after the well-occupied days at the opening of the Jena campaign, he could write on October 13 from Gera to the Empress as follows:

GERA, October 13, 1806, 2 a.m.

I am to-day at Gera, *ma bonne amie*, and things are going very well, quite as I hoped they would ... I am in excellent health and have already increased in weight since my departure. Yet I travel from twenty to twenty-five leagues a day, on horseback, in my carriage, etc. I retire to rest at eight o'clock and rise at midnight. I imagine sometimes that you have not yet retired to rest. Ever thine.

Activity—activity in command—there we have one of the secrets of victory!

Such activity can only be shown by men who still possess the sacred fire and vigour of youth.

We have followed in detail the Emperor's life at headquarters, which was reduced in his case to a private room, serving the purpose of a study.

When he was not there he was on the roads or travelling across country "on horseback, in his carriage, etc.," as he wrote in October 1806 to the Empress. In this new form of activity Napoleon again sought to get the most he could out of his time.

The methods of transport employed by Napoleon in time of war were, according to circumstances, either horse or carriage. In proximity to the enemy, when the marches became manoeuvres or reconnaissances, the Emperor was on horseback in the midst of his troops.

When far from the enemy, he remained at headquarters, waiting until his marching corps were near the positions he had indicated. Economical of his time, he calculated the hour of his departure in such a manner as to be at the head of his corps at the very moment when his presence became necessary; on such occasions he travelled there rapidly in his carriage.[56] When with his army the Emperor had two kinds of carriages: post-chaise and a light calash.[57] The first was used for long journeys, the second to carry him from one corps to another, or to travel in a few hours over ground which the troops would take a day to cover.[58]

The interior of the post-chaise was arranged in such a manner that the Emperor could stretch himself out in it on mattresses and sleep as though in a bed, thus enabling him to travel at night without fatigue. A large lantern, hooked on to the back of the carriage, made it possible for him to work at night as though in his study. As we see, everything was so arranged that time spent on the road was not lost.

When he wished to show himself to the troops and follow the movements of the army nearer at hand, the Emperor rode on horseback. Badly seated on his steed, riding without any leg action and with loose reins, Napoleon was a mediocre horseman; but until 1809, the year in which he covered on horseback in five hours, at the rate of twenty-five kilometres an hour, the road from Valladolid to Burgos, he may be described as an indefatigable rider. In 1812 he had become stout, his vigour had diminished, and he no longer left his carriage until the last moment. He was not only an indefatigable but a very bold horseman;[59] he rode at a break-neck pace. When it was necessary to cover great distances on horseback, all the saddle horses were divided into brigades of nine.[60] These brigades were then placed at intervals in advance on the road to be followed, so that the Emperor always found fresh horses every ten or fifteen kilometres.

When the Emperor left his headquarters on horseback he was followed by a numerous staff. Amidst the crowd which pressed on his footsteps, Napoleon's simplicity and calm, and the gentle gravity of his face formed a strange contrast with the animation of his generals, the richness of their uniforms, and the elegance of their horses.[61] Behind the Emperor were the Chief of the Staff and the Grand Equerry, who carried a map of the district attached to a button of his coat—a map which was conveniently folded, in order that it might be consulted by Napoleon at any moment. Quite near followed a page, carrying a telescope in a case slung across his shoulders, and a soldier of the escort, on whose back was slung a leather bag containing a map, a writing-case, and a compass.[62] About fifty feet in front walked two orderly officers, preceded by a dozen horsemen of the squadron of cavalry on duty, commanded by a lieutenant. At a certain distance behind the Emperor's group came four squadrons, selected from each of the regiments of the Guard, chasseurs, Polish light horse, dragoons, and grenadiers. This escort was commanded by a general aide-de-camp.

All these officers, who pressed on Napoleon's footsteps, moving about and treading on each other's heels, in order to remain as close as possible to the Master, created a veritable obstruction. In 1813 an order regulated the formation of the suite which was to accompany the Emperor to the battlefield.

According to this order,[63] the staff which was allowed to follow immediately behind the Emperor included the Chief of the Staff, the Marshal on duty, the Grand Equerry, the two aides-de-camp and the two orderly officers whose turn it was to be on duty, the page, Roustan, an officer connected with the stables, and an officer-interpreter.

All the other aides-de-camp, orderly officers, generals, etc., came after the first squadron of the escort, which kept at a distance of fifteen hundred metres from the Emperor.

A conscript[64] of Geneva, Pierre Louis Meyer, who was enrolled in the 35th regiment of the line, has given in his *Memoirs*, published at Geneva in 1907, a striking picture of the Emperor passing in front of the columns of the army. His graphic description is as follows:

"For three days we saw young men leading magnificent Piedmontese asses, each of which carried two barrels of wine for the Emperor's household. Lieutenant Soyez, who was very friendly towards me, said, 'The Emperor will be passing soon—would you like to see him?' which question naturally 'pleased me.' He led me to the side of the road and, after waiting half an hour, we heard a confused murmur of 'Long live the Emperor!' at the same time perceiving in the distance a cloud of dust such as I have never seen before. The noise rapidly drew nearer and all the soldiers, raising their shakos on

the points of their bayonets, shouted 'Vive l'Emperor!' We saw the whole
Imperial staff arrive, a number of at least eighty, all on horseback, each one
more beautiful than the last and all covered with gold. The lieutenant had
only time to say to me 'There he is!' His white horse never galloped, for it had
been trained to go only at a quick trot. The marshals and generals, however,
came galloping forward. He wore his green coat of a chasseur of the guard,
with a little star and his cross of honour on his breast. There we have the way
in which this extraordinary man distinguished himself by his simplicity."

What importance did Napoleon attach to love during all his journeys across
Europe? To him it was an amusement, of which he did not deprive himself,
but which was ever kept subordinate to serious matters. "The Emperor was
very fond of women, but never allowed them to obtain any influence over
his mind. He looked upon love as a diversion, and in this respect he could
not have been more material, for the object of his affections of yesterday was
as nothing to him on the morrow."[65] Whilst on campaign Duroc, Murat,
Berthier, and Talleyrand, "the latter of whom," said the Emperor,[66] "had
always plenty of mistresses," undertook to satisfy Napoleon's passing fancies.

There was Mme. Fourès in Egypt, and Grassini at Milan before Marengo;
and there was also Mme. Walewska at Warsaw and at Finkenstein in 1807,
and at Schoenbrunn in 1809. But the last-named was not an amour of the
moment, but his left-handed wife—his Polish wife. In his journeys across
Europe we find still many other love adventures, momentary fancies for
which he paid two hundred louis, but which a captain of his army could have
obtained for twenty francs.[67]

What is important to note in all this is that at an age at which many clever
men compromised their work on account of the eternal feminine, Napoleon
had the will-power to resist this seduction. He himself drew attention to
Murat's example, and pointed out how he had committed many faults whilst
on campaign, owing to the fact that he liked to have his headquarters every
evening in a château where there was a pretty woman.

"I never ran after women," said the Emperor at St. Helena. "At the time of
my second Italian campaign I told Berthier to send for Grassini, who could
never understand why I had disdained her during my first campaign, when she
was only sixteen. But I had other matters to attend to then. What would have
become of a general-in-chief of twenty-five if he had run after the fair sex? All
the women of Italy were on their knees before the liberator of their country."

NOTES

1 Headquarters was itself divided into the headquarters of the Staff and that of the General Commissary of Stores.

2 Mme. Visconti, the wife of Marquis Francesco Visconti (Ambassador of the Cisalpine Republic in Paris; died in 1808), was "tall and beautiful," writes Desaix in his journal; she was the widow of Jean Sopransi, the friend of Mme. Bonaparte. All her contemporaries praise the beauty of her face and figure. Although she openly received Berthier, and his infatuation for her was the subject of the laughter of all the young officers of the staff, he loved her to the end, and in 1814 made her a settlement of 40,000 francs a year. The portrait of Mme. Visconti, who has justly been called "Berthier's folly," was painted by Gerard and is in the Louvre. (Note in *Journal de voyage du General Desaix, en Suisse et en Italie* (1797), edited by Arthur Chuquet. Plon, Nourrit et Cie, 8, rue Garanoière, Paris.)

3 *Mémoires militaires de Grabowski,* a Polish officer attached to the General Staff of Napoleon I 1812, 1813, 1814, p. 219.

4 *Mémoires du baron Fain,* p. 241.

5 *Relation circonstanciée de la campagne de 1813 en Saxe,* by Odeleben, a Saxon officer attached to the Imperial Staff, p. 198.

6 *Mémoires de Mme. de Rémusat,* vol. iii. p. 317.

7 *Ibid,* vol. i. p. 121.

8 *Journal de Castellane,* p. 85.

9 The Grand Marshal was the chief of the prefects of the Palace. His coat was amaranthe coloured, and was entirely embroidered with silver down to the waist. The prefects of the Palace wore the same colour with less embroidery.

10 Imbert de Saint-Amand's *La Cour de d'Impératrice Josephine,* p. 75.

11 *Journal de Castellane,* p. 93.

12 Odeleben's *Relation circonstanciée de la camipagne de 1813 en Saxe,* pp. 83 and 147.

13 "Gallant, amiable, joining the forms of the old court to the more real value of the men of the military court of the Emperor," says Mlle. Avrillon in her *Mémoires,* "Caulaincourt had a durable *liaison* with the beautiful Mme. de Canisy, a lady of the Empress's palace and wife of the Emperor's Equerry" (*Mémoires de Mile. Avrillon,* vol. ii. p. 38 *et seq.*).

14 Imperial decree of the 30th Vendémiaire, year XIII. (October 22, 1804), creating two *secrétaires de cabinet* and stating their functions.

15 It will be remembered that during the first Italian campaign, Clarke was delegated by the Directory to spy on Bonaparte. Instead of doing this, he colluded with him.

16 A letter from Napoleon to Davout, Paris, December 2, 1811.

17 Masson's *Napoléon chez lui,* p. 100.

18 *Mémoires du baron Fain,* p. 235.

19 *Vie de Planat,* p. 204.

20 In 1813 the uniform of the superior civil employees of Napoleon's household, such as chamberlains and equerries, was the same as that of orderly officers: light blue coat with elegant and rich silver embroidery and a black plumed hat (Odeleben).

21 *Mémoires du baron Fain,* p. 254.

22 Masson's *Les Cavaliers de Napoléon,* p. 175.

23 Odeleben's *Relation de la campagne de Saxe en 1813,* p. 180.

24 Charles Duplessis' *L'Equitation en France.*

25 The uniform of the head *valet-de-chambre* was: "A French coat of green cloth with facings and collar enriched with gold embroidery, a waistcoat of white kerseymere, black breeches, and silk stockings." Green was the Emperor's colour and was worn by the whole of his personal staff.

26   Odeleben's *Relation circonstanciée de la campagne de Saxe en 1813*, p. 140.

27   Note written in the Emperor's hand on a copy of the *Mémoires de Fleury de Chabouton*.

28   *Journal in édit de Gourgaud à Sainte-Hélene*, p. 565.

29   Masson's *Napoléon chez lui*.

30   Odeleben's, *Relation circonstanciée de la campapne de Saxe en 1813*, pp. 157 and 158.

31   *Ibid.*

32   *Mémoires du baron de Méneval*, vol. iii. p. 42.

33   Odeleben's *Relation circonstanciée de la campagne de Saxe en 1813*.

34   *Mémoires du baron de Fain*, p. 40.

35   Circular from the Chief of the Staff to the Chiefs of the Staffs of the army corps, Würsburg, September 29, 1806: "… I order you (also) always to send me, without delay, the position of your cantonments when any change has been made in them, His Majesty having *expressly* ordered me to hand him daily a detailed report relating to the position of the Grand Army" (Foucart's *Campagne de Prusse … Jéna*, p. 192).

36   Méneval, vol. i. p. 402.

37   *Mémoires du baron de Fain*, pp. 82 and 83.

38   Méneval, vol. i. p. 402.

39   *Mémoires de Fouché*, vol. i. p. 339.

40   See *L'Espionnage militaire sous Napoléon Ier* by Paul Müller.

41   *Mémoires du baron de Fain*, p. 84.

42   *Mémoires du baron de Méneval* , vol. i. p. 420. Napoleon had a poor memory for proper names, which he often altered. He said, for example, Caligula for Kalouga, Macon for Mouton, Glogau instead of Gourgaud.

43   The whole of this passage is taken almost textually from Foucart's precious work *La Campagne de Prusse* (Jéna, p. 880), from which we have taken many of the elements for this study.

44   Format double elephant is 0.320 x 0,195; little elephant is 0,230 x 0,185.

45   Odeleben's *Relation circonstanciée de la campagne de Saxe en 1813*.

46   Las.Cases' *Souvenirs*, p. 231.

47   *Journal de Castellane*, p. 66.

48   The brigade consisted of nine horses, two of which were for the Emperor and seven for his suite.

49   In Paris, as on campaign, the Emperor "lived anyhow," as he used to say; there was no regularity whatever in his habits. Excess of work kept him in his study and at home; he never dined out, rarely went to the theatre, and hardly ever appeared except at times and in places when and where he was not expected … To this manner of living he attributed the fact that he had escaped numerous attempts on his life (Las-Cases' *Souvenirs de l'Emperor Napoléon*, vol. i. p. 192).

50   According to the Polish general, Roman Soltyk, attached to Napoleon's staff in 1812.

51   *Mémoires de Mme. de Rémusat*, vol. i. pp. 125 and 266; vol. iii. p. 237.

52   Méneval's *Mémoires*, vol. iii. p. 48.

53   Fain's *Mémoires*, p. 238.

54   Odeleben's *Relation circonstanciée de la campagne de Saxe en 1813*.

55   According to Méneval's *Mémoires* and Odeleben's *Relation circonstanciée de la campagne de Saxe en 1813*.

56   Gourgaud's *Examen critique de l'ouvrage du comte de Ségur*.

57   Fain's *Mémoires*, p. 230.

58   "Dressed in his uniform and with his head covered with a checkered handkerchief, the Emperor could sleep in his carriage as though in his bed. In the interior of his carriage were a number of drawers with locks and keys, containing news from Paris, reports, and books. Opposite Napoleon was placed a list of the relays. A large lantern hung at the back of the carriage and lit up the interior, whilst four other lanterns illuminated the road. The

mattresses, which Roustan arranged, were skilfully packed into the carriage, and beneath the basket were stored a small reserve of torches. Roustan was alone on the box, and six powerful Limousine horses, driven by two coachmen, drew the coach, which was simple, green, supplied with two seats, and well suspended. There was a difference between the Emperor's seat and Berthier's, inasmuch as the one who accompanied Napoleon could not lie down "(Odeleben's *Campagne de 1813 en Saxe*, p. 185).

When the Emperor left his post-chaise to move with his troops, the vehicle was left with the rear-guard and the baggage-carts of the Imperial household. These were what were called "les gros equipages." This section, in charge of an equerry and under the escort of a picked detachment of gendarmerie of the Guard, followed at a distance of two or three days' journey.

59 Napoleon rode like a butcher. He held the bridle in his right hand, with the left arm pendent. He looked as though he were suspended on his saddle. Whilst galloping, his body rolled backwards and forwards and sideways, according to the speed of his horse. As soon as the animal stepped aside, its rider lost his seat, and as we know Napoleon more than once was thrown" (Odeleben's *Relation circonstanciée de la campagne de Saxe en 1813*).

"He (Napoleon) rode competently but without grace. Arabian horses were trained for him; he preferred them because they could stop suddenly. But as they also started suddenly, and as he held his bridle carelessly, he would often have fallen if the necessary precautions had not been taken. He liked to gallop down steep slopes, at the risk of breaking the necks of those following him. He had several falls which were never mentioned, because it would have displeased him" (*Mémoires de Mme. de Rémusat*, vol. iii. p. 230).

"The Emperor never used the spur, nor the pressure of the calves to set off his horse at a gallop; he started it with a touch of his whip "(Chlapowski's *Mémoires*, p. 128).

"The horses which the Emperor usually rode were Arabians; of small size, greyish-white coat, good-tempered, gentle gallopers, and easy amblers" (Pain's *Mémoires*, p. 248).

"The horses, very well broken in, were trained with the greatest care by the groom Jardin, who accustomed them to all sorts of sounds and to the sight of all kinds of objects. They even went as far as driving dogs or pigs between the horses' legs" (*Mémoires de Constant*).

60 "In each brigade there was a horse for the Emperor, one for the Grand Equerry, one for the equerry on duty, one for the secretary, one for the surgeon, one for the page, one for Houston, one for the groom and one for a servant. Spare horses were grouped around the brigade for the special use of the Prince of Neuchâtel, aides-de-camp and orderly officers" (Baron Fain's *Mémoires*, p. 238).

61 *Souvenirs du general baron Paulin*, p. 21.

62 Fain's *Mémoires*, p. 236

63 Quoted by Pierron in *Méthodes de guerre*, vol. i. p. 461.

64 Swiss soldiers in the pay of a foreign Power (taken from *Le Temps*, January 1, 1908).

65 *Mémoires de Mlle. Avrillon*, vol. ii. p. 282.

66 *Ibid.*

67 See Frederic Masson's *Napoléon et les femmes*.

V

Imperial Headquarters: The Staff

Berthier's staff—Cabinet of the Chief of the Staff: its composition and duties—Private staff and aides-de-camp of the Chief of the Staff; composition of the General Staff—Officers entrusted with army orders at the General Staff; offices of the General Staff and their duties—The great Imperial quarters; the small headquarters of the Emperor—Essential difference between the role of the General Staff and the armies of the First Empire and that of the German Army of 1870—Restricted role of the Imperial Staff corresponding to the essentially personal method of command of Napoleon—Missions—Transmission of orders—Conclusions.

S IDE BY SIDE WITH THE Emperor's household, and forming, as Fain tells us, "a world apart," was what we may call Berthier's staff. It was also an organization lacking in unity and with more or less perfect departments, very different from the great General Staff of a modern army. What we call Berthier's staff consisted of the private staff of the Chief of the Staff, the offices or cabinet of the Chief of the Staff, and finally the General Staff properly so called. The last named was itself divided into two categories of officers: the officers of the General Staff entrusted with army orders and the officers of the *offices of the General Staff*, offices quite distinct from those designated above under the appellation *offices of the Chief of the Staff*.

As we have already said, the role of the Chief of the Staff and his assistants was simply to transmit the Emperor's orders and see to the *details* of the army. "The Emperor alone gave movement, he alone directed all the departments."[1] We will see how the work was divided amongst the various organs of Berthier's staff.

We must first of all recall the fact that until August 9, 1807, Berthier was at one and the same time Chief of the Staff and Minister of War.

During campaigns he was replaced at the Ministry in Paris by a general secretary. For a long time this official was M. Denniée *père*, who had had Napoleon's confidence and Berthier's friendship since 1957.

As long as he was Minister, Berthier reserved to himself, whilst on campaign, the work of the staff, the division of the funds of his department, the sending out of the orders given by the Emperor concerning movements, operations, the offices of the artillery and engineers and the prisoners of war.

All this part of the work was attended to by the "offices of the Chief of the Staff," which were also called the "cabinet of the Chief of the Staff." This cabinet was composed of a dozen civil employees or non-combatants—modest and indefatigable workers of tried zeal and conscience. We would name Muster-Master-General Le Duc, Berthier's private secretary, who was trusted with his personal correspondence, and the safeguard of the archives and safe of the General Staff.

Sub-Inspector of Reviews Dufresne was head of the book-keeping department and interior administration of the Chief of the Staff.

As Minister of War and Chief of the Staff, Berthier had funds at his disposal and passed orders for payment, and in accordance with the Emperor's orders he delegated his powers either to marshals or to heads of departments.

He sent all applications for money to M. Dufresne, the chief accountant, who after examining them was in a position to decide. M. Dufresne was entrusted with all the correspondence concerning funds (credits, pay, etc.) with the Minister Director of the Army administration, the Commissary of Stores, the heads of departments, the Paymaster-General, and the Receiver-General of Public Taxes. M. Dufresne, with an employee under his orders, had also to do with the army staff as regards promotions, decorations, pensions, etc., decrees, *lettres de service*, and notices.

A retired captain, "whose serious wounds and a bullet in his thigh did not prevent him being at his hard work both night and day,"[2] M. Salamon, saw to the movement of troops, a duty which he had carried out in the office of the Chief of the Staff during all the campaigns from 1805 to 1814.

By "movement of troops" is meant all the Emperor's orders concerning movements, the sending out of orders to marshals, heads of departments, etc. (minutes; sending out of orders; notices to all the authorities who were expected to know the movements ordered; registration), the writing out of orders concerning new organizations (army corps, divisions, etc.), reports to the Emperor informing him in detail of the sending out of his orders and asking him for his instructions regarding questions submitted to the Chief of the Staff, the recapitulations demanded by the Emperor presenting the state of such and such a part of a department in regard to the execution of his orders, the condition of the troops rejoining the army, and the sending to the Ministry in Paris all the work intended for it.

Marshals and generals commanding army corps, governors, commanders of ports, and various heads of departments addressed their reports and requests to the Chief of the Staff, who presented them to the Emperor; moreover, they wrote direct to the Emperor when he had written to them, or when they considered it necessary to communicate with him, but this direct correspondence did not exempt them from detailed reports to the Chief of the Staff.

The correspondence through the channel of the Chief of the Staff was the essence of the organization of the Grand Army.[3] With the aid of a few employees, the indefatigable Salamon attended to the whole of this work.

Outside the cabinet, the Chief of the Staff had near him a certain number of general and superior officers who were personally attached to him and who, with his aides-de-camp, formed what was called the private staff of the Chief of the Staff. These generals, colonels, and adjutant-majors were, in reality, although not bearing the title, Berthier's chief aides-de-camp. He entrusted them with missions which could only be committed to the charge of officers of high rank.

This private staff was under the orders of one of the general aides-de-camp. On October 2, 1806, it was Colonel of Engineers Blein who carried out the duties of assistant Chief of the Staff. At the same time he was in charge of the secret section of the cabinet, the classification of reconnaissances, and the Marshals' correspondence.[4]

The number of the aides-de-camp of the Chief of the Staff varied at different periods; there were six in 1805, as many as thirteen in 1807, and nine in 1812. They ranged in rank from colonel to sub-lieutenant. "They were distinguished more by their personal courage and the elegance of their manners," says Baron Fain,[5] "than by the red trousers which formed the salient colour of their uniform." On December 8, 1808, the Emperor made his solemn entry into Madrid, and a review was held on the Prado. Berthier's aides-de-camp were noticed for the elegance and beauty of their appearance. "Almost all possessed fine figures and agreeable faces. They wore crosswise a Hungarian pelisse of black cloth, a white dolman with gold braid and fur, broad trousers, and a shako of scarlet cloth surmounted by a white aigrette of heron's feathers. These clothes were enriched by galloons and numerous twisted fringes and gold buttons. A fine black silk and gold waistbelt, a small cartridge-box, a sabretache, and a Damascus sabre completed the costume. The parade horses were grey-white Arabians, with long silky flowing manes, and carried a bridle *à la hussarde*, with gold galloons and tassels, whilst a panther skin, festooned with scarlet and gold, covered the saddle."[6]

In 1812, in the midst of Berthier's aides-de-camp, one might have imagined oneself, according to Fezensac, in a drawing-room of the Faubourg St. Germain. The companions of Fezensac, who was then aide-de-camp to the Chief of the Staff, were MM. de Girardin, de Flahaut, de Noailles, de

Montesquiou, Le Couteulx, and d'Astorg. In the account-book for February 1807, thirteen officers are inscribed as aides-de-camp of the Chief of the Staff, among them being the son of Mme. Visconti, Captain Sopransy, whom poor Berthier wished to make into a hero,[7] and "handsome Canouville," the favourite lover of Princess Pauline Borghèse.

In 1813 we find, amongst this gilded youth, two brothers, the Ducs de Bauffremont, Berthier, brother of the Prince of Neuchâtel, and Laczinski, brother of Mme. Waleska. As can be seen, Berthier was easily affected by recommendations. With the character we know he possessed could it have been otherwise?

However, these aides-de-camp were only employed like those of the Emperor, on outside missions or mere copying work, without any connection with what one can call the work of the staff. There was nothing arduous, as Fezensac tells us, in their work. They were rarely on journeys, on which the officers of the staff were usually sent. In camp two of them were on duty daily: one to carry orders, the other to receive despatches and officers sent out on missions. Each one's turn came only once every four or five days. This little aristocratic clan naturally did not show boundless devotion to the Emperor. In 1812, at Moscow, criticisms and even insulting remarks against the Emperor always came from the Prince of Neuchâtel's. The Emperor was aware of it and did not like Berthier's staff.[8]

The General Staff was quite distinct from Berthier's cabinet and private staff; it was much further removed from the Chief of the Staff and was housed apart, whereas Berthier had his cabinet near him, in the same house as the Emperor. "The Emperor made his appearance fairly frequently in the Prince's office," writes M. Deniée *fils*, the inspector of reviews who belonged to the cabinet of the Chief of the Staff in 1812, "and never left without showing kindness to one of us; the most absolute silence was observed, and entrance was forbidden even to the aides-de-camp on duty" who were in the *salon de service*.

Unlike the cabinet, the staff was constituted only of officers.

Three assistant Chiefs of the Staff divided the work of the General Staff.

The first assistant Chief of the Staff bore the title of Chief of the General Staff and directed the work as a whole. Berthier gave him his orders in writing, just as the Chief of the General Staff submitted questions to Berthier in the form of letters or reports.

As special work, the head assistant Chief of the Staff directed all the details of the work and was in direct correspondence regarding them with the Chiefs of the Staff of the Army Corps. He organized the communications and rear of the army—the work of the troops, detachments of recruits, convoys, and evacuations. He regulated the outside work of officers and the office work of the General Staff. General Andréossy (1805), Adjutant-Major Hastrel (1806),

General Lecamus (1809), and General Count Monthyon (1812–13) successively carried out the duties of Chief of the General Staff.

The second assistant Chief of the Staff was in charge of camps, marches, and cantonments. His duties were clearly set forth in the following letter addressed from Boulogne by Berthier on the 14th of Fructidore; year XIII, to Major General Mathieu Dumas:

To Major-General Dumas

BOULOGNE, 14 of Fructidor, year XIII.

I beg to inform you, General, that the Emperor has chosen you for employment on the General Staff of the Grand Army immediately under my orders as Chief-of-the-Staff and with the title of Assistant Chief-of-the-Staff, Quartermaster of the Army. Camps, marches and cantonments will be entrusted to you. Under your orders will be an adjudant-major and four assistants.

I have ordered that each General-in-Chief (commanding an army corps) shall appoint in his army an adjudant-major, charged exclusively with the same duties as those entrusted to you on the General Staff. These officers will correspond direct to you, receive your instructions and be responsible to you.—I beg to remain with the highest regard,

MARSHAL BERTHIER

Another letter written by Berthier at the beginning of the campaign of 1805 will give us an idea of the work required from the second assistant Chief of the Staff.

Marshal Berthier to General Mathieu Dumas

(Without either address or date)

I beg you, General, to find me immediately a route for Marshal Murat, who is leaving Stuttgard for Goettingen.

See if that can be done in a day's march. Find me a route for Marshal Ney from Stuttgard to Heidenheim, via Esslingen, Gceppingen, and Weissenstein, leaving on the 12th and arriving on the 15th.

Trace another route for Marshal Lannes from Ludwigsbourg to Aalen, via Schorndorf and Gmund, leaving on the 12th and arriving on the 16th. Mark on the map, in accordance with your knowledge of the country, the day's marches.

I desire General Dumas to hand me this work in half an hour.

(Signed) MARSHAL BERTHIER

Routes were only roughly sketched out, great latitude being left to commanders of army corps in the choice of roads, cantonments, or bivouacs. Sometimes this latitude was not without inconveniences. To establish order in the movements of the columns, Mathieu Dumas was constantly on the road, rushing from one column to another, in order to recognize and fix the routes in conjunction with the marshals.

The third assistant Chief of the Staff was specially entrusted with the topographical department. During the greater part of the campaigns of the Empire; General Sanson was at the head of this office. He had ten officers and geographical engineers under his orders. His duties were to draw up each day a plan of the positions occupied by the army, to direct reconnaissances, collect topographical information, survey positions, battlefields, and, if necessary, draw up a map of the districts conquered or occupied. All these maps and reports on reconnaissances, necessary for operations and kept in the Emperor's topographical office, were preserved in duplicate at the topographical office of the General Staff.

Under the orders of the assistant Chiefs of the Staff, officers of various ranks—adjutants, commanders, majors, assistant captains of the staff[9]—were employed at the General Staff, either inside or outside the office, according to the category to which they belonged. These, when holding the rank of adjutant-commander, were employed in reconnaissances, visits, and temporary commands of frontier towns; when majors, they were also put in provisional command of frontier towns and co-operated with captains in carrying orders; when assistant captains, "entrusted at the General Staff with army orders," their principal duty was to assure, concurrently with aides-de-camp of inferior rank and orderly officers, the transmission of orders.

The officers of the "offices of the General Staff" formed a category quite distinct from the preceding one, and this specialization of officers is a characteristic of the Imperial Staff. These officers were also sent at times on missions and tours of inspection, but they were not employed to carry orders.

In 1806 the offices of the General Staff comprised three adjutant-majors, a major, seven captains, and, in addition, for General Sanson's topographical office, three commandants and six geographical engineers. The organization of October 2, 1806, made known the questions examined in the offices of the General Staff, questions almost exclusively of an administrative order.

The organization of October 2, 1806 divided the work between three divisions, exclusive of the topographical office. Although this separation into divisions was not maintained, we find in the statement of this organization the enumeration of business treated in the offices of the General Staff.

First division: general supervision of work, orders of the day, watchwords, dispatching of orders, letters and packets, officers' *ordres de service*, movements, muster-rolls, information, commandants of fortresses and general correspondence.

Second division: accommodation for chief headquarters, police, gendarmerie, subsistence, distributions, and hospitals.

Third division: prisoners of war and deserters, *requisitionnaires* and conscripts, military justice.

The Emperor's household and Berthier's staff constituted but a small part of the Imperial quarters. "To form an idea of the population of Imperial headquarters," writes Baron Fain, "you must add to the household of the Emperor and that of the Prince of Neuchâtel:

"That of the minister, the Secretary of State;

"That of the General Commissary of army stores;

"That of the Treasurer;

"That of the Commander-in-Chief of the artillery;

"That of the Commander-in-Chief of engineers;

"That of the *colonels generaux* of the Guard;

"Sometimes even that of the Minister of Foreign Affairs; finally the whole of the Imperial Guard in the midst of which the Emperor usually lived."[10]

"When the Prince of Neuchâtel," Fezensae tells us, "reviewed the grand Imperial headquarters at Vilna in 1812 one might, at a distance, have taken it for troops in battle array. Picture the gathering together at the same spot of everything composing that staff, imagine the prodigious number of servants, led horses, and baggage of all kinds which it dragged after it, and you have some idea of the spectacle presented by chief headquarters."[11]

When in movement this numerous staff divided itself into fractions according to needs. The little vanguard, which was also called little headquarters, followed the Emperor. It was the battle staff. The rest of the grand Imperial headquarters remained in the rear, often at a distance of several days' journey, and sometimes itself divided into several parts.

For example, in 1812, at the opening of the campaign, the headquarters of the General Staff, which included, with the general staff, the staffs of the artillery and the engineers, and a part of the administration, rejoined at Schippenheil the Emperor's little headquarters, whilst the headquarters of the commissary of stores was at Koenigsberg, the centre for supplies.

To move and to encamp so huge a body as the grand Imperial headquarters the following arrangements were made.

An assistant Chief of the Staff held chief command over grand headquarters. His duties consisted in seeing everything that happened, in maintaining order, and in looking after the safety of headquarters, and in inspecting detachments proceeding either to the army or to the hospitals. He was the common centre of all who came and went. He had no authority, however, over the Emperor's Guard and household, which possessed a special organization. A general baggage-master of the army was responsible for everything connected with vehicles.

In brief, the commanding staff of grand headquarters was strongly constituted; that was indispensable for the maintenance of something like order in such a body, composed of so many heterogeneous elements.

Having taken this general view of grand headquarters, let us return to the staff. In modern armies, the staff is the service whose mission it is to formulate and to transmit the wishes of the Commander-in-Chief. But this is only part of its role; another part, and not the least important is to collect, group, and submit to the Commander-in-Chief in a concrete form the information of all sorts which serves as a basis for his decision. The staff also works in close collaboration with the Commander-in-Chief, who remains, however, entirely responsible for the decisions come to. This conception of the role of the staff was bequeathed to us by the German army, in which it was applied with the success we know of during the Franco-German war of 1870. Under the nominal command of King William, the German armies were in reality commanded by General von Moltke, Chief of the Staff, who was above all entrusted with the strategical department. Side by side with General von Moltke, the chief staff comprised in all fifteen officers, of whom three were aides-de-camp. There was first of all General von Podbielski, Quartermaster-General, that is to say, under-chief of the General Staff, and in this capacity entrusted with details; then three lieutenant-colonels, *chefs de section*: Bronsart von Schellendorf, operations; von Brandenstein, conveyance and marches; Verdy du Vernois, information concerning the French army. Finally, Major Blume, head of the *bureau des opérations*, especially occupied himself with the drawing up and transmission of orders. The other officers carried out the duties of assistants. These five officers—Podbielski, Bronsart, Brandenstein, Verdy, and Blumewere for General von Moltke not only precious auxiliaries, but veritable collaborators.

The work, Verdy[12] tells us, was arranged as follows:
"We met each morning at General von Moltke's to study the situation and the steps which it called for. There were present at this meeting the quartermaster-general, the *chefs de section*, the general commissary of stores (Lieutenant-General von Stock), the head of the *bureau des operations*, the chief aide-de-camp, and often also the director of the telegraph.

"Following this meeting, General von Moltke submitted to King William his proposals as well as the means of execution ... This staff consisted entirely of friends, each of whom zealously carried out his duty without either envy or jealousy ... There was such unity of view, in particular, between the three *chefs de section* that if one of them was obliged to break off in the drawing up of an order intended for any army whatsoever, he was immediately replaced by one of the two others without any one supposing that the writer had been changed."

When an important despatch arrived in the middle of the night the council immediately met at General von Moltke's, and decisions ensued from the examination together of the situation.

How different, as we have just seen, were the methods of work and command of Napoleon. He alone, as it were, thought, desired, and decided, nay, he went still further in his monopolization of work by dictating the orders for operations. The staff was a machine for copying or making certain of details. What a diversity of wheels in that complicated machine! There was the Emperor's cabinet, the cabinet of the Chief of the Staff, the offices of the General Staff, so many separate compartments in which men of divers origins, most of them quite ignorant of the science of war, divided the work; and by a singular anomaly the offices of the General Staff, the only ones which were formed with staff officers, took no part to speak of in the elaboration of *ordres d'opérations*. "The role of the staff officers was almost reduced," wrote Thiebaut, "to the drawing up of the positions of the army constantly demanded by Napoleon." The Emperor himself said that the General Staff was the least necessary part of grand headquarters. The administrative part of headquarters was necessary for the upkeep of the army, but it seems as though the Emperor could alone, if need be, have set it in motion, put it into cantonments, and sent it forth to battle.

The defective organization of the material work of the staff and the technical incompetence of those who took part in it, were the cause of numerous errors in the orders,—errors a few of which have been noted in history.

Here are a few instances. In 1806 an order of September 19, for the mustering of the Grand Army was insufficiently collated: Bamberg was written instead of Nuremberg, with the result that there was a crossing of the first and third corps, and a delay of twenty-four hours in the movement of the latter.

A letter of September 24, 1806, relative to movements to be carried out by various corps, is full of material errors, and on certain points in contradiction with orders sent on September 30.[13]

In 1805 Berthier's staff did not succeed, for the departure of the camps of the Ocean, in tracing an independent route for the corps of Davout, Soult, and Ney. But for the vigilance of Davout, who pointed out the error in time, the orders given would have caused a crossing between the third and fourth corps.

"In 1809," relates Jomini, "the various corps were assembled on Ile Lobau. By a *very detailed* order in thirty-one paragraphs, the Emperor arranged for the crossing by these corps of the left arm of the Danube, and their formation on the plain of Enzersdorf. Nevertheless, the Chief of the Staff did not perceive, on sending out the ten duplicates of the famous decree, that by mistake the central bridge had been assigned to Davout, although he was to form the right wing, whilst the bridge on the right had been assigned to Oudinot, who was to form the centre. These two corps crossed in the night, and but for the intelligence of the regiments and their leaders, the most horrible disorder would have happened. The error doubtless had escaped Napoleon, but Berthier had not rectified it."

In a letter dated from Strasburg on September 30, 1805, the Chief of the Staff sent to Murat instructions full of contradictions and omissions regarding essential points. Murat wrote to Berthier to point out the errors and added:

"With the best will in the world, it is impossible under these circumstances to execute properly His Majesty's orders ... I beg you, *Monsieur le Maréchal*, to explain yourself more clearly. You do not mention the Hautpoul division. Is it still under my orders?"

These examples suffice to justify that reproach which was addressed by the Emperor to Berthier in 1812: "The staff is organized in such a manner that nothing is foreseen."

These errors in orders arose to a great extent, in our opinion, from the fact that the material work of the staff was not animated by activity of mind. No intellectual life quickened those heterogeneous offices, which worked independently of one another, without either unity of principles or direction. The officers or functionaries composing the staff furnished the commanders-in-chief in their office-work with but a precarious assistance, because they had not been prepared for their role, and the whirlwind which carried them along did not allow them to acquire the instruction in which they were lacking. A staff capable of thinking in unison with a Commander-in-Chief is an institution which can only be created in time of peace by a long and methodical training.

If the aides-de-camp and officers of the General Staff did not participate in the work of the cabinet as regards the progress of operations except in a very limited way, they were, on the other hand, employed to the very fullest extent on the outside duties of the staff. They were veritably the Emperor's *missi dominici*. He sent them on missions and journeys in every direction to obtain information, to control the execution of his orders, and to throw light by their reports on what he could not see himself. The young officers of the Imperial Staff were often very inexperienced when judging alone situations which they were expected to understand.[14] There, again, their lack of anterior preparation was felt; but generally they showed, in the accomplishment of their missions, a zeal, vigour, celerity, and a faculty of making the best of things which merit all our admiration.

Moreover, Napoleon, as we shall soon see, possessed a talent for awakening the zeal and redoubling the energy of all those young officers who surrounded him. What would a colonel of thirty-five years of age not have done when he received from the Emperor such a confidential mission as that which was given to Lejeune, Berthier's aide-de-camp on February 15, 1810?

"Set out for Spain. See everything in detail, men, and *matériel*, and note everything. Return without loss of time, and act in such a way that when I speak to you I shall believe I have seen things for myself." Then, when dismissing him, the Emperor graciously added: "Go and win your spurs."

Officers of the staff of lower rank were also employed in carrying orders. "They were," says General Edouard Colbert, "veritable couriers with epaulettes, carriers of orders from whom, owing to their intelligence and zeal, they required much more celerity than from a professional courier." During the wars of the Revolution the generals had couriers who were paid by the State to carry their despatches, but the Emperor, finding that these men were incapable of giving any explanation concerning what they had seen, put them on half pay and ordered that in future despatches should be carried by aides-de-camp and officers of the staff. The lack of maps, with which the marshals themselves were sometimes insufficiently provided, the almost general ignorance of foreign languages,[15] the limited development of cross-country routes, and the bad state of the roads rendered the transmission of orders and despatches difficult. This department was so much the more difficult because the leaders took no trouble whatever to guide their officers.

The narratives of Fezensac, the former aide-decamp of Ney and Berthier, leave no doubt on that point. "On October 11, 1806,"he writes,[16] "I was on duty at Schleiz. Hardly had I arrived than the Marshal (Ney) handed me a movement order to carry to General Colbert.[17] I wanted to ask him in which direction to go. But he replied: 'No remarks, I don't like them.' We were never told of the position of the troops. No movement order or report was communicated to us. We had to find out as best we could, or rather guess. In my particular case—aide-de-camp of a general who did not reflect for a moment whether my horse was in a condition to support such fatigue, or whether I understood my new duties[18]—they entrusted me, at dead of night, when everything was of great importance, with an *ordre de mouvement*, and would not allow me to ask even where I was to go." Speaking in a more general manner, Fezensac adds: "They did not inquire, when it was a question of going at full gallop, whether our horses were in a condition even to walk, whether we knew the country, or whether we possessed maps, which we were always without. The order had to be carried out and they did not trouble themselves about the means ... This method of attempting everything with the most feeble resources; this determination to regard nothing as impossible; this boundless confidence in success which at first had been one of the causes of our superiority, ended by becoming fatal to us."[19] In this respect the working of the staff also left something to be desired.

In short, it is certain that the staffs were a weak point in the armies of the First Empire, and this defect contributed to the disasters of Napoleon's last campaigns.

As Jomini says, a good staff can foresee many errors in war, and many errors were committed at that time in consequence of incomplete reconnaissances and orders either badly drawn up or badly transmitted. Nowadays the role of the staff has increased in importance; the officers of the staff must be the enlightened assistants of the Commander-in-Chief, and consequently continually acquainted with his intentions; their mission is to prepare his decisions and rid him of all the details which might cause him anxiety, and thus obscure those general views which are the basis of the decisions of a supreme head. "Let one alone command, for several minds weaken an army." This maxim of Machiavelli is truer to-day than ever. "Every one must remain within the boundaries of his duties, otherwise everything will be confusion."[20] With an army, the unity of command—I would even say the unity of inspiration must dominate all decisions. But this primordial condition having been fulfilled, our desire should be that, on the various steps of the military ladder, every one should be allowed to see clearly in his sphere of action, to put his intellectual forces to use, and to fight, subordinately, not only with his arm and his heart, but also with his science and his mind.

NOTES

1   *Itinéraire général de l'empereur Napoléon pendant la campagne de 1812*, by M. Denniée fits, inspector of reviews, who belonged to the cabinet of the Chief of the Staff.
2   *Mémoires de Lejeune.*
3   Everything which is here said concerning the cabinet of the Chief of the Staff is taken textually from Foucart's *Campagne de 1806* (Prentzlow and Lübeek).
4   *Ibid.*
5   *Mémoires*, pp. 239, 240.
6   *Mémoires du baron Lejeune*, who was Berthier's aide-de-camp, and designed the uniform described above.
7   After the battle of Marengo, Berthier drew up a report in which Sopransy was mentioned five times. He was the son of Mme. Visconti, a youth of sixteen, and Berthier attributed the winning of the battle to him! Sopransy did this and did that, he wrote, all to please Mme. Visconti (Napoleon to Gourgaud, Gourgaud's *Journal de Sainte-Hélène*, vol. i. p. 307).

8   Planat de la Faye, aide-de-camp to General de la Laraboisière in 1812, *Vie de Planat*, p. 93.

9   The uniform of the assistants of the Staff was as follows: a blue coat with red collar and gold epaulettes, white breeches and hat ornamented with white feathers.

    The civil employees of the offices of the Grand General Staff, that is to say, the offices of Berthier and the Emperor, wore a blue coat *à la française*, with the button of the General Staff.

10 *Mémoires du baron Fain*, p. 241.

11 Fezensac's *Souvenirs*, p. 226.

12 At grand headquarters 1870-71. *Personal Recollections*, by Verdy du Vernois, p. 37.

13 Bonnal's *Manoeuvre d'Iéna*, p. 197.

14 Ségur's *Histoire et Mémoires*, vol. ii. p. 218.

15 In Germany, for instance, hardly any but the Polish officers knew the language of the country (Grabowski's *Mémoires*, p. 69).

16 Fezensac's *Souvenirs militaires*, p. 110.

17 General Colbert commanded the cavalry brigade of Ney's corps.

18 Fezensac had entered on his duties as aide-de-camp that very day.

19 Fezensac's *Souvenirs militaires*, p. 129.

20 Bonaparte to Pille, Nice, June 16, 1796.

VI

Superintendence of Execution

The Emperor's inspections—His reviews—A review in Poland in 1807—Control of effective forces—Visits to the outposts—The positions, elements of control and information—Missions of inspection entrusted to aides-de-camp and officers of the staff.

O NCE A DECISION HAS BEEN come to and orders have been given, a Commander-in-Chief has fulfilled but half his role. No order is valuable without the act which springs from it. A Commander-in-Chief, whilst allowing every one reasonable initiative, must take part in the execution of orders, so as to give the army the impetus necessary for great efforts. How is this impulsion which forces men on to heroic sacrifices to be given? It is by keeping an eye on them, by awakening and sustaining their ardour by rewards of all kinds, and also by repressing, by means of penalties, the laziness and inertia of stragglers.

This stimulating influence of the "Master's eye" was perhaps never greater than in the armies of Napoleon. "Orders are nothing," he wrote to Berthier in 1812, "unless one is sure that they are carried out." The act—ever the act—that was his aim; constantly, and by the shortest path, he proceeded towards his goal, a definite and determined act. "Ideology was his *bête noir*; he disliked it not only through selfish calculation but also and much more through an instinctive love of the truth."[1]

"Day and night," writes Ségur, "the Emperor, far from being satisfied that he had done everything, like other leaders, when he had given his orders, himself watched over the exact and complete accomplishment of all his commands."[2] Every day, when on campaign, and no matter what the weather might be, he went out. Sometimes he made short excursions to visit his army corps, or else strategical positions. On reaching the cantonment the first thing he did was to inspect the site of the camp around his dwelling, in order to see if the soldiers had plenty to eat, and if there were easy means of communication among them. To him, war was not a game of chess played merely in the privacy of his study; his activity outside was no less great than his intellectual activity.

When the army was at the Ocean camps, he was seen to display extraordinary activity not only in inspecting the troops but in superintending the work undertaken with a view to invading England. He had rented, near Boulogne, the little château called Pont-de-Briques, on the road to Paris. He generally arrived there when least expected by his corps, and immediately mounted his horse; and he was back again at Saint Cloud when thought to be still in the midst of his troops. "I made several of these journeys with him in his carriages," says the Duc de Rovigo. "He generally left in the evening, lunched at the Chantilly post-house, supped at Abbeville, and reached Pont-de-Briques very early. A moment later he was on horseback, and he often did not leave the saddle until night. Not until he had seen the lowest soldier and the most ordinary workshop did he return. He descended into the docks and ascertained the depth reached since his previous visit. He generally took back with him to dinner, at seven or eight o'clock, Admiral Bruix, General Soult (the commander of the Boulogne camp), Saganzin, the engineer in charge of the work connected with bridges and roads, General Faultrier, who was in command of the artillery stores, and finally the officer in charge of the victualling department, so that before retiring to rest he knew more about the state of his affairs than if he had read volumes of reports."[3]

We here see the ardent desire which Napoleon showed in all his undertakings—a desire to see things for himself, to follow them up closely, and to continue his examination until they were brought to fruition.

"Deciding that Pont-de-Briques was still not near enough to the scene of his operations, he chose a site on an elevation called Tour d'Ordre, dominating the sea. From this point he could see the English squadron, and take in at a glance the various divisions of his flotilla. Here Napoleon had had built a temporary dwelling composed of several rooms, in which he often lived for many days. In one of these rooms was a big telescope, directed seawards, enabling him to see distinctly what happened out at sea, and even the English coast."[4]

In the course of operations the Emperor passed a part of his troops in review almost daily. He paid as much attention to a regiment or a mere detachment as to an entire army corps.

In October and November 1806 he reviewed successively, at Berlin, the 3rd, 7th, and 4th corps of the Grand Army, the cavalry reserve, the Guard, the great artillery parks, and the corps of engineers.

In 1809, in the courtyard of the Castle of Schœnbrunn, there was daily a grand parade to which Napoleon summoned successively men who were leaving the hospitals, as well as all the regiments which had the most suffered, in order to see for himself if they were being well attended to, and if his forces were being increased.

In 1812 the Emperor spent a fortnight at Vitepsk. Every morning he was present at the parade of the Guard in front of his palace; and he insisted on everybody being there ... In the presence of the General Staff and the Guard, he entered into the minutest administrative details. Muster-masters-general and officers were summoned, and called upon to state in what condition the supplies were, how the sick were being attended to in the hospitals, and how many dressings had been prepared for the wounded. They often received reprimands or very severe reproaches—sometimes undeserved.[5]

The Emperor generally reviewed all the detachments which joined the army, and which always received a route obliging them to pass by grand Imperial headquarters, unless the position of their corps obliged them to make a countermarch. The assistant chief of the staff received orders from the Chief of the Staff or the aide-de-camp on duty as to the hour the Emperor was to see the troops. The Chief of the Staff noted in his green pocket-book the Emperor's orders and observations, which were written out clearly on a simple piece of paper of small size by one of his secretaries. The Chief of the Staff handed to the Emperor a report giving the result of the review, and had the various orders sent to his office. Following on reviews came orders of the day, in which observations were by no means spared.

The work of the review was submitted to the Emperor the very next day; the night was spent over it, and the corps had to make out their memoranda of proposals immediately. Moreover, when an army corps was to be reviewed by the Emperor, the Marshal always ordered the colonels to prepare in advance and bring with them the memoranda of proposals for promotion and the Legion of Honour.

The Emperor's review was, as we see, not a mere ceremonious display at which the Commander-in-Chief was content with galloping more or less brilliantly in front of the troops: it was a serious operation, a veritable act of control, immediately followed by rewards or punishments. Without the slightest doubt these reviews exercised quite a different influence over a soldier's mind than those of our own day.

Let us form a clear idea of the spectacle presented by one of the Emperor's reviews by reproducing the narrative of an eye-witness. In his *Souvenirs,*[6] Colonel de Gonneville, then sub-lieutenant in the 6th Cuirassiers, has left us a picture of a review of a division of the Cuirassiers of General Espagne (the 4th, 6th, 7th, and 8th Cuirassiers), then, in the spring of 1807, cantoned on the Passarge. This is what he says:

"... The division to which we belonged was assembled to be passed in review by the Emperor. I had never seen the Emperor and so I reached the ground greatly agitated. At last, for the first time, I was to see near at hand the author of the immortal campaigns of Italy and Egypt, the conqueror of Austerlitz!

"After the regiments, arranged in single line, had been waiting for an hour, a group of horsemen appeared on the horizon and was soon near us. At its head, fifty paces in front of a brilliant staff, was outlined a man with the most martial face and bearing. He wore a knightly tunic, covered with embroidery, white trousers, and fairly strong riding boots; a sable cap with a red crown, surmounted by black ostrich feathers, covered his head; whilst, worn saltierwise on his left breast, was an ancient sword whose handle, enriched with precious stones, glittered in the sun. I thought that it was the Emperor, but it was only Murat, Grand Duke of Berg, who, in his capacity as commander of the whole of the cavalry, came to pay the honours of his division to the Emperor. He passed at a gallop from the left to the right, then returned at a walking pace along the whole line, stopped on the left, and waited.

"We had not long to wait, for, soon, from the extremity of the plain by which he had arrived there debouched a much more numerous group. First of all came the Mamelukes, covered with gold, whose superb horses, although held in hand as if wild, bounded; then the aides-de-camp; and, a hundred paces behind, the Emperor followed by his immense staff. In the rear was a squadron of chasseurs of the Guard. The Emperor was far from having the terribly martial bearing of the personage whom, in my ignorance, I had mistaken for him. He wore a grey redingote of the most simple appearance, and a small hat with a black cord, without any other ornament but its cocade. His unbuttoned redingote enabled one to see the epaulettes of a colonel on the undress uniform of the chasseurs of his Guard, the only uniform which, since the Empire, he ever wore on campaign. He wore a white vest, white breeches, and soft riding boots, and was astride an admirable light grey Arabian horse. His saddle cloth and holster-cap were edged with a rich bullion fringe, and the stirrups, as well as the bit and buckles of the bridle, were gold-plated."

Picture to yourself, then, amidst the monotony of a plain in Poland, that long line of cuirassiers (who "wore the short blue Imperial coat with turned-down collar and red or yellow trimmings according to the regiments, white breeches, high boots, breastplate, and steel helmet with brass crest and flowing horsehair"[7]) with Murat, in his dazzling uniform on the left, and the Emperor, in legendary dress, arriving in the midst of his brilliant cortege, and you will have before your mind's eye a picture of this review worthy of the brush of a painter. But this is only the scenery; we now come to the effective action, the work of control.

"The Emperor," continues Colonel de Gonneville, "passed in front of us towards the right. On reaching the end he ordered that they should command 'divisions to the right,' that they should form into companies, and dismount. At this time, and until the fall of the Empire, regiments consisted of eight companies, forming four squadrons; the officers, also on foot, were placed in the order of their rank to the right of their companies. On arriving at each regiment, the Emperor received the muster-roll, which he handed to the Chief of the Staff. He then asked the colonel the following questions: 'What is your effective force?' 'How many men have you in hospital, at the depot, how many sick in camp or absent for any other cause?' He repeated the same questions to the captains, and woe betide those whose memory or ignorance led them astray! Severe words, accompanied by looks which did not promise future favours, left them with sad reflections. This is what happened to Colonel Merlin, who was in command of the 8th Cuirassiers; he became so confused in his replies that there was an immense difference between the number of his effective force and that formed by the various categories. When the Emperor reached my company, after having questioned my captain, on the left of whom I stood, he stopped opposite me and asked the colonel why the accoutrement of my horse was not uniform. The colonel replied that, returning from the enemy's prisons, I had not been able to procure the accoutrement. The Emperor did not like to be caught, especially in cavalry matters, so, looking at me angrily, he cried, ' But your division has not yet seen the enemy.' I did not dare to speak, and those irritated eyes fixed imperturbably upon me made me very ill at ease. The colonel was beginning to explain how things had happened when Lieutenant-General Espagne, who, on my return from captivity, had received me very badly, advanced, and unstintingly praised my conduct on the occasion in question. During this recital the Emperor's face underwent a complete change, and when he had heard everything he made me a gracious and profound salute.

"We filed past at a trot in squadrons, and on arriving in front of the Emperor we raised our swords in the air with a cry of 'Vive l'Empereur.' The shouts were formidable, and the review appeared to have satisfied the than in whose honour it had been held.

"On leaving our regiment, he said to Colonel d'Avenay, 'Colonel, at the first engagement a bullet, or a general's cross!'"

One of the Emperor's greatest anxieties whilst on campaign was to maintain the greatest possible number of combatants. Better than any one else did he know with what rapidity effective forces dwindle. By every means within his power he sought to reduce the number of valueless units. The first question when he spoke to a leader was always, "How many are at present under arms?" And they hardly ever sought to deceive him, for it was known that he was distrustful and verified accounts.

In 1805, at Braun, when on one of those incessant journeys which he made to visit positions and army corps, he perceived the light cavalry of his

Guard. Thanks to his experienced eye, he estimated the number of horsemen and found it very reduced. He took from his pocket a small note-book, in which the effective forces of the various corps were inscribed, and having run through it summoned General Morland to him. "Your regiment," he said in a severe tone, "is down in my notes as having 1200 men, and although you have not yet had an engagement with the enemy, you have not more than 800 horsemen there. What has become of the others?"

To have a clear understanding, and fearing complaisance towards Morland, he ordered Marbot, Augereau's aide-de-camp, who happened to be at head-quarters, to count the chasseurs, and inform him of their number. There were four hundred missing. Marbot relates, in his *Mémoires*, the subterfuges he employed to hide the truth from the Emperor, and his anxiety at the thought of the inexactitude of his report being discovered.[8]

If Napoleon, when on his daily outings, met a detachment he questioned its leader, interrogated him regarding his effective force and destination, made him show the movement orders, and rectified errors.

During the day and also at night he went on his rounds to the outposts. Pictures have popularized Napoleon's action in taking the gun of a sleeping sentinel and mounting guard until the soldier's awakening—a striking object-lesson which depicts the attitude of the "Little Corporal" towards his soldiers. More than one piece of negligence in the duty of the outposts had he thus to repress. "His Majesty," we read in an order of the day dated from Scheenbrunn, on November 14, 1805, "noticed, whilst on the tour of inspection which he made at two o'clock in the morning, a good deal of negligence in the work of the outposts. He discovered that it was not done with, the rigorous exactitude required by military decrees and rules. Generals and colonels must be at their outposts before daybreak, and the line must be under arms until the return of the reconnoitring parties. It must always be taken for granted that the enemy has manoeuvred during the night in order to attack at daybreak."

One can easily understand how such vigilance kept the army on the alert and the moral effect it produced on the troops. Every soldier was convinced that the Emperor had his eye upon him. Thus, in 1812, when troopers were dying of hunger on the roads of Russia, they did not think of placing the blame on Napoleon. "It is most unfortunate," they said, accusing only the zeal and sometimes the probity of administrators; "yet the Emperor is looking after us all the same."

Another of Napoleon's methods of control was the attentive, the very attentive study of the muster-rolls. "The fine condition of my armies," he wrote to his brother Joseph on August 6, 1806, "arises from the fact that I occupy myself with it one or two hours every day; and when, every month, they send me the muster-rolls of my troops and fleets—rolls which form twenty thick volumes—I leave everything else to read them in detail, in order to see the difference there is between one month and another. I take more pleasure in this perusal than a young girl does in reading a novel." At the Tuileries these thick account books, bound in red morocco, were always standing in a pile at a corner of the Emperor's desk. In the case of the army there were several models, containing various information: account books in which each regiment had its sheet and was arranged in its numerical order; account books for each military division, giving all the details of the military forces of which each division was composed; account books for the army corps in which the fighting units were counted and subdivided as in their camps; an account book for the staffs of the generals, another for the artillery, another for the engineers, and finally an account book in which the levies of troops in each department were set down,—the black book of the prefects as Fain calls it.[9]

On campaign the great muster-rolls were renewed every fortnight, and in addition the Emperor received a summary muster-roll every five days.

In spite of the care with which the muster-rolls were made out, Napoleon discovered errors in them and did not fail to point these out to the Minister of War. "I have found in the muster-rolls," he wrote on February 2, 1812, "seventeen companies of the train of artillery back from Spain, but you find only nine. That shows the error committed by the office which draws up the muster-rolls when they set down as *carried out* movements which are only *ordered*. I have already several times pointed out similar errors, and this shakes my confidence in the work of this office. I approve and I desire that it should write its observations and the indication of *orders given* in red ink, but it must risk nothing and only set down in black ink what exists."[10]

An order given is not an order executed; between the two there is the whole distance which separates the word from the deed, and like a true man of action the Emperor was careful to see that, in his army, there was no confusion on that point. To verify the execution of orders given is one of the greatest obligations of a commander. A general-in-chief cannot be present at the carrying out of all the orders given in his name, but the examination of the muster-rolls handed to him enable him to detect certain errors and to impress his subordinates with his vigilance. On this subject also let us quote a letter of February 28, 1806, from the Emperor to Prince Eugène: "The high treasurer complains that the 67th regiment has not reached Genoa. These complaints would not be made if the Chief of your Staff carried out his duty and if, after having sent an order to a corps, he communicated its route to the Minister of War. The minister never misses sending me these documents and

I am in a position to verify the carrying out of my orders, but the Chief of your Staff does nothing."

On campaign, the primary information which Napoleon looked for in the muster-rolls was the number of combatants in the army, the basis of his strategical and tactical conception. On September 22, 1806, he wrote from St. Cloud to the Chief of the Staff:

"You estimate that there are 28,000 horses in the Grand Army. But you include in them neither the 4th dragoons, nor the 20th chasseurs. You do not count, either, a thousand men who have left Paris and are about to join the army, which will then consist of 30,000 men. But you are wrong if you think that all those are troopers' horses. The officers' horses are included therein; and you know that a lieutenant has two horses, a captain three, a major and a colonel more, which very much increases the number of non-combatants. This, therefore, must be distinguished with greater clearness by setting down the officers' horses in one column and those of the soldiery in another …"

By means of the muster-rolls and the detailed statement of the position[11] of the army corps which Berthier handed him daily the Emperor was accurately informed regarding the strength and position of his troops.

What Napoleon could not see for himself or extract from the muster-rolls, he learnt by asking the officers of the staff.

He constantly employed aides-de-camp and staff officers on missions, the object of which was "to look after established order and the observation of military laws and regulations in the various branches of the service. Missions concerning a single and well-determined object," writes Thiébaut in his *Manuel général du service des États-majors*, "were called visits." Thus, on September 27, 1805, AssistantMajor Lomet, of the General Staff, was sent to Strasburg to visit the army boot stores, to question the commissary on the subject of the amount of provisions and to verify.

Under other circumstances missions were inspections of greater extent and were called tours of inspection. On December 16, 1805, at Schœnbrunn, the Emperor summoned his aide-de-camp General Rapp, who had just been slightly wounded at Austerlitz, and said to him, "Are you in a condition to travel?" "Yes, sire." "In that case, go and tell Marmont the details of the battle of Austerlitz, so that he will be enraged at not having come, and observe the effect it has produced on the Italians. Here are your instructions:

> You will proceed to Gratz. You will remain there sufficient time to inform
> General Marmont of the details of the battle of Austerlitz, to tell him that
> negotiations have been opened but that nothing is decided, that he must
> hold himself in readiness for anything that happens; you will make yourself

acquainted with General Marmont's situation; you will tell him that I wish him to send spies to Hungary, and that he must inform me of everything he learns. You will continue your journeyto Laybach, where you will find Marshal Masséna 's corps, the 8th army corps, the exact condition of which you will report to me ... You will then go to Palmanova, after having strongly urged Marshal Masséna to arm and victual this fortified town thoroughly, and you will inform me of its condition. Thence you will proceed opposite Venice, see the positions we occupy and the situation of our troops. From there you will reach General Saint-Cyr's army, which is marching on Naples, and observe its composition and strength. You will return via Klagenfurth, where you will see Marshal Ney, and then rejoin me.

Take care to write to me from every stopping-place; send estafettes to me from Gratz, Laybach, Palmanova, Venice, and the place where you find the Naples army. Thereupon I pray God to keep you in His safe keeping.

NAPOLEON

Mere captains, such as Castellane, aide-de-camp to General Mouton, who was himself the Emperor's aide-de-camp, were entrusted with similar missions. On July 21, 1809, at Schcenbrunn, Castellane was summoned to the Emperor's presence and received the following order in which his misspelt name was written in Napoleon's own hand.

Aide-de-camp "Castelan" will proceed to Linz, where he will hand the adjoining letter to the Duke of Dantzig. Thence he will go to Bayreuth to take the letter to the Duke of Abrantes. At Bayreuth he will note the name of the troops composing the corps of the Austrian General Kienmayer and the positions they occupy. He will also bring me the muster-rolls of the Duke of Abrantes' corps—infantry, cavalry, and artillery. On his return he will see the fortifications of Passau, Linz, and Molk, and place himself in a position to inform me about the works. On the way he will receive General Bourcier's despatches.

(Signed) NAPOLEON
SCHŒNBRUNN, July 21, 1809.

In addition, on dismissing him, the Emperor ordered Castellane to send him a report on the troops and hospitals.

Castellano has left us the narrative of his tour of inspection. He travelled day and night in a *chariot de poste*, stopping at each place only during the strictly indispensable time. On July 22 he was at Linz, and on the 25th at Bayreuth, where Junot, by special favour and repressing his customary rudeness towards inferiors, received him at his table with perfect politeness. At

Ratisbonne he visited the hospitals, and in order to lose no time sacrificed a lady's favours. He then visited, on July 28, the fortifications of Passau, on the 29th the bridge head of Linz, and on the night of the 29th to the 30th, by moonlight, the fortifications of Milk. Back at Schœnbrunn on July 30, he sent in, on the following day, his report to the Emperor, who found it the best he had received during that campaign.[12]

To be complimented by Napoleon, it was necessary on these tours of inspection "to see everything in detail, to note everything, to return without loss of time, and to give the Emperor, after he had read the report, the impression that he had seen things for himself."[13]

In order to give a still clearer idea of the care shown by Napoleon in avoiding, by active supervision, any inertia in the execution of his orders, we will also give the narration of a mission entrusted to aide-de-camp Philippe de Ségur.

At the end of June 1803 the First Consul had made a nineteen days' journey from the mouth of the Somme to Flushing with the object of seeing whether the orders given for the organization of the camps of the Ocean were to the purpose, to complete these orders, superintend them, and hasten their accomplishment.

On the following 23rd of August, a few weeks after his return to St. Cloud, he considered it necessary to send Ségur to remake this same journey, step by step, to ascertain if all the work ordered had been carried out, and to send him from each place, in the most minute detail, a statement as to the exact stage of advancement of this work. The written order given to Ségur concludes with the enunciation of this elementary rule to be observed in every report:

"This officer must set down nothing by hearsay. He must see everything with his own eyes, say nothing but what he has seen, and when he is obliged to say something he has not seen, say he has not seen it."

On Ségur's return the First Consul received him at St. Cloud in his study whilst he was having his luncheon. He welcomed the aide-de-camp playfully. "After a hundred questions," relates Ségur, "as, listening to my replies, he had spilt his coffee over the white revers of his coat (on that day he was wearing the uniform of a grenadier of the Guard), he complained of having spoilt his fine uniform. Then he asked me if I had lunched, and I verily believe that, satisfied with my reports and replies, he was ready to pour me out a cup of that coffee which he took but twice a day and never more, whatever may have been said. 'I have seen all your reports on armaments,' he said to me; 'they are correct. However, you forgot two cannons at Ostend.' He had ordered the placing of these two guns behind the town on an embankment in case of a surprise. The order had not been carried out."[14] Ségur left, overcome with astonishment at Napoleon's memory. General Duroc told him afterwards that, ministerial reports, compared with his, having been found inaccurate, two Ministers had been severely rebuked for these differences.

Such were the means employed by Napoleon when watching over the good condition of his armies and the execution of his orders. In spite of the vast difference which exists in their constitution between the Imperial army and a modern army, Napoleon's method of work may, in its main lines, serve as a model. The chief of a modern army must allow his subordinates to show much greater initiative than that enjoyed by the marshals of the Empire, but we must beware of thinking that this initiative must involve, in the course of the execution of orders, the abdication of the supreme command.

Initiative, if it is to be fruitful, must be directed into the right channel and controlled; initiative is only fruitful when there is unity of action, and this unity of action can only be maintained by incessant rectifications by a chief who has indicated the object to be attained and the general direction to be followed. Like the Emperor, the leader of an army, despite means of rapid transport, cannot see everything with his own eyes, he must use other means of control, and in particular employ many officers of the staff. These missions for the purpose of verification are one of the most delicate but also one of the most important parts of their role. We would add, with Thiébault, that these officers, although possessing no quality in themselves, have, however, according to the nature of their mission and the capabilities it presupposes, the right to make themselves heard; they ought to be able to use it if need be to submit to the general to whom they are sent on mission the reflections which they consider useful. Without doubt they ought to do this with circumspection and discretion, with the respectful attentions which differences of rank and age impose, but with the frankness and courage that the safeguarding of the general interest commands. They must show themselves worthy of the confidence placed in them by their zeal and intelligence, and the uprightness and firmness of their character. "Such a mission offers an officer of the staff the opportunity of showing the extent of his capacity and morality, or of his inability or baseness—the opportunity to cover himself with honour or with shame."

As, in spite of everything, rank and age naturally confer additional authority, it is to be desired that, as under the First Empire, the General-in-Chief should have at his immediate disposal a few generals in community of ideas with him, and who, in consequence of their personal position, will be better qualified to speak and act in his name in the most important circumstances.

NOTES

1 Taine's *Le Régime modern*, pp. 28, 29.
2 Ségur's *Histoire et Mémoires*, vol. i. p. 180.
3 *Mémoires du due de Rovigo*, vol. i. pp. 3, 5 *et seq.*
4 Méneval's *Mémoires*, vol. i. p. 344.
5 Fezensac's *Mémoires militaires*, pp. 240, 241.
6 *Souvenirs du colonel de Gonneville*, p. 60.
7 Description of the uniform given by Henry Houssaye's *1815: Waterloo*, p. 115.
8 Marbot's *Mémoires*, vol i. p. 246.
9 Baron Fain's *Mémoires*, p. 80.
10 Napoleon to General Clarke, Minister of War, February 2, 1812.
11 For the drawing-up of this detailed statement of the position of the army corps, the chiefs of the staff of the corps had to send to the Chief of the Staff "without delay" the list of their cantonments in the form of a table, of which the following is a model:

STATEMENT OF CANTONMENTS

....ARMY CORPS   ....DIVISION

Date.	Position of Headquarters.	Desigantion of the Regiments.	Marches and Cantonments.	Topographical and Military Notes: Resources of the Country.

12 *Mémoires de Castellane*, pp. 68 and 69.
13 *Mémoires de Lejeune*, Berthier'e aide-de-camp.
14 Ségur's *Histoire et Mémoires*, vol. ii. p. 232.

VII

Rewards and Penalties: Napoleon and his Generals

Napoleon's egoism in command—His contempt of man—His
attitude towards his generals—Hostility of certain generals towards
Bonaparte at the opening of his career, and how he established his
authority—Penalties: his premeditated anger, imperial upbraidings—
Material rewards: promotions, dotations, titles of nobility,
gratuities—Moral rewards: the Legion of Honour, mentions, praise,
orders of the day, marks of satisfaction of various kinds—The
Emperor's systematic partiality—The bulletins—Jealousy and
servility of his generals—Weakness of the system—Napoleon's
judgment on his marshals—Qualities of a general-in-chief—Lannes,
Suchet, Masséna, Soult, Davout, Gouvion-Saint-Cyr.

THE ART OF HANDLING MEN constitutes, without doubt, one of the most
important and most delicate parts of the function of supreme command.
The ideal is to possess an army in which everyone, from the generalin-chief
to the common soldier, is ready to make the greatest effort, and sacrifice his
life out of a sense of duty and patriotism; it is this noble ideal which should
be set before all the citizens of a free nation, these elevated feelings which the
educators of a nation ought to endeavour to inculcate into the hearts of the
youth of the country. These were the feelings which animated the armies of
the French Revolution.

The incentives which Napoleon employed to give an impetus to his army
were, we must recognize, of a different order.

"Napoleon's being was certainly formed," as Nietzsche has said,[1] "by faith
in himself and in his star, and by the contempt of Man which proceeded
from it." In Napoleon's opinion there were two levers by which men could
be moved: fear and interest.[2] His great general principle, which he applied
in all manner of ways in big as in little things, was that no one showed zeal
unless he was anxious.[3] Consequently he did not place all his confidence
in anybody, he excited rivalry, and kept those who were serving him on
the alert. Beneath every good action or good feeling he sought to discover

personal interest. "At the time of the Egyptian expedition, Talleyrand had spontaneously lent him a sum of ten thousand francs which he needed to remove the obstacles placed in his way by secret enemies. Returning later, in a conversation with Talleyrand, to the subject of this service rendered, he said to him: 'What personal interest could you then have had in lending me this money? I have cudgelled my brains a hundred times and never have I been able to see your object clearly.' And when the Prince de Bénévent— diplomat that he was—replied that he had had none, that he had done him this service without ulterior design, Bonaparte added: 'In that case, if you really acted without prevision, your action was that of a gull.'"[4] Talleyrand could not confess that he had staked ten thousand francs on the future of the young conqueror of Italy, but, despite his apparent ignorance, Napoleon was not deceived. However, what did the ulterior motives and calculations of Talleyrand matter to him provided he was useful to him; for "he liked only those men who were useful to him and as long as they were so."[5] Man's value from the point of view of character and intelligence mattered little to him; one may even say that it gave him offence. "A strange man in everything, he considered himself vastly superior to the rest of the world, and yet he feared every form of superiority. Who, among those who were near him, has not heard him say that he preferred mediocre people? Who has not observed, when he employed a man of eminence, that he found it necessary, before granting him his confidence, to discover first of all his weak side, the secret of which he generally hastened to divulge?"[6]

The quality which he valued the most was, accompanied by zeal in his service, an absolute and blind devotion to his person. "The officers of my Guard," he said at St. Helena, "had not the best of educations, but they suited my system: they were all old soldiers, born of peasant or artisan parents. Parisian society had no influence over them: They depended entirely on me; I had them better in hand and was surer of them than if they had been well-bred men."[7]

In everything he thought first of himself, and of France afterwards. "Do not forget," he wrote to his brother Joseph, "that your first duty is towards me, your second towards France, and your third towards Spain." In 1815, after his abdication, he said of Davout bitterly: "I thought that Davout loved me, but he loved only France."

We must not run away with the idea that there was any narrowness or meanness in this absorbing egoism; nobody knew better than Napoleon how to recompense those who aided in establishing his power and in consolidating his throne. He bound the fortune of France to his own, which he desired should be ever higher. "To rise higher, ever higher, was the law and fatality of his nature."[8] This boundless ambition, aided by extraordinary faculties, opened up for him a prodigious career as a conqueror, but it went so far that it ended in being the cause of his ruin.

To return to the subject under consideration, Napoleon's attitude towards his generals was naturally in concordance with the general system of government he had adopted. From the day on which he was appointed General-in-Chief of the Army of the Interior (October 20, 1795), he began to keep all his old comrades at a respectful distance. "The obsequious officer of the day before, the *tutoyeur* of the Midi, gave place to a chief who would allow no companionship."[9] Later, as Emperor, when he was in a good humour, it came to pass that he spoke familiarly to his generals, but this familiarity was such that all idea of reciprocity was excluded. "A momentary effusion," writes Mme. de Rémusat,[10] "with one of those who were in close relations with him was instantly followed by a change of manner—the Master felt it necessary to point out that he had come to the end of his role as a good-natured man. Suddenly his face changed, smiles gave place to a look of gravity, he raised his severe-looking eyes which always seemed to increase his small stature, and gave some insignificant order or other with all the abruptness of an absolute master who does not wish to lose an opportunity of commanding when he so desires." Until the end of his days he wished to be the Emperor. "In coming here," he said to Gourgaud at St. Helena, "you thought you would be my companion. But I am no one's. Nobody can have ascendency over me."

General "Vendémiaire" did not succeed all at once in attaining that indisputable authority which the Emperor Napoleon had later. Time and method were necessary for the establishment of his domination. Even after the first Italian campaign and the Egyptian campaign, certain generals, such as Masséna , MacDonald, Augereau, Bernadotte, Lecourbe, and Delmas, retained a sincere love of republicanism, and blamed both Bonaparte's ambition and his dictatorial bearing; they regretted that he did not possess the modified authority, the disinterested patriotism, the easy access, and the simple communicative mind which they liked in Moreau, his former rival. Consequently, soon after Marengo, Bonaparte set to work to destroy every trace of independence in his old companions. He succeeded, subjugating some by means of fear and the hope of favours, and setting aside others who resisted the offered temptations. Henceforward he would have only subjects.

He himself explained, as follows, the reasons for his haughty conduct:

"I was young when I attained command of armies. My first campaign astonished Europe; the ineptness of the Directory could no longer support me in the position I had reached. I undertook a gigantic expedition to occupy people's minds and to increase my glory. My former friends disappeared owing to their inactivity or were dishonoured through reverses. When I saw

France at the last extremity, I returned and found the path to the throne open in all directions. I mounted it as the last hope of the nation.

"Hardly had I been seated than I saw that some had pretensions. Moreau, Bernadotte, and Masséna could no longer pardon my successes. It was my duty not to fear but to subdue them, and my plan regarding them was quickly made.

"They tried several times either to overthrow me or share with me. As division was less adventurous, twelve generals hatched a plot to divide France into twelve provinces. As my share they generously left me Paris and the suburbs! The agreement was signed at Ruel. Masséna was appointed to hand it to me. But he refused, saying that he would leave the Tuileries only to be shot by my guard. He knew me well. Pichegru and Moreau came to conspire in Paris. We know how their intrigues ended. My position was not an ordinary one, consequently my conduct had to be in accordance.

"Fear and the hope of fortune and favours could alone exist between them and me. I was lavish with both. I have made courtiers; I have never pretended to make friends."

General Edouard Colbert has narrated that at the beginning of the Egyptian expedition there was much murmuring in the higher ranks of the army against Bonaparte and the expedition in which he had engaged the army. Informed of the discontent of certain general officers; among whom was Murat, Bonaparte instructed General Dugua to invite them to dinner, and addressed the following words to them in an appropriate tone:

"I know that several generals are dissatisfied and preach revolt. Let them take care. The distance from a general or a drummer-boy to me is the same under certain circumstances, and if one of these circumstances presents itself I shall shoot one like the other."

Nothing can resist such language when it is known that he who uses it is ready to pass from words to deeds.

Having thus established, at the beginning, his sovereign power, Napoleon strove, during the whole of his career, to maintain it. To those at his feet he distributed favours and glory, but knowingly. Thus, after Auerstädt, he said to the Empress, who had expressed astonishment at the great honours accorded to Davout: "Davout is a man to whom I can distribute glory without inconvenience; he will never know how to bear it."[11]

"The annoyances which Napoleon experienced very often resulted in fits of anger, from which those in his private circle were, however, saved, because he had always need of witnesses. One might have said that he could do nothing without set purpose. It was, therefore, always in public that he showed his discontentment by means of reprimands, sometimes very hard ones, but limited to words. He considered that these scenes were necessary to maintain vigilance and stimulate zeal, which it was necessary should increase with the difficulties of the circumstances."[12]

If a general sought to escape from his authority or neglected to observe rules, he was called to order in a manner which admitted of no reply. One morning Gouvion-Saint-Cyr, on his return from Naples, where he had been replaced in his command, attended the levee at the Tuileries. "You have doubtless received the permission of the Minister of War?" asked Napoleon. "No, sire," replied Saint-Cyr. "But there was nothing for me to do at Naples." "If, within two hours," said the Emperor, "you are not on the road back to Naples, you will be shot before noon on the plain of Grenelle."

He treated General Loison in the same manner because he had left Liége, where he was in command, in order to spend two days in Paris, whence he was called by urgent business. To forget for one moment that he was the master was to him high treason.

Consequently we can readily believe Chaptal, when he tells us that, with the exception of two or three generals who had known him in his youth and had retained a certain liberty in his presence, all the others trembled when they approached him.

We must not conclude, however, that this harshness was habitual to Napoleon. Although, owing to his southern temperament, he was naturally irritable, his outbursts of violence were, as we have just seen, rather calculated demonstrations than explosions of blind anger. He was Italian, and by nature essentially a diplomatist and practical. Consequently, in many cases he closed his eyes to his generals' irregularities purposely, and also, in the end, through lassitude. It was thus that, at the Eylau cemetery in 1807, he replied merely with a gesture of disdain to the invectives of Augereau, who came to him full of anger and despair after the routing of his army corps.

"The name of the conqueror of Castiglione," he said to those around him afterwards, "is national property and must be respected."[13]

In 1812 Napoleon instructed Montbrun to proceed rapidly to Vilna with his army corps in order to prevent the Russians destroying the large stores they had accumulated there. Murat, wishing to appropriate the credit of the operation, stopped Montbrun on his march and thus caused him to arrive late. This intervention produced a scene which gives a striking idea of the character of the men who appeared in it.

"Seeing Montbrun at the head of his army corps, the Emperor, furious, dashed towards him, addressed him in that violent manner which he adopted only too often, and threatened to send him to the rear as good for nothing. The commander of the 2nd cavalry corps attempted to explain. 'Silence!' cried Napoleon. 'But, sire …' 'Will you be silent?' 'But, sire …' and

Montbrun, with a look, sought Murat's aid. But Murat spoke not a word, whilst Napoleon, getting more and more heated, continued his threats. It was then that Montbrun, overflowing with anger, drew his sword, seized it by the point, and hurled it behind him over his head—and whilst this sword, whistling through the air, fell more than forty feet away, he set off his horse at a gallop, shouting, 'Go to h—, all of you!' and dashed to his tent, where he remained, awaiting arrest. For a few moments Napoleon did not move; then, white with anger and astonishment, he set off again without a word ... All the witnesses of this painful scene expected to see Montbrun summoned before a courtmartial, or imprisoned, or at least dismissed from the army. But none of these things happened, and the affair was hushed up. Perhaps Murat, when *tête-à-tête* with his powerful brother-in-law, confessed the truth. ... Montbrun retained command of his army corps, but this scene explains the little regret which was expressed, three months later, in the bulletin of the battle of Moskowa, at his death."[14]

In the same way Bernadotte, who plotted against the First Consul at Rennes, and who compromised the movements of the army at Auerstädt and Wagram, profited by special indulgence because he was Joseph's brother-in-law.

We must not, therefore, expect to find any distributive justice in the manner in which Napoleon treated his generals; his conduct towards them depended essentially on personal consideration and momentary circumstances. Exceedingly hard, after Baylen, on Dupont, whom he thought of shooting, whom he imprisoned, without trial, after having cashiered him, struck him off the rolls of the Legion of Honour, deprived him of all his dotations and his title of count; he showed much more indulgent towards MacDonald after Katzbach, for Vandamme after the capitulation of Kulm, and for Gouvion-Saint-Cyr after that of Dresden. In 1813 he was no longer the same man.

The customary punishment for errors was a sharp upbraiding expressed in Napoleon's particularly vehement tone; he "heartily rated" blunderers or those who, were thoughtless. His severity was generally limited to that.

In 1805, when Murat advanced too rapidly on Vienna, he wrote to him, on November 11, from Molk, as follows:

"Cousin, I cannot approve of your manner of marching. You are acting thoughtlessly and do not attentively examine the orders I give you ... You have thought only of the vain glory of entering Vienna ... Glory exists only where danger lies—there is none to be had in entering a defenceless capital."

On the following 16th of November he once more reprimanded Murat in the following terms:

"It is impossible for me to find adequate words to express my dissatisfaction. You command but my vanguard and you have no right to make an armistice without my orders. You are making me lose the fruits of a campaign. Break the armistice immediately and advance on the enemy ... This was but a stratagem ... The aide-de-camp of the Emperor of Russia is a scamp. Officers are nothing when without authority, and this one had none whatever ... You have allowed yourself to be tricked by an aide-de-camp of the Emperor, and I cannot conceive how you ban have consented to be so deceived."

In 1808, in reply to a reprimand of the same type, Murat expressed the sorrow it had caused him.

"The Grand Duke of Berg must allow me to express my mind to him," wrote Napoleon. "When he does well I shall say nothing. When he, does something which displeases me, I shall tell him. That is my custom."[15]

There we have the tone and declarations which characterize the bearing of a leader towards his subordinates. From this point of view the following letter sent to Berthier on February 10, 1806, on the subject of his brother Leopold's journey to Paris is no less suggestive:

"I am annoyed that you have sent your brother to Paris. I did not wish to see him and I shall not do so. Write to him to leave immediately. Your brother has made two millions in Hanover and he must not give himself airs. If, now that he is rich, he wishes to escape from his duties he will find himself in queer street.

"I regard a general who leaves his troops as dishonoured. As to a woman's confinement, I am not going to enter into those details. My wife might have died at Munich or at Strasburg before I would have altered by a quarter of an hour the execution of my plans or views ... Military men are becoming quite feminine, and I intend to be inflexible. If General Berthier had come without orders he would have been arrested."

From the point of view of deviations from probity Napoleon was excessively indulgent. Several of his generals, such as Soult and Masséna, were peculators and pillagers. When things went too far he made them disgorge, but without otherwise punishing them. In 1806 he seized at a Leghorn banker's a sum of 3,000,000, the illicit earnings of Masséna , but shortly afterwards he consoled him with the title of the Duke of Rivoli and an income of three hundred thousand francs.[16] All this was, we must admit, of doubtful morality, and confirms our opinion that Napoleon cared nothing about keeping his generals to a belief in pure patriotism and military duty accomplished disinterestedly.

After penalties, we must obtain an idea of the Emperor's methods of recompensing his soldiers. No one distributed more open-handedly what Marshal Bugeaud in his picturesque phrase called "the feed of oats," but, as in the case of penalties, recompenses were dealt out systematically. "Napoleon sought to govern men by imagination, vanity, and interest ... As his extraordinary faculties made him capable of great and splendid things, he employed them in captivating the imagination of France, the world, and posterity ... Hence the truly admirable part of his power and life, and if we only consider that we cannot place him too high. However, a severe observer will perceive that it is the intelligence of the imagination, and imagination itself more than the purely moral sentiment of what is just and right which did everything. Take for instance religion: it was not its truth but its influence and prestige which prompted what he did for it, and so with everything else."[17]

The first method of reward was promotion. On the constitution of the Empire, Napoleon created for his companions eighteen marshalships, four of which were reserved for old servants—Kellermann, Lefebvre, Pérignon, and Séruriei. The fourteen other marshals Were Berthier, Murat, Moncey, Jourdan, Masséna , Augereau, Bernadotte; Soult, Brune, Lannes, Mortier, Ney, Davout, and Bessieres. Most of these were men who had been associated with Napoleon's fortunes for some time—companions of his Italian and Egyptian days, and men of Brumaire. Other generals of value—Saint-Cyr, Lecourbe, Grenier, and Vandamme—were left on one 'side because their devotion to the new state of things was uncertain.

He provided all his marshals with magnificent positions. To those who, like Murat, Bernadotte, and Berthier, were closest to him through family alliances or the nature of their services, he gave sovereign principalities; to others he distributed, with the title of Prince or Duke, large dotations, taken from the immense domains which he carved at will from conquered countries. Berthier became Vice-Constable, Master of the Hounds, Prince of Wagram, Duke of Valengin, and Sovereign Prince of Neufchâtel. He possessed an income of 1,354,000 francs, without counting the revenue from his Neufchâtel principality.

Murat was Grand Admiral, Grand Duke of Cleves and of Berg, and then *passe-roy* of Naples, as the old soldiers of the Guard used to call him.

Masséna, the Duke of Rivoli, and Prince of Essling, had an income of 800,000 francs without counting his salary of 200,000 francs as Marshal and leader of an army corps; Davout, Duke of Auerstädt and Prince of Eckmuhl, had an income of 900,000 francs; and so with the others.

He also gave them fine hotels in Paris and magnificent estates in the suburbs of the capital: Grosbois to Berthier, Savigny-sur-Orge to Davout, Grignon to Bessieres, La Houssaye to Augereau, Polangis to Oudinot, Rueil to Masséna, and Les Coudreux to Ney.

In addition to the title of Prince or Duke, which commemorated decisive battles (Castiglione, Rivoli, Montebello, Elchingen, Auerstädt, Essling, Wagram, and Moskowa), other duchies, granting no territorial authority but provided with an annual dotation of 60,000 francs, were distributed to mar-shals or generals. These were Dalmatia,[18] Istria, Bellune, Trevise, Feltre, Padua, Rovigo, Tarente, Reggio, Raguse, Vicence, Frioul, etc. Brune and Jourdan were the only marshals who did not receive titles of nobility. In order to bind his companions-in-arms still more firmly to the maintenance of his throne and dynasty he went still further; he married them to women of his own choice, selected from amongst the richest heiresses in France, thus founding families which, to use his own expression, would be "centres of support" for the great Empire.

The marshals were not the only ones who were thus generously rewarded; generals, colonels, and other officers also received "dotations which, joined to the title of count, baron, or chevalier, were to recall throughout the ages the recollection of the glorious ancestor, the companion of the new Caesar. These dotations were rarely below 4000 francs a year, and often reached 40,000 or 50,000 francs. Alright, the Emperor's cousin, and doubtless favoured on that account, received from 1808 to 1812 an annual dotation of 288,000 francs from the Emperor's extraordinary Domain, and in addition—like many oth-ers—a dotation from the Mont-de-Milan and the Domain of the kingdom of Italy. Baraguey d'Hilliers had an annual dotation of 20,000 francs, Beaumont 30,000 francs, Belliard 53,012 francs, Lasalle 50,000 francs, Colbert 10,000 francs, Corbineau 10,000 francs, Junot 80,000 francs, Milhaud 30,000 francs, Montbrun 24,000 francs, Rapp 110,882 francs, Savary 162,055 francs, etc."[19] One can see the inequality of the positions and understand the feeling of jealousy which resulted.

In addition to these magnificent incomes, the Emperor distributed numer-ous intermittent rewards. On September 23, 1807, he gave 11,000,000 francs in gratuities to marshals and generals of division. "Every general who returns with the army will receive a thousand, two thousand, or three thousand louis with which to amuse himself during a few days in Paris; it is on that account that the Vice-Constable distributes these gratuities to them."[20]

Promotion, titles of nobility, and much money—these, then, were the allurements held before every one in the army. Every one—generals, officers, and soldiers—could aspire to them, for, every bit as much as Masséna, the son of a publican, and for fourteen years a soldier and non-commissioned officer; as Ney, the son of a cooper; as Lefebvre, a miller's son who was the first to receive from Napoleon a title of nobility because he had been a sim-ple soldier whom every one in Paris[21] had known as a sergeant in the French Guards; as Murat, the son of an innkeeper; as Lannes, the son of a stableman; and as Augereau, the son of a mason and a fruit-seller,—all, every bit as much as these could, in principle, reach the summit of the ladder. Every one per-

ceived above him, on a higher rung, a former comrade, and said to himself
that he was as good as he was; not to be on the same level was torture to him,
so he strove to rise higher. But, however high he rose, he still found other
occupants who had formerly been his equal; consequently no rank obtained
by him came up to his expectations. "Look at Masséna ," said Napoleon a few
days before Wagram, "he has acquired sufficient glory and honour, yet is not
content. He wishes to be a prince like Murat and Bernadotte, and will kill
himself to-morrow to obtain his desire."[22]

"To these substantial rewards of position and money Napoleon added, as
a means of recompensing his army, others in which imagination and public
opinion played a leading part."[23] In the first place there was the Legion of
Honour, in which civil and military merit mingled in a national brotherhood.

The various ranks in the Legion admitted of a flotation, but this was only
an accessory. In Napoleon's mind "the Legion of Honour was a moral institution which added strength and activity to that spring of honour which so
powerfully moves the French nation ... It was the creation of a new money
of a very different value from that which came from the public treasury, a
money the value of which was unchangeable, and the source of which could
not be exhausted since it was founded in French honour, a money, in short,
which could alone be a reward for actions regarded as above reward."[24] The
Legion of Honour was not only a reward, it was a political institution; in this
sense it was intended, in the mind of its creator, to constitute, "in the new
society whose elements were scattered, without system and without cohesion"[25] a "granite block," the flower of the nation which would take the place
of the privileged persons of former days.

This new aristocracy was to be recruited principally from the army.

To those who made the objection that crosses and ribbons were baubles
worthy of a monarchy, the First Consul vivaciously replied:

"... I defy you to show me an ancient or modern republic in which
there were no distinctions: You call these baubles, well, it is with baubles
men are led."[26]

Ranks in the Legion of Honour were high rewards which, if they were
to retain their value in the eyes of public opinion, must not be distributed indiscriminately. Bulletins, orders of the day, words of praise, a more
affectionate manner or a smile—one of those charming smiles which won
the hearts of generals as much as those of simple grenadiers—were still
other means adopted by Napoleon to give his army a final increase of
energy, incentive, and dash. These were distributed in carefully measured
doses by a master in the art of leading men at the very right moment and
in the manner best suited to the occasion.

The bulletin of October 15, 1806, recognized Davout as possessing "distinguished bravery and great firmness of character, the first qualification of a man of war." The Emperor was sparing in his praise, Méneval tells us. The victory of Auerstädt was worth more, however, than this mention in the bulletin Consequently he granted the 3rd corps the honour of being the first to enter Berlin, he passed it in review, loaded it with rewards, and sent it the following order of the day:

> Generals, officers, non-commissioned officers, and soldiers of my 3rd army corps—
> I wished to assemble you in order personally to testify to my satisfaction in your splendid conduct in the battle of the 14th.
> I have lost brave men, and I regret them as I would my own children. But, like true soldiers that they were, they have died on the field of honour.
> You rendered me on that occasion signal service. It is to the brilliant conduct of the 3rd corps that we owe the results you see before you.
> Soldiers, I have been satisfied with your courage, and you, generals, officers, and non-commissioned officers, you have for ever gained the right to my gratitude and favours.

This simple eloquence and these measured words, added, it is true, to numerous promotions and decorations, electrified the 3rd corps. To judge of the effect produced, one has only to read Davout's letters to his wife.

"Yesterday the Emperor passed the 3rd corps in review," he wrote on November 29, 1806, "and every one will remember it eternally. He made numerous promotions, granted decorations to more than five hundred soldiers, and completed his favours by the praise and proofs of satisfaction he bestowed."

In the letter which followed this, he expressed himself as follows:

"I am very delighted, *ma petite aimée*, with the impression which the Emperor's praise of my conduct has made upon you. I shall always be electrified and superior to myself every time there is a question of meriting the favours he has bestowed upon me and, in short, of serving him."

However, the imperial egoism and the restrictions of the system appeared once more on this occasion. Davout had won a victory at Auerstädt which was quite distinct from the Emperor's victory at Jena; he had given battle to the chief Prussian army, whereas the Emperor had only routed Hohenlohe's rearguard. Auerstädt had been the decisive battle, but at first the Emperor would not make a distinction between the two fights. He wished the day of October 14, 1806, to bear but a single name—the battle of Jena. It was not until March 1, 1808, that he decided to recognize the rival victory publicly, by giving Davout the title of Duke of Auerstädt.

Words of praise and personal gifts were also, we have said, amongst the means of influence of General Bonaparte, or the Emperor Napoleon, over his subordinates.

The following is the letter which he wrote to Major Auguste Colbert, who was wounded in the Syrian expedition:

> HEADQUARTERS, CAIRO, July 12, 1799.
> I send you, Citizen, a pair of pistols to replace those you have lost. I cannot give them to any one who will make better use of them.

On May 21, 1800, he again wrote to Colbert as follows:

> I have received, Citizen, your letter of the 15th (Floreal) in which you inform me of your return from Egypt. Never shall I forget the bravery you displayed in Syria. Welcome!

Such attention filled Colbert with enthusiasm, as the following letter to his mother shows:

> Yesterday I received a letter from General Bonaparte in reply to the one I wrote him on my arrival here. It is very honourable tome: he says that he will never forget the bravery I displayed in Syria and he welcomes me. Behold, my dear mother, my great man, the one to whom I can devote myself. It is a long time since, for the first time, he awakened in my soul the desire for glory. To merit his esteem will ever be my finest victory. The more I have seen of this man, the greater I have found him.

Did Colbert, when writing this letter, realize that even at that time one of Bonaparte's greatest powers was the knowledge of how to secure the attachment of men of his ability? A knowledge of the human heart, the faculty of winning hearts by a letter, a word, an attention,—a precious qualification for a general, especially when he commands men so sensitive as Frenchmen,—was, as we see, one of Napoleon's powers.

Many other similar instances of moral rewards of various kinds devised by the Emperor aught be given. We will conclude our enumeration with the following narrative.

In 1807, in the month of June, Ney's 6th army corps, attacked on the Alle by vastly superior forces, cleverly escaped from the enemy's clutches by retreating for two days. Napoleon, with imposing forces, rejoined the 6th corps at Deppen, but by that time it was quite out of danger. The Emperor, proceeding to Ney's bivouac, congratulated him in front of the whole army for his splendid conduct; after which he made the whole of the reinforcements, the guard, Lannes' corps, and the cavalry division of Lasalle, Grouchy and Nansouty file off in front of the 6th corps. What finer homage could be paid to bravery? What a feeling of pride and noble emulation can thus be awakened in man's heart and imagination!

As in the case of the distribution of great positions, many special considerations presided over that of rewards. Certain services were purposely unrecognized, because those who had rendered them did not please.

This systematic partiality was particularly apparent in the bulletins. "The Emperor composed his bulletins with the very greatest liberty, paying attention, first of all, to his desire to efface everything and establish his infallibility, then seeking for the kind of effect he wished to produce on foreigners and the French public, and finally yielding to his views regarding his lieutenants—to his good-will or illwill towards them. Truth came a long way behind all this."[27] Consequently nothing could equal his generals' surprise when they read the bulletins received from Paris; and yet it was little they asked for, so well had the Emperor succeeded in curbing their vanity. But if, when face to face with the master, they held their tongues, they did not hesitate to cry out against the injustice they suffered when his back was turned. On the evening of Marengo, Kellermann, coming into the presence of Bonaparte, who was surrounded by a large number of officers, received this cold reception: "You made a fairly good charge," and to increase the effect produced the First Consul, turning at the same time to Bessieres, the Commander of the Consular Guard, said to him: "Bessieres, the Guard covered itself with glory." In the third edition of the Marengo bulletin, published in 1806, Kellermann's name was not even mentioned. Despite his decisive charge, he received no promotion after Marengo. "Would you believe it, friend," he wrote to Lasalle, "Bonaparte has not made me a general of division—I who have just placed the crown on his head."[28]

Vandamme, who during the whole of the Empire, in spite of his brilliant services, waited in vain for his marshal's baton, was less guarded in expressing his anger. "He is a mean-spirited fellow, a forger and a liar," he exclaimed one day in the presence of thirty generals and superior officers, the majority of them Württembergers or foreigners, "and but for me, Vandamme, he would still be keeping pigs in Corsica."[29]

Many others, just as discontented but more prudent, said nothing, so as not to retard the moment when a majorat in Westphalia made them part of the privileged class.[30] This state of things created around Napoleon an atmosphere of anxiety, servility and jealousy, which far from displeased him. Divide ut imperes" might have been his motto every bit as much as it was Louis XI's and Catherine de Médicis'.

Even those of his lieutenants who were on the friendliest terms with him, such as Lannes, were jealous of a favour granted to a neighbour. When Lannes received no mention in the bulletin after the capitulation of Prentzlow, he bitterly complained of the omission and was consoled by Napoleon in the following caressing words:

"You and your soldiers are children! Do you believe that I am not aware of all you have done to second the cavalry? There is glory for every one. Another day it will be your turn to fill the bulletin of the Grand Army with your name."

Completely brought round by this paternal scolding, Lannes hastened to reply:

"Yesterday I had Your Majesty's proclamation read in front of the troops. Its final words produced a deep impression on the hearts of the soldiers. They all began to shout: 'Long live the Emperor of the West!' It is impossible for me to tell Your Majesty how much these brave men love you; truly a mistress could not be more beloved than you are in their eyes. I beg Your Majesty to inform me if, in future, you wish me to address my despatch to the Emperor of the West, and I ask this in the name of my Army Corps." This clumsy flattery pleased the Emperor, for "he loved praise from whatever mouth it came. Moreover, he was known to have been more than once imposed upon by it. Constant admiration was ever successful even when it was expressed somewhat foolishly."[31] The following facts show to what an extent the servility of generals was carried and Napoleon's complaisance in receiving the most vulgar homage.

In 1806, on leaving Berlin for the campaign in Poland, a proclamation was addressed to the army promising it fresh triumphs and declaring all the Emperor's love for his soldiers. On this occasion Marshal Brune, Commander of the Boulogne reserve, issued the following order of the day, which was published in the Monitewr, where everything was printed by order.

> Soldiers, for fifteen days in succession read in your dormitories the sublime proclamation of His Majesty the Emperor and King to the Grand Army. Learn it by heart. Every one of you, touched to the heart, will shed tears and will be carried away by that irresistible enthusiasm which inspires heroism.[32]

Almost everybody adopted this servile attitude, for to remain a man in his presence, that is to say to preserve independence of character and thought, was to run a risk.

In brief, the Imperial Army was influenced solely by the passion to please a single man who dazzled with his prestige and omnipotence, and who distributed riches and glory just as he thought fit. The impulsion thus given was for a time irresistible. But on the day when the master's prestige and power declined, his generals' sacred fire began to die down, the motor slackened its speed, and that enormous machine, the army, got out of order. Thus, every system of exploiting men which has only private interests in view is inevitably doomed to early ruin. But what art was shown in handling these men, in influencing them, in turning them, in forming them into the finest army of the world!—and also what a pity it is that this art was not placed at the service of a noble and just ideal. In that case, however, Bonaparte would not have become Napoleon and the history of Europe would have been quite different.

In spite of the personal point of view which he adopted in distributing glory, honours, ranks, and even high positions of command according to his own fancy, Napoleon had a definite opinion regarding the intrinsic value of his marshals, and he certainly established differences amongst them, a gradation with regard to intelligence, character, and aptitude for chief command. But he never clearly expressed his private opinion. He did not wish any one around him to look consequential. Desaix was the only man of whom he spoke with a sort of enthusiasm during the whole of his life. But Desaix died at Marengo on June 14, 1800.[33] Even at St. Helena, where human greatness held forth no further hopes for him, he spoke to posterity solely in the interest of his glory and dynasty.

"I think I may be permitted to affirm,"writes Mme. de Rémusat, "that the Emperor did not love one of his generals. He said ill of them fairly often and sometimes rather serious ill. He accused them all of great greediness, which he purposely encouraged by infinite liberality. One day, when he was passing them in review before me, he pronounced against Davout this sort of judgment: 'Davout is a man to whom I can distribute glory without inconvenience; he will never know how to bear it.' Speaking of Marshal Ney, he said, ' he possesses a thankless and factious disposition. If I am destined to die by the hand of a Marshal, the odds are that, that hand will be his.' Of that discourse I have kept in mind that Moncey, Brune, Bessières, Victor, and Oudinot appeared to him to be only mediocre men, destined to remain but titled soldiers all their lives; and that Masséna was somewhat a used-up man of whom one saw he had been jealous. Soult sometimes disquieted him. Skilful, rough, and proud, he negotiated with the Master and disputed his conditions. The Emperor overawed Augereau, who had more rusticity than true firmness in his manners. He was fully aware of Marmont's vain pretentions and wounded him generally with impunity, and he was also acquainted with MacDonald's customary bad temper. Lannes had been his comrade, and sometimes this marshal wished to remind him of it. He was prudently called to order. Bernadotte showed more spirit than the others; he was ceaselessly complaining and, in truth, was often harshly dealt with."[34]

These interesting appreciations give us but an incomplete idea of the military value attributed in Napoleon's mind to his marshals. Most of them were, strictly speaking, only men for immediate use—handy men, fighters. At the head of this glorious phalanx marched Ney, the brave of the brave, and Murat, whom Napoleon called at one and the same time a simpleton and a hero. Lannes was an excellent commander of an army corps. "He was wise, prudent, audacious, and possessed imperturbable coolness when face to face with the enemy. Napoleon, who had seen the progress of his understanding, often expressed surprise at it. He was superior to all the generals of the French army on the field of battle when it was a question of manoeuvring 25,000 infantry men. He was still young and would have improved; he would perhaps have even become qualified to undertake great tactical movements, which he did not yet understand."[35]

Lannes, therefore, was not yet the complete General-in-Chief whose portrait has been drawn for us by Napoleon as follows:

"Firmness, which is, moreover, a gift from heaven, is an essential quality of a general.[36] But for a general to be complete there must be perfect equilibrium between his perspicacity and his character, or moral courage. This is what Napoleon called 'being square as much at the base as at the top.'"[37] If his courage is much superior, a general oversteps his ideas, and, on the contrary, he does not dare to carry them out if his character or his courage are inferior to his intellect. The mind, added Napoleon, taking a sailing ship as a means of comparison, is the sail, and character the draught of water. If the latter is considerable and the masts are weak, the vessel makes little progress, but it resists the violence of the waves; if, on the contrary, the sails are strong and high and the draught of water small, the vessel can navigate in fine weather, but at the first storm it is submerged. To sail well the draught of water and the suit of sails must be in exact proportions.[38]

The sort of moral courage which he appreciated the most was that which he called "two o'clock in the morning courage," that is to say, the courage of an *improviste* who, despite the most sudden events, retains, nevertheless, his habitual liberty of mind, judgment, and decision.[39] On this subject Napoleon said that he had observed that he possessed this sort of courage more than any other and that he had met few men to equal him in that respect. He declared that the faculty of retaining coolness in the midst of the most serious events was indispensable to the man in command of armies, and he expressed himself on this point in the following terms:

"The first quality of a General-in-Chief is to possess a cool head, which receives correct impressions of things, which never gets overheated, does not allow itself to be dazzled or excited by good or bad news, so that the successive or simultaneous impressions which he receives in the course of a day class themselves in his brain and are accepted at their true value; for common sense and reason are the result of the comparison of several sensations taken into equal consideration. There are men who, owing to their physical and moral constitution, form a picture out of everything: whatever knowledge, intellect, courage and other good qualities they may have, nature has not fitted them for the command of armies and the directing of great military operations."[40]

In the case of we Frenchmen, it is these qualities of moral courage and *sangfroid* which ought especially to be sought for in our generals, for "in France we shall never lack men of intellect or makers of plans, but we shall never have enough men of great character and vigour, in brief, men possessing the sacred fire."[41]

"Men who do not possess much character but are highly intellectual are the least fitted for war: they are ships whose masts are disproportioned to their ballast; it is better to have a good deal of character and little intellect. Men who are intellectually mediocre and whose character is in proportion often succeed in this profession."[42] Napoleon mentioned Prince Eugène de Beauharnais, in whose case this equilibrium between character and intellect was the sole merit, and which nevertheless sufficed to make him a very distinguished man.[43] He added that people formed a very imperfect idea of the strength of character necessary to wage, with a full knowledge of its consequences, one of those great battles whence depended the fate of an army, a country, and the possession of a throne. Consequently, observed he, one rarely found generals who were in a hurry to wage battle. "They took their position into careful consideration, they formed their combinations and meditated upon them, but there began their indecision, and nothing was more difficult and yet more precious than to know how to decide."[44]

The generals who possessed intellect and character in the same high degree were Caesar, Hannibal, Turenne, Prince Eugène of Savoy, and Frederic.[45] In his opinion, Maréchal de Saxe and Wellington had more character than intellect. Of all the generals of the Revolution, Desaix and Hoche were the only ones whom he considered might have gone far.[46] Desaix possessed in a very high degree that precious equilibrium defined above. Kleber was endowed with the greatest talent, but was only a man of the moment. He sought glory as the only road to pleasure. Moreover, he was in no way national in his outlook and could just as easily have served a foreign nation.

He began his military career in his youth under the Prussians, a fact of which he was very proud.

Moreau did not amount to much in the front rank of generals ... nature had not finished its work in him, with the result that he had more instinct than genius.

In the case of Lannes, courage was at first superior to intellect, but later intellect increased daily to form a balance. He had become very great at the time of his death. "He was a pigmy when I took him, a giant when I lost him." In the case of another whom he mentioned at St. Helena, intellect, on the contrary, surpassed character: one could not assuredly refuse to recognize his bravery, but nevertheless he thought, like many others, of the bullets.

Speaking of ardour and courage, the Emperor said:

"There is not one of my generals whose watergauge, as I call it, I do not know. Some, he said, fitting gesture to words, are up to the waist, others up to the chin, and others, finally, are over head and ears—and the number of those, I assure you, is very small."

Suchet was "one whose character and intellect had grown surprisingly."

Masséna was a very superior man who, thanks to a very special privilege, did not possess the muchdesired equilibrium until he was under fire; it grew in his case in the midst of danger. His distinguishing characteristic was stubbornness. He was never discouraged.[47] He prepared for an attack rather badly, and his conversation was not over-interesting, but at the first cannon shot, in the midst of the bullets and danger, his thought acquired strength and clearness.[48]

In Soult's case, his talent as a general was not precisely his strongest point; he was much more an excellent orderer, a good Minister of War ... however, the whole of his campaign in the south of France was very fine.

What is difficult for us to believe is that this man, whose appearance and attitude indicated great character, was a slave in his household[49] ... He was a very ambitious man led by his wife.

To complete this gallery of marshals who appear to have been the best fitted to assume chief command we have still to give the Emperor's opinion regarding two leaders whose cold and severe qualities certainly placed them amongst Napoleon's most skilful lieutenants, namely, Marshals Davout and Gouvion-Saint-Cyr.

Napoleon was a man of the Midi and in that quality he was especially fond of "those gaseous who carried their heads high and feared nothing."[50] We are sometimes astonished, writes General Bertrand, to see the Emperor prefer this officer to that, who in many respects possessed superior qualities, but the fact of the matter was the Emperor had a leaning towards venturous men.[51] Davout was cold, methodical, circumspect, and fastidious; whilst being animated with the idea of acting on the offensive at all cost, an attitude which characterized all his military operations, he left nothing to chance. His suspicious, hard, and pitiless character was not calculated to attract sympathy. Napoleon called him "a vigorous policeman." At the time of the Egyptian campaign, he refused to acknowledge that he possessed intellect, and the Staff repeated the phrase attributed to the General-in-Chief, i.e. "Davout is a stupid ass." If we recall that other description of his—"Davout is a man to whom I can give glory without inconvenience; he will never know how to bear it"—we can believe that that first impression was never completely effaced. However, Davout's brilliant military operations compelled the Emperor to show his esteem. Auerstädt was a revelation, and the bulletin of October 15, 1806, had to state that the Marshal had displayed "distinguished bravery and great firmness of character, the first quality in a soldier." The fine Ratisbonne manoeuvre and his services at Eylau and Wagram could only magnify Davout in the Emperor's mind; consequently, in 1812, in view of war with Russia, he spoke of giving him command of a vanguard army of 200,000 men. He asked him for a report on the organization of this army, explained his plan of operations to him and added, as a mark of supreme confidence in his military talents, "ponder over your maps in the light of all these suppositions and make your objections to me."[52] However, in the course of the campaign, zeal shown by Davout, who, it is said, "wished to foresee everything, order everything, and carry everything out,"[53] once more prejudiced the Emperor. This regrettable impression grew, estranged from his confidence a bold, tenacious and wise soldier, and favoured his leaning towards Murat, whose temerity flattered his hopes still more.[54] Nevertheless, in the end, Napoleon recognized that the Prince of Eckmuhl possessed "a strong and very superior mind" and proclaimed him, at St. Helena, "one of the purest glories of France."

To that firmness of character which characterized the whole of his career, Marshal Gouvion-Saint-Cyr joined great intelligence. Marbot, who was under his orders in 1812, speaks of him in the following terms: "He was one of the most capable military men in Europe. I have never known any one who directed his troops better on the field of battle. It was impossible to find a calmer man. Whatever might happen, he was as though made of ice. One can imagine what such a character, seconded by a taste for study and meditation, gave this general officer."[55] There, indeed, it would seem we have a man who possessed in a high degree the necessary mental qualities and character of a General-inChief, yet he was always given the second place by Napoleon. This was chiefly owing to political reasons. Gouvion-Saint-Cyr showed the same firmness of character in political opinions as in his military work. He openly disapproved of the 18th of Brumaire; on the proclamation of the Empire, he abstained from sending his adhesion to the new state of affairs; and Napoleon never entirely forgave him for this independent spirit and moral courage. To this essential reason must be added the antipathy of two contrary temperaments: on the one hand, daring, impetuosity, the rapidity of lightning, brilliant actions, and fiery words; on the other, prudence, method, well-thought out combinations, and a horror of anything theatrical. Napoleonic warfare, made up of violence and audacity, furious entries into campaign, and tremendous thunderclaps, which destroyed the military power of a country at one blow, was not according to Gouvion-Saint-Cyr's manner. "Moderation," says his historian, Baron Gay de Vernon, "was so much his guide in all things that he seemed to avoid even excess of well-doing, preferring good solid actions to those which were too brilliant and which, though they struck like lightning, disappeared as rapidly, and placing perhaps much above the glory of conquering to the bitter end the surer merit of being never conquered."[56] Saint-Cyr himself wrote that he would never advise any one to adopt Napoleon's method of warfare. "I have always thought that, if it often gave him a great advantage, it was the result of his character more than method itself, which ever appeared to me, even at the time of his most brilliant victories, to be too hazardous to be followed by generals of a less extraordinary temper."[57] Such a doctrine could not win for Saint-Cyr the Emperor's confidence. However, Daru has related that in 1813, after Saint-Cyr's capitulation at Dresden, Napoleon uttered the following eulogistic appreciation: "The Allies have violated the rights of man, not in order to deprive me of 20,000 to 25,000 soldiers, but to make Saint-Cyr prisoner. He is the first of us all in defensive warfare." Then, after a moment's silence, he added: "But I am superior to him in attack."[58]

But at this period, when misfortune was knocking at his door, Napoleon was all gentleness towards his generals. At St. Helena he told another tale. He reproached Saint-Cyr "with never going into action, with seeing nothing for himself, and with leaving his comrades to fight alone … I was wrong in employing Saint-Cyr … Comte Lobau was to blame for that. He was always talking to me about him … He was liked by those who served under him because he rarely fought and spared his men." Gouvion-Saint-Cyr appears to us to be a skilful strategist who only lacked the divine spark to be a great soldier approaching Napoleon.

One day, at St. Helena, Dr. O'Meara asked the Emperor who was the most skilful French general. Napoleon made him the following reply, with which we will conclude this only too brief chapter:

"That is difficult to say, but it seems to me that it is Suchet. Formerly, it was Masséna, but we may regard him as dead. Suchet, Clausel, and Gerard are, in my opinion, the best French generals."

NOTES

1   Nietzsche's *Humain, trop humain. Aphorisme*, p. 164.
2   Gourgaud's *Journal de Sainte-Hélène*, vol. ii. p. 414.
3   *Mémoires de Mme. de Rémusat.*
4   *Ibid.*
5   Gourgaud's *Journal de Sainte-Hélène*, vol. i. p. 44.
6   *Mémoires de Mme. de Rémusat*, vol. iii. p. 46
7   Gourgaud's *Journal de Sainte-Hélène*, vol. i. p. 44.
8   Vandant's *L'Avènement de Bonaparte.*
9   Yung's *Bonaparte et son temps*, p. 101.
10 Mémoires de Mme. de Rémusat. vol. i. p. 393.
11 *Ibid*, vol. ii. p. 370.
12 Méneval's *Mémoires*, vol. i. p. 265.
13 Ségur's *Histoire et Mémoires*, vol. iii. p. 163.
14 Narrative of an eyewitness, set down by General Thoumas in *Les Grande Cavaliers du premier Empire.*
15 Quoted by General Thoumas in *Les Grands Cavaliers du premier Empire*, p. 465.
16 *Mémoires de Marbot*, vol. iii. p. 19.
17 *Mémoires de Mme. de Rémusat*, preface, vol. iii. p. xi.
18 "Soult was exceedingly vexed at receiving the title of Duke of Dalmatia and being thus placed on the footing of the Dukes of Vicence, Bassano, Bénévent, and many others, whose new names were no more significant than the old ones. He wished and hoped to be made Duke of Austerlitz. The battle of this name was indeed his finest feat of arms and the time at which it was fought the finest of his military career. But Bonaparte would not share the honour of this splendid victory with any one."—Saint-Chaman's *Mémoires*, p. 104.
19 Frédéric Masson's *Cavaliers de Napoléon*, p. 51 *et seq.*
20 *Mémoires de Metternich.*
21 *Commentaires de Napoléon Ier*, vol. v. p. 335.
22 Taine's *Le Régime Moderne*, p. 344.
23 *Ibid*, p. 338.
24 Report of Counsellor of State, Rœderer, instructed to present to the Council of State a bill for the creation of the order of the Legion of Honour.
25 Bonaparte's speech before the Council of State (May 4, 1802).
26 Delaitre's *La Légion d'Honneur.*
27 *Mémoires de Mme. de Rémusat*, vol. ii. p. 207.
28 *Mémoires de Bourrienne*, vol. iv. p. 146.
29 *Mémoires de MacDonald*, Introduction, p. 47.
30 *Souvenirs d'un officier de la Grande Armée*, by Elzéar Blaze, p. 123.
31 *Mémoires de Mme. de Rémusat*, vol. iii. p. 201.
32 *Ibid.*
33 Mémoires de Mme. de Rémusat, vol. ii. p. 207 note 1.
34 Speaking of courage and physical courage the Emperor said on the subject of physical courage that it was impossible for Murat and Ney not to be brave but that no one had less brains than they bad, especially the former.—*Mémorial.*
35 *Commentaires de Napoléon*, tenth note on the art of war, vol. iv. p. 112.
36 Gourgaud's *Journal de Sainte Hélène*, vol. ii. p. 126.
37 *Mémorial de Sainte Hélène*
38 Gouvion-Saint-Cyr's *Mémoires*, vol. iii. p. 49.
39 *Mémoires de Sainte Hélène*, vol ii p. 17.

40 *Commentaires de Napoléon Iᵉʳ*, vol. vi. p. 353.

41 Gourgaud's *Journal de Sainte-Hélène*, vol. i. p. 200.

42 *Mémoires dictés au Général Bertrand*

43 *Mémorial.*

44 *Ibid.*

45 *Mémoires dictés au Général Bertrand.*

46 Gourgaud's *Journal de Sainte Hélène*, p. 62.

47 *Commentaires de Napoléon*, vol. i. p. 178.

48 *Mémorial.*

49 *Ibid.*

50 General Bertrand's *Campagne d'Égypte at de Syrie*, Preface, p. 38.

51 General Bertrand's *Campagne d'Égypte at de Syrie.*

52 *Correspondance de Napoléon*, letter 17,621.

53 Ségur's *Histoire de Napoléon et de la Grande Armée*, p. 127.

54 *Ibid.*

55 Marbot's *Mémoires*, vol. iii. p. 177.

56 Baron Gay de Vernon's *Vie de Maréchal Gouvion-Saint-Cyr.*

57 Gouvion-Saint-Cyr's *Mémoires*, vol. iv. p. 225.

58 Baron Gay de Vernon's *Vie de Maréchal Gouvion-Sain-Cyr*, p. 380.

VIII

Rewards and Penalties: Napoleon and his Soldiers

Napoleon as an exciter of energy—His means of influencing his soldiers: promotion, honorary distinctions, hierarchy among the troops—Retirement of old soldiers—His moral means: prestige, familiarity with the common soldier, noble words, allocutions, proclamations—Napoleon's solicitude for the common soldier—Penalties—The Emperor's indulgence and appeals to self-esteem in the repression of faults—Conclusion.

THE GREAT NAPOLEONIC VICTORIES MUST not be exclusively attributed to the Emperor's strategic combinations and tactics; they were also largely due[1]—half due, said Napoleon—to the value of his soldiers. What would have become of the finest military ideas without that sacred fire and that endurance which impelled the common soldier to rush to the fight, despite the fatigue of camp-life and forced marches, and which caused him to face death twenty times when storming positions? But the common soldier, the one who fought in Italy and Egypt as much as the legendary old soldier of the Empire, was he not also—in part at least—a creation of the leader's genius? He was formed, it is true, from that good and fine human clay, the French race, but the genius of the artist was also needed to fashion with this choice material the splendid soldier we know.

In describing Skobelev, Vicomte Melchior de Vogüé has eloquently said that "this singular man was above all a mesmerizer of crowds, an inveigler of hopes. In all the affairs of which he was in command, we shall search in vain for one of those strategical movements which are classical in schools of war; but he had a mysterious gift: everything about him communicated military madness to his soldiers. His presence, wrote one of the combatants at Geok-Tepe, brought about a special excitement of our whole nervous system." With a genius for combinations in addition, the Little Corporal possessed, like Skobelev, the power of animating the common soldier and filling him with enthusiasm, the fluid which is communicated from the leader to the trooper, that magnetic power without which every great general is incomplete; he was, in the highest degree, an exciter of energy.

The imperial soldier stands before us with a characteristic physiognomy. He was frank in bearing and speech, spirited in action, and disdainful of danger—all qualities of his race; but he also possessed that virtue which people are often pleased to refuse Frenchmen—perseverance. What bravely supported suffering those brilliant victories, of which we now only see the splendour, represent! How did the Emperor succeed in obtaining this extraordinary result from his army? This is what we will now endeavour to make clear.

"Whilst the Emperor knew how to stay his generals' pretensions with a firm hand, he spared no pains to encourage and satisfy his soldiers."[2] With this object in view, he employed all the material and moral means at his disposal: promotion, honorary distinctions, material advantages of all sorts, the skilful exploitation of all feelings which impel men to action—pride, vanity, emulation, sense of military honour—and a rational employment of that personal influence which confers on certain men the gift of subjugating armies and crowds.

One of his principal means of action was to maintain in the hearts of his soldiers the hope of reaching, solely by their own efforts, the highest rungs of the military ladder. Every soldier, said he, carried a marshal's baton in his knapsack. A pure illusion, doubtless, but one which sufficed to arouse energy and provoke emulation, the source of great efforts. "Every head was turned by Bernadotte's example," wrote Elzéar Blaze. "Such a marshal was going to become a king and such a grenadier a corporal—a very natural conclusion for us to come to. We each of us thought that there was a sceptre in the scabbard of our sword. A soldier had become a king; every one thought that he also would become one! "Napoleon took care to foster this illusion and to give reality to this bait by promoting, from time to time, old non-commissioned officers devoid of any instruction to the rank of officers. Whilst saying that the best commanded army would be that in which each officer would know how to act for himself, according to circumstances, he desired that "the multitude of ignorant and incapable men should be represented in the ranks."[3]

He sought to appear as a tutelar divinity who, by his will alone, transformed boundless hopes into reality.

To impress simple imaginations all the more, he had a fondness for personally distributing promotions and rewards in front of the troops. Often, when passing an army corps in review, or even on the field of battle, the Emperor stopped in front of a regiment, and calling the officers around him, spoke to them by name. He ordered them to point out those amongst them whom they considered as the most worthy of obtaining either promotion or a decoration; after which he passed to the soldiers. These testimonies, given by their peers, united the corps by bonds of esteem and confidence, and these promotions, discerned by the troops themselves, increased their value in their eyes. At one of these distributions of military rewards, which resembled family scenes, a non-commissioned officer was pointed out to the Emperor as being the best and bravest. The colonel, whilst admitting that he possessed the necessary qualities to make a good officer, added that, in rendering him this justice, he regretted that he could not propose him because of a serious hindrance. "What is it?" asked Napoleon, sharply. "Sire, he can neither read nor write." "I make him an officer," was the retort. "Colonel, you will see that he is recognized in that quality."[4]

He thus sometimes took pleasure, in order to make himself popular, in upholding against the colonels the rights of old soldiers to promotion. "A few days before Leipzig," relates Saint-Chamans, "the Emperor filled all the vacant places in my corps, and there were a good many of them. After having presented to him the officers whom I proposed for the ranks of colonel, major, captain, and lieutenant, I brought forward a few young men to be made into sub-lieutenants. 'That's not what I want,' he said to me, somewhat vivaciously; 'they are too young. Give me some good terrorists.' Not understanding, I opened my eyes in astonishment. 'Yes,' he added, 'give me our brave fellows of '93.' I then brought forward a few old quartermasters, who were as stupid and incapable as they were old. He was delighted with them, and without a question at once promoted them."

This momentary predilection for the Terrorists was only make-believe, an intentional move, a democratic attitude intended to make the old soldiers believe that, "if the Tondu was the cause of people being killed, he also knew how to recompense them." In his conscience, far from liking the Jacobins, Napoleon, as Emperor, was rather disposed by nature to favour the aristocrats. He laid it down as a principal that, in a strongly established government, you ought to give at most a quarter or a fifth of officers' posts to men from the rank and file. Consequently, at a period when his power was greatest, he was lavish in his distribution of promotions to the sons of generals, high officials, and nobles who had rallied to him—to all those who had an attachment for the court. Young Grouchy, after being a sublieutenant for a few months, was made lieutenant; Mme. Walewska's brother, a worthless fellow, was promoted from the rank of lieutenant to that of colonel; Prince Borghèse, the Emperor's brotherin-law, despite his well-known inferiority in military matters, rapidly became a general; and in 1806 two-thirds of the gendarmes, who during the whole war had been in but a single engagement and suffered inconsiderable losses, received their epaulettes.

We find the basis of his thought in this reply to his aide-de-camp, Mouton, who, entrusted with the preparation of a promotion list, expressed astonishment, with his customary frankness, at the promotion of Raoul de Montmorency, who was almost always ill: "One does not govern an Empire, M. Mouton, as one leads a regiment."[5]

Because unjustified choices were made fairly often, one must not conclude that the whole system of promotion was based on political, dynastic, or personal considerations; we must regard those cases merely as favours necessitated by the establishment of a new *régime*. This allowance having been made, we must recognize that the Emperor strove to furnish his army with a sound complement of officers. It was necessary to remain for a fixed time in each rank before being proposed for promotion. In 1805 this period was for a captain five years, for a lieutenant four years, and for a sub-lieutenant four years. No sergeant or quarter-master could be presented for the rank of sub-lieutenant if he had not served for six years, and held his rank for four years, unless he had come from the Fontainebleau military school, or from Saint Cyr.

When an officer was proposed for the rank of major or colonel, he did not receive his commission until he had been presented to the Emperor and had commanded manoeuvres at a review. "As the Emperor knew all the officers personally, his choice was made with discernment. Whilst with the army and on the occasion of the passage of corps through Paris, he held frequent reviews, which were something more than sterile displays. He questioned the officers who were new to him, and ordered them to command manoeuvres in his presence. Those which departed from ordinary routine sometimes embarrassed officers who had not made a sufficiently deep study of their profession. Napoleon imposed on officers with whom he was not entirely satisfied the obligation of studying those manœuvres by placing them under the superintendence of colonels and generals. He never lost an opportunity of making certain for himself if they had profited by this addition to their military education."[6]

It was thus that, in 1805, he wrote to Berthier: "You will note that the Emperor, having put the 58th at Cologne through manoeuvres was satisfied with the officers' and soldiers' appearance, but observed with chagrin that the major had no knowledge of his manoeuvres, that consequently he has ordered that he be suspended for three months, and sent for that time to a camp to receive instruction, and that he will not be reinstated until he has shown that he knows the manoeuvres in the greatest detail."[7]

The military instruction of officers consisting only of the practice of their profession, the majority of the brave old fellows who became officers were entirely lacking in culture. Elzéar Blaze has given us a caricature in that officer, an instructor at the Fontainebleau school, who regarded the platoon school as the best book for the formation of youth and confiscated the logarithms tables as being novels printed in figures.[8]

On campaign, promotion was given on principle only to those who fought and to those especially who fought under the Emperor's eyes. In his opinion, absent ones were always in the wrong. "The Emperor," writes Castellane, "always refused promotion to absent officers, even although wounded; he wished by this method to encourage presence under the flags."

In the Spanish armies, which were far away from him, promotion could only be obtained in cases in which it was impossible to refuse, and it was no rare thing to see captains who had served for fifteen years. This was due, it was said, to the Emperor's fear of giving too much importance to that war in the eyes of France and Europe. Happy, indeed, were those who in battle attracted the Emperor's attention! At that epoch, as at all times, promotion was largely due to chance. Honorary distinctions were distributed in the same manner as promotions. First of all, there were, under the Consulate, presentation arms, a system which he instituted on September 25, 1799. These consisted of guns, axes, bugles, etc., bearing the names of the soldiers to whom they were granted and the names of the actions in which they were won. Swords of honour were also given to officers and soldiers who had distinguished themselves by deeds of extraordinary bravery or who had rendered extremely important services. These rewards were not purely honorary; they carried with them a high stipend. Their number was limited; there were only two hundred swords of honour for the whole army. On the occasion of the distribution of these presentation arms, the First Consul took pleasure in giving to the humblest recipients a special proof of his esteem; he treated them as comrades in arms and in such a manner as to double the value of their reward. "When the First Consul," writes Constant, "made a distribution of arms of honour, there was given at the Tuileries a banquet to which all who had shared in these rewards were admitted indiscriminately whatever might be their rank. There were sometimes two hundred guests at these dinners. General Duroc was the master of the ceremonies and the First Consul took care to recommend him to mix simple soldiers, colonels, and generals together. He ordered the servants to see that the first especially had plenty to eat and drink. These were the longest meals at which I saw the Emperor, who showed there perfect amiability and freedom ... He got them to relate the brave deeds which had brought them national recognition and sometimes roared with laughter at their singular narratives. He pressed them to eat their fill and sometimes drank to their health. But in some cases his encouragement failed to overcome their timidity, and the waiters took away their plates one after the other without them having touched them. This constraint did not prevent them from being full of joy and enthusiasm on leaving the table. '*Au revoir*, my brave fellows,' said the First Consul to them, 'be quick and baptize for me those newborn ones there.'"[9]

On May 14, 1802, arms of honour—exclusively military rewards—were replaced by the institution of the Legion of Honour, intended to recompense both civic virtues and military services. The object of this double character given to the Legion of Honour was to awaken a noble emulation amongst all those who did honour to the country or contributed to its prosperity and glory. "The soldiers who knew neither how to read nor write were proud, as the price of having shed their blood for their country, of wearing the same decoration as men of great civilian talent, and these, on the other hand, attached all the more value to this reward for their work as it was the decoration worn by the brave."[10] And, indeed, the crosses of the Legion of Honour, lavished on military men, were given but parsimoniously outside the army. In 1814, out of 48,000 nominations in the legion, since its creation, only 1200 were civilians. Non-commissioned officers and simple soldiers had their share of these crosses, which were the cause of much envy and jealousy." At the close of each fight and each victory, the regiments received them, and from the Emperor's hand, which increased their value."After Wertingen, he summoned forth one dragoon per regiment and decorated him. After Elchingen; he asked to see the two brave men of the 10th Chasseurs who had captured the flags. "What are you?" he said to the first. "Brigadier, Sire." "Here is the cross." "And you?" he asked the second. "Sire, shoe-maker." "Give him ten louis." Such was his tone and manner.

To still further excite a feeling of emulation in the army, the Emperor established a sort of hierarchy among his troops. The corps were composed of main companies and picked companies. In the battalions, the two picked companies were distinguished from one another: side by side with the light-infantry soldiers, who were pigmies, one saw giants, the grenadiers. "If he had had men of different colour in his army he would have composed black and white companies; in a country in which there were cyclops and hunchbacks, he would have utilized companies, composed some of cyclops and others of hunchbacks."[11] In these words of the Emperor at St. Helena clearly appears the whole of his system, so different from the tendency of modern armies to make everything uniform.

Above the picked companies came the Guards. The young Guard received high pay and shared the magic of its elder, the Old Guard, whose soldiers, nick-named "the Immortals," because they were rarely sent into action, were better paid, better fed, and better clothed than the common soldier. All the regiments were jealous of this sacred body of troops, which, in addition to their material advantages and fascinating renown, had the honour of daily watching over the security of the great man and of being his supreme resource in battle.

Although more particularly benevolent to men who were actually in his service, Napoleon also took an interest in the lot of his old soldiers. According to whether they were still more or less good for work, they could, with protection and good luck, obtain either a place at the Invalides or a modest employment in some administration—forestry, postal, tobacco, or revenue departments—or a small pension, or again, a few *arpents* of land in a conquered country. They could also be admitted into a company of veterans in garrison in a fortress. But nothing was more uncertain than the obtaining of these rewards, the limited number of which was insufficient for all the candidates. The wrecks of the Grand Armies were too numerous to be all sheltered, and more than one brave old soldier, enticed by the Emperor towards a mirage of promotion and glory, found but poverty in his declining days.

The hope of gaining a prize in this lottery of material rewards may partly explain the power and continuity of the effort made by the soldier of the Empire. However, the hope of greater well-being and of greater consideration cannot be regarded as the sole motive which caused these electrified crowds to follow Napoleon's footsteps. The majority of the conscripts, sons of the people, were enrolled by force, and left their village without enthusiasm for warlike deeds. Yet these coerced men, carried away by a powerful influence, were quickly transformed into the splendid soldiers we know. "Duped, the soldier was by Napoleon, as the weak are by the strong, and yet he never ceased to become enthusiastic about him, to come under his charm, and to obey his will; nay, he even loved him, especially when he was no longer there."[12]

What was the secret of Napoleon's mysterious power to create such a state of mind? "The study of the human heart,"replies Méneval, "had taught him the art of attaching men to him and subjugating them. His presence and words aroused enthusiasm. His eloquence was earnest and rapid; his words were energetic, profound, and often sublime. His simple exterior, heightened by an air of grandeur and the habit of command, and the fascination of his look, whose quiet and severe expression penetrated to the depths of the heart, inspired respect, mingled with fear and affection. No leader was more popular in history, and yet never would he consent to humble himself to acquire that popularity."[13]

To these purely exterior causes is to be added the prestige of glory, benevolent familiarity, and a natural and reciprocal sympathy which daily life in common establishes, especially when on campaign, between every chief worthy of that name and his soldiersa sympathy which synthetizes a host of actions and reactions more or less perceptible and many of which escape analysis.

At the beginning he showed, first of all, the prestige of the man who knows what he wants, and whose successes confirm his superiority. At the siege of Toulon he established his authority by means of his character, talent, and bravery. "His attitude was not that of pride, but one recognised in it the assurance of a man who knows what he wants and feels he is in his right place."[14] Soon, the Italian victories produced a halo of glory for this young general of twenty-five whom the soldiers saw walking in their midst, sharing their fatigues and dangers, dashing into the thick of the fight with flag in hand, as at the bridge of Arcola, and crying, "Follow your General!" He appeared to them then, at once as a comrade, whom they themselves advanced in rank with every battle, and as a superior being who had command over events. Their confidence rapidly grew into a sort of cult for this familiar and tutelar god. Although later, they could, at certain moments, grumble about him, the moment the battle came he was ever providence in their eyes and infallibly brought victory.

That which contributed to conquer the soldier's heart was the fact that this great man did not hold himself aloof in his grandeur: he was a familiar genius who spoke to them like a father to his children, and so much so that they imagined that they belonged to him. If he sometimes dazzled them by great military spectacles, like that splendid review at the Boulogne camp where he was seen seated on Dagobert's throne distributing, amidst the beating of a thousand drums, the roar of 3000 pieces of artillery, and the uproar of 100,000 cries of "Long live the Emperor," decorations which he took from the helmets and shields of Bayard and Duguesclin, he also knew how to speak to them in a simple affectionate tone, and with the eloquence of the heart.

A sergeant of grenadiers of the 32nd demi-brigade, Leon Aune, wrote from Toulon to the First Consul to recall himself to his "tutelar god." The brave fellow enumerated his exploits—five brilliant actions, resulting in five wounds. Bonaparte replied to him as follows:

> To BRAVE LÉON,—I have received your letter, brave comrade. You have no need to tell me of your actions. Since the death of brave Benezette, you are the bravest grenadier in the army. You possess one of the hundred swords which I am distributing to the army. All the soldiers agree that you are the model of the regiment. I have a great desire to see you, and the Minister of War is sending you the order. I love you like my own son.
>
> (Signed) BONAPARTE[15]

A sub-lieutenant's commission in the Consular Guard accompanied this letter, which of its kind is quite typical.

In the course of his daily reviews he questioned the soldiers, asked them their names, the enumeration of their campaigns and wounds, showed particular attention to veterans by a friendly pat on the cheek or a pinch of the ear, spoke to them as he would to old comrades, and theed and thoued them with a familiarity that charmed them. "It is thus," said he, "that men are led."[16]

On the eve of battle, in spite of his many anxieties, he redoubled his attention to the common soldier.

"In 1805, on the Danube, he hastily visited the regiments, spoke ardent words to them, formed them into a ring in the midst of the thickly falling snow and with mud up to their knees, told them of the enemy's position, and said that he counted on them. During the three days preceding Austerlitz, he ceaselessly visited all the camps, speaking sometimes to the soldiers, sometimes to the leaders."[17]

On November 29, 1805, Napoleon, after his interview with Dolgorouki, returned along the Briinn to Olmutz road on foot. Carabineers of the 17th Light Horse were stationed as far as the first infantry post of his army. Irritated by the boasting of Alexander's aide-de-camp, he showed his ill-humour by striking the ground with his whip. The sentinel, an old soldier, observed him, then, putting himself at his ease, with his gun between his legs, began to fill his pipe. When Napoleon passed in front of him, he looked at him and said:

"Those fellows there think that they have nothing more to do than to swallow us!

"Oh! oh!" replied the old soldier immediately; "they'll find they're very mistaken, for we shall have something to say about that!"

This answer, adds Savary, made the Emperor laugh; he resumed his serenity, mounted on horseback, and returned to headquarters.

This little campaign scene shows us how familiar and cordial were the relations between the leader and the humble companions who shared his glory. He himself said: "My soldiers were very free with me. I have met many who theed and thoued me. They were instinctively sympathetic; they knew that I was their protector and avenger."[18]

"Bonaparte," writes General Desaix in his diary, "never saw a demi-brigade without persuading it that he considered it the best in his army; he often spoke to them and ever had something vigorous to say. He gave to each demi-brigade magnificent flags on which, in large letters of gold, the names of the battles in which they had distinguished themselves were inscribed. They added the words of praise uttered by their general. The 57th was 'the terrible 57th'; the 18th inspired the phrase, 'I know you well, 18th, you will beat the enemy'; whilst the 32nd called forth the words, 'I was easy in my mind, for the 32nd was there.'"

On becoming Emperor he continued, successfully, to employ the same plan.

On November 30, 1805, he addressed to the 17th infantry regiment, which he had entrusted with the defence of Santon, a speech full of fire and energy. After having pointed out the great importance of this position in the battle he foresaw, he reminded the 17th of the numerous actions in which it had distinguished itself during the Italian campaign, and impressed upon it the necessity of retaining its old reputation. The regiment, after having sworn to die at its post rather than surrender, proceeded to the spot and ardently set to work to fortify itself.[19]

During the battle of Lutzen, the Emperor, whilst proceeding to the right wing, met the Compans Division, composed of marines, entering into line. Galloping in front of them, the Emperor shouted these inspiriting words: "Forward, marines! show that you also are soldiers of my Grand Army."

A thousand enthusiastic shouts responded to this appeal, and these soldiers fought as valiantly as our best infantry.[20]

Finally, by his celebrated proclamations, which every one will remember, he addressed himself to the whole army, he excited its emulation by quickening its pride, its anger against the enemy, and by promising it glory, rest, and material enjoyments. These warlike orations, as the Institute then proclaimed, constituted a new form of eloquence which was lacking in French literature. "Napoleon instinctively discovered a model military eloquence, he adapted the oration to the use of French valour, and in such a way as to electrify it. Henry IV uttered some witty and happy things which Crillon and the noblemen repeated, but in this case an eloquence adequate for great operations and in proportion to those armies which had sprung from the people was needed—an eloquence which was brief, serious, familiar, and monumental. From the very first amongst the number of his means of conducting great military operations, Napoleon found it."[21]

It was not only by speech that he captured the soldier's heart, but also by his attitudes and his manner, sometimes sharing his fatigue and watching over his needs. He was seen on the eve of Jena to take a lantern to aid the gunners in their work, and at Eylau to assist in the working and pointing of cannon. The next day but one after Friedland, at the crossing of the Pregel, he himself lent a hand to the pontonniers to encourage them. At his incessant and interminable reviews, which often lasted six hours in succession, he walked slowly along the ranks putting innumerable questions, collecting petitions stuck on the ramrods of the guns, and rendering justice to demands. On his visits to bivouacs he tasted the soldier's bread and drank from his gourd. On the morning of Eylau, he was seen to ask, in the case of one company, for a potato per squadron, and, seated on a truss of straw, to cook them in his fire, turning them over with the end of a stick. All this, it may be said, is the bluff of a great leader, but this bluff made a strong impression on Napoleon's men.

Probably no leader of an army gave more orders than Napoleon to assure the upkeep and subsistence of his armies. The rapidity of the movements and the defective organization and working of the administration often resulted in these orders—which were sometimes, moreover, inexecutable—not being carried out, but the soldiers, seeing the Emperor full of solicitude for them, did not dream of reproaching him with their privations and suffering. One must confess, moreover, that he did not hesitate to throw on to others, with evident injustice, the responsibility. But his object was attained; he was and remained in the eyes of the soldier the "tutelar and infallible god."

Moral and material rewards gave to the Grand Army an impulsion which for a long time was irresistible, but the offensive inspiration, however powerful it may be, is not sufficient to make an army out of a collection of men. In such an agglomeration there are multitudinous elements of disorder against which one must react. To assure cohesion and concordance of efforts, discipline is necessary. One must, doubtless, aim at creating in an army a moral discipline which impels each individual to sacrifice his personal interests for the general good; that is an ideal at which one should ever aim. But it is never attained. The maintenance of order necessitates the application of penalties intended to repress inevitable errors and weakness.

The methods to be employed to assure discipline differ very considerably according to the nationality of armies. "Armies are, in their good as in their bad qualities, the faithful representation of the nations whence they proceed, one must, consequently, judge and lead each of them with views and by means which are appropriate. This doctrine is especially applicable to the French army whose constitution is peculiar and whose originality exceeds that of other armies."[22] Differences of temperament, general education and civilization are some of the conditions one must take into account.

"If I were in command of Frenchmen," Frederic II said one day, "I would make them into the finest soldiers in the world. To pass over a few thoughtless acts, never to worry them unnecessarily, to encourage the natural gaiety of their minds, to be scrupulously just towards them, and to inflict no minutiae upon them—such would be my secret in rendering them invincible."

It was in this way, so well adapted to their national character, that Napoleon himself conceived French discipline. Provided he was brave whilst under fire and resisted fatigue, the soldier could commit many faults without exhausting the Emperor's indulgence.

"Every act of repression was an exception and was ordered merely for the sake of example. When they fought amongst themselves or went marauding, when they pillaged or violated, they had to be born under a very unlucky star to receive the punishment proscribed by the regulations."[23]

Even during the finest period—in 1805 and 1806 —the imperial armies were undisciplined. Davout's corps, in which order was maintained with remarkable firmness, formed a contrast with the remainder of the troops. In the Urn campaign the soldiers openly gave themselves up to marauding. After Jena, discipline was relaxed to such a point that the lives of the officers were no longer safe.[24] After Eylau, 60,000 men, almost all marauders, were missing from the army.[25] On the evening of Wagram, the whole French army was drunk. One could write a volume on the acts of indiscipline tolerated in the armies of the Republic and the Empire.[26]

Napoleon closed his eyes so long as he judged that the success of his operations was not compromised by disorder, but on the approach of battle he sometimes decided to make examples in order to bring his men together.

In 1796, on leaving Nice for Italy, a battalion claimed its pay, complained of being without boots, and refused to set off. Bonaparte forced it to start, then, ordering it to stop, sent it ignominiously to the rear. The same day the major was placed on trial, the battalion broken up, the officers disbanded, the non-commissioned officers dismissed, and the soldiers scattered by fives in other corps.[27] At the opening of the 1796 campaign the troops were in the greatest destitution, and disorders recommenced. By an order of April 22, 1796, major-generals were authorized to shoot there and then officers or soldiers who by their example incited others to pillage and destroyed discipline.

But these examples of severity were exceptional; they were not according to Napoleon's habitual manner. His system was above all to appeal to moral means to lead back his soldiers to the observation of discipline. In November 1796, Vaubois, forced into the Haut-Adige, was obliged to abandon Trente, and beat a precipitous retreat towards Rivoli. Two demi-brigades, the 39th and 85th, had given way without being able to be rallied. Bonaparte gathered the whole division on the plateau of Rivoli and spoke to it in these words:

"Soldiers, I am not pleased with you. You have shown neither discipline, nor constancy, nor bravery. No position could rally you. The 39th and 85th, you are not French soldiers. Chief of the Staff, have inscribed on their flags, 'They no longer belong to the army of Italy.'"

This speech, delivered in a severe tone, drew tears from those old soldiers, and several grenadiers, who possessed arms of honour, cried: "General we have been slandered. Place us in the vanguard and you will see whether the 39th and 85th belong to the army of Italy." Having thus produced the desired effect, Napoleon addressed a few words of consolation to them. A few days afterwards these two regiments covered themselves with glory.[28]

By these means Napoleon was able to inculcate in his soldiers so great a feeling of self-respect that they themselves saw to the repression of misdeeds which might tarnish their glory. After Ulm, the stragglers of the army, reassembled at Braunau, had to submit, on returning to their companies, to the affront of a search, in which each of them, deprived of the booty he had pillaged, was handed over to the joyous and severe fustigations of his comrades.[29]

The day after a battle, squads could be seen forming themselves into courts and summoning before them soldiers who had been absent from the fight. Their defence was heard and a decision without appeal either acquitted them or meted out a fraternal punishment, inflicted there and then. The officers closed their eyes to this and sometimes even encouraged this salutary penalty. "Recommend the colonels," wrote Davout to Gudin after Eylau, "to encourage the soldiers to give the slipper and to lay it on hard in the case of all those who did not appear at the battle, or who were absent without legitimate motive."

It was thus that, despite disorder whilst on the march, and in camp, a special discipline, inspired by emulation, a point of honour, and a cult for the Emperor resulted in the French army of this epoch being able to march and fight in a marvellous manner, although most of the time it was badly fed, badly maintained, and badly paid.

There is here ample matter for reflection for those who will have the honour of leading our national army to battle. Certainly everything is not to be imitated in Napoleon's method. In exploiting all the resources of the country to the fullest extent, he had especially in view the establishment of the supremacy of his power in the world and the surpassing in glory of the illustrious captains of all time. But, setting aside his excessive ambition, one cannot help admiring the power of suggestion which this extraordinary man acquired over his soldiers. Can we by the same means once more lead our soldiers to the same glorious destiny in the battles of the future? "There is nothing," the Emperor said, "that one cannot obtain from Frenchmen by offering them the allurement of danger; it seems to put spirit into them: it is their Gallic heritage. Valour and a love of glory are with Frenchmen an instinct, a sort of sixth sense. How many times, in the thick of the battle, have I stopped to watch my young conscripts throwing themselves into the fight for the first time! Honour and courage issued from every pore."[30] The race has not changed during the last hundred years. Are not Frenchmen to-day in the vanguard of nations which dash towards the perilous conquest of the air? And when we see the superb disdain of death which animates new generations, have we not a right to conclude that it will suffice to know how to lead them with the military tact of Napoleon to renew, when necessary, the exploits of the Imperial epoch?

NOTES

1   Gourgaud's *Journal de Sainte Hélène*, vol. ii. p. 485.
2   *Mémoires de Mme. de Rémusat,* vol. ii. p. 110.
3   Pierre Cantal's *Etudes sur l'armée revolutionnaire*, p. 44.
4   Méneval's *Mémoires*, vol. ii. p. 206.
5   Castellane's *Mémoires,* p. 81.
6   Méneval's *Mémoires*, vol. ii. p. 312.
7   *Correspondence*, 8023.
8   *Souvenirs d'un officier de la Grande Armée*, p. 14.
9   *Mémoires de Constant*, vol. i. p. 160.
10 *Commentaires de Napoléon*, vol. ii. p. 153.
11 Jean Morvan's *Le Soldat imperial*, vol. ii. p. 474.
12 *Mémoires de Méneval* vol. iii. p. 8.
13 *Ibid.*
14 *Souvenirs d'un sexagénaire*, vol. iii. P. 10.
15 *Correspondance de Napoléon*, vol. vi. 4529.
16 Gourgaud's *Journal de Sainte Hélène*, p. 580.
17 Jean Morvan's *Le Soldat imperial*, vol. ii. p. 311.
18 *Mémorial de Sainte Hélène*.
19 *Journal d'opérations du 5ᵉ corps.*
20 *Vie de Planat de la Faye*, p. 131.
21 Sainte Beuve's *Causeries du lundi*, vol. i.
22 General Trochu.
23 Jean Morvan's *Le Soldat imperial*, vol. ii. p. 495.
24 Letter of Marshal Ney, October 18, 1806.
25 Fezensac's *Souvenirs militaires*, p. 163.
26 Pierre Cantal's *Etude sur l'armée révolutionnaire*, p. 118.
27 Ségur's *Histoire et Memoires*, vol. i. p. 190.
28 *Commentaires de Napoléon Iᵉʳ*, vol. i. p. 250.
29 Ségur's *Histoire et Mémoires*, vol. ii. p. 428.
30 *Mémorial de Sainte Hélène*.

IX[1]
Napoleon on the Battlefield: On the Eve of the Fight

Napoleon's activity on the eve of battle—Napoleon two days before
and on the eve of Jena—The day of October 12, 1806: awaiting
information before coming to a decision; political action on the
enemy, letter to the King of Prussia, proclamation to the Saxons—
Rallying of the troops left in the rear and revictualling—The night
of October 12–13: lack of information on October 12 due to the
absence of cavalry exploration on the left flank—Day of October
13: arrival of information; dispositions taken at 9 a.m.—Departure
from Gera at 10—Dispositions taken at 11.30 and at 3.30—The
Emperor's arrival on the heights above Jena at 4 o'clock; the first
reconnaissance of the enemy—The night of October 13–14:
superintendence of execution—Order to Davout at 10 p.m.—
Second reconnaissance of the enemy on October 14 at 1 a.m.—
Conclusions.

A BATTLE IS THE ESSENTIAL act of warfare. In Napoleon's strategy, all
combinations aimed exclusively at a decisive battle, with the destruc-
tion of the adversary as its immediate consequence. The Emperor knew
better than any one that, in this act of violence, victory belonged to the
one of two opposing parties who brought into operation the greater mass
not only of material but also of intellectual and moral forces. It was with
the object of attaining this superiority of living force that the whole of the
Emperor's mental activity was directed in the course of a campaign; and on
the eve of battle this activity, at all times prodigious, redoubled in intensity.
He then lived only for the realization of his object, towards which he strove
with a force of will which has doubtless never been equalled.

How many battles have been lost through the heedlessness and torpor of
generals-in-chief!

"At Vittoria," said Napoleon to Gourgaud, "we were beaten because Joseph
slept too long. If I had slept on the night of Eckmühl, I should never have
carried out that superb manoeuvre, which was the finest I ever made. With

50,000 men I beat 120,000. Thanks to my activity, I was here, there, and everywhere. I awakened Lannes by kicking him, he was so fast asleep. A general-in-chief ought never to sleep."

He added that if he had not been so fatigued at Waterloo he would have ridden on horseback the whole night. As a matter of fact, Napoleon made a rule of spending the day and night preceding a battle in reconnoitring the forces and position of the enemy, in studying the field of battle, in visiting the bivouacs, and in giving orders.

Face to face with such a method of action, which is quite within the reach of all those entrusted with the direction of an army, what are we to say of the criminal negligence of generals who desert their duties at the decisive moment and who cannot be dragged from their criminal quietude either by the pressing appeal of their subordinates or by the cannon itself? Let us repeat once more—activity! activity! thou art one of the essential elements of victory!

We are going to give an instance of this activity on the part of the Emperor. We are going to follow him step by step during the two days preceding Jena, before accompanying him on to the field of battle, which will be the subject of the last chapter of this study.

In a preceding chapter we left the Emperor at his Auma headquarters, on October 12, at 5 a.m., at the very moment he had given orders for his army to wheel about to the left, bringing the corps of the first line on the Saale, from Naumburg to Kahla.

We will go back to Napoleon at Imperial headquarters at that same hour on October 12, and attach ourselves to his footsteps up to the eve of the battle of Jena (October 14).

After having dictated a few letters during the morning, the Emperor mounted on horseback at Auma on October 12 at 8.30 a.m., to proceed to Gera, where Imperial headquarters were to be established. *En route*, between Auma and Mittel, shortly after 9 o'clock, he passed in front of the Gudin division, which was about to march to Naumburg, and was accorded military honours. The distance from Auma to Gera is thirty kilometres, and can be easily covered by a horseman in a little under four hours. Napoleon reached Gera about noon, and took up his quarters at the Ducal palace.

What was his opinion of the situation at that time?

The bulletins and his letters to the marshals and Talleyrand have handed it down to us as follows:

"The Prussian army occupies Eisenach, Gotha, Erfurt, and Weimar; it is striving to reunite its columns at Erfurt; the king's council is divided by different opinions, it is ever deliberating and never in agreement." In such a state of mind, what resolution could this council come to? It could decide on one of three things: take the offensive from Erfurt on Jena,[2] remain at Erfurt on the defensive,[3] or retreat behind Ilm and the Saale.[4]

The position of the French army on October 12 enabled a reply to be made to these three hypotheses: Three corps in the first line on the Saale, Davout at Naumburg, Lannes at Jena, Augereau at Kahla; then, a march in the rear, the Guard, Soult, and Ney; finally, on the right flank, a short march from Naumburg and watching the road from Leipzig, Bernadotte and Murat, with part of the cavalry reserve. The remainder of the cavalry reserve (3 divisions), the Imperial mounted Guard, the parks of artillery, and the engineers were in the rear, and needed still one or two days to rejoin the mass of the army.

Before ordering fresh movements, Napoleon wished to obtain more precise information regarding the enemy. He impatiently awaited it.[5] Meanwhile, in the afternoon, he wrote the following letter to the king of Prussia—a letter so noble in its tone, so full of apparent moderation, and also so Machiavelian, inasmuch as its object was to show the King's Council that the division in its ranks and the uncertainty of its plans were known, that we reproduce it in its entirety:

The Emperor to the King of Prussia

IMPERIAL CAMP, GERA, Oct. 12, 1806.

MONSIEUR MON FRÈRE—I did not receive Your Majesty's letter of September 25 until the 7th. I am grieved that they made you sign that sort of a pamphlet.

I reply to it merely to protest that never shall I attribute to you the things it contains; everything in it is contrary to your character and the honour of both. I pity and disdain the authors of such a work. Immediately afterwards I received the note of your minister of October 1. It fixed a rendezvous with me for the 8th. Like a good knight, I kept my word with him. I am in the middle of Saxony. Believe me, I possess such forces that all yours cannot hold the victory in the scales for long. But why shed so much blood? With what object? I use to Your Majesty the same language that I addressed to the Emperor Alexander two days before the battle of Austerlitz. May heaven grant that traitors or fanatics, more the enemies of you and your throne than they are of me and my nation, will not give him the same advice to arrive at the same result! Sire, I have been your friend for six years. I do not wish to profit by this sort of frenzy which animates your councils, and which makes you commit political errors at which Europe is still quite astonished, and military errors of the enormity of which Europe will not be long in hearing. If, in your note, you had asked me for possible things, I should have granted them; but you demand my dishonour, and you may be certain of my reply. War then is between us, and our affiance broken for ever. But why send our subjects to the slaughter? I do not value a victory which will be purchased by the lives of a large number of my children. If I were at the beginning of my military career and had to fear the hazards of battle, this language would be quite out of place. Sire, Your Majesty will be beaten; you will have compromised the repose of your days and the existence of your subjects without the shadow of a pretext. To-day you are intact and can treat with me in a manner that is in conformity with your rank; before a month you will treat in a different situation. You have given way to irritation, for which they cunningly calculated and prepared. You say that you have often rendered me services. Well, I wish to prove to you that I remember them. You are in a position to save your subjects from the ravages and misfortunes of war. Hardly begun, you can end it, and you will take a step for which Europe will be grateful to you. If you listen to the madmen who, fourteen years ago, wished to take Paris, and who have now embarked you on a war and immediately afterwards *on offensive plans which are equally inconceivable*, you will do an injury to your people which you will be unable to remedy during the remainder of your days. Sire, I have nothing to gain against Your Majesty. I want nothing and have never wished for anything from you. The present war is an imprudent one.

I feel that perhaps by this letter I am irritating a certain susceptibility natural to every sovereign, but circumstances will not permit me to speak with deference. I speak as I think. Moreover, Your Majesty must permit me to tell him that it is not a great discovery for Europe to learn that France is three times more populous than Your Majesty's states, and quite as brave and as warlike. I have given you no real motive for war. May you order this band of malevolent and imprudent men to be silent in the presence of your throne and the respect which is due to it—may you restore tranquillity to yourself and your states. If you never again have an ally in me, you will find a man desirous of only waging wars indispensable to the policy of my people, and of avoiding the shedding of blood in a struggle with sovereigns who are in no way opposed to me industrially, commercially, and politically. I beg Your Majesty to see in this letter only my desire to spare human blood, and to spare a nation which, geographically, ought not to be an enemy of mine, the bitter repentance of having lent too willing an ear to ephemeral sentiments which become excited and calm down with so much ease among nations.

Whereupon, monsieur mon frere, I pray God to hold you in his holy and worthy keeping.—Your Majesty's good brother,

NAPOLEON

Continuing his political manoeuvres, the Emperor prepared, that afternoon at Gera, a proclamation to the Saxons with the object of detaching them from the Prussian cause.

At the same time, he thought of the troops in the rear, which it was necessary to bring up, and of the important question of re-victualling on the approach of the battle. He also had, without the slightest doubt, an interview with Soult, who was at Gera with his headquarters and one of his divisions.

Such was the way in which that afternoon of October 12 at Gera was employed. In the evening the Emperor went to bed as usual at eight o'clock and rose about midnight. It was then that he came to the important decision to give his army a rest on the 13th.

Only one corps, that of Ney, was to move: from Auma it was to go to Roda, where it would be about three leagues from Jena and in a position to assist Lannes in case of an attack.[6]

For what reason did he give the army this rest?

"One does not make forced marches with an entire army in order to rest a day afterwards."[7] The reason given by the Emperor was "to give the troops time to come up,"[8] to enable the corps "to procure provisions with which to fill the caissons, to rally the stragglers, and to put the arms in condition,"[9] but it is permissible to believe that he had another unconfessed motive—namely, that, in the early hours of October 13, he was uncertain as to the direction in which his corps were to be sent. The information which he required to enable him to come to a decision could not reach him until eight o'clock in the morning of that day.[10]

However that may be, correspondence was continued on October 13 at one in the morning: letters to Commissary of Stores Villemanzy concerning revictualling and the establishment of a hospital at Auma, to Duroc on the subject of the revictualling of the Guard, to Prince Jerome, Nansouty, d'Hautpoil, Klein, and others, instructing them to advance the troops in the rear, to Ney ordering him to Roda, and to other Marshals telling them to give their troops a rest. At 2 a.m. the Emperor wrote to the Empress as follows:

I am to-day at Gera, *ma bonne amie*, and things are going very well, quite as I hoped they would. With the aid of God, the situation, in a few days, will have assumed a very terrible character, I believe, for the poor King of Prussia, whom, personally, I pity because he is good. The Queen is at Erfurt with the King. If she wishes to see a battle, she will have that cruel pleasure. I am in excellent health and have already increased in weight since my departure. Yet I travel from twenty to twenty-five leagues a day, on horseback, in my carriage, etc. I retire to rest at eight o'clock and rise at midnight. I imagine sometimes that you have not retired to rest.—Ever thine.[11]

He then addressed to Talleyrand the third bulletin of the Grand Army which had been dictated during the night.

This bulletin shows us Napoleon's idea of the position of the enemy on the night of the 12th to the 13th.

"The enemy, cut off from Dresden, was still at Erfurt on the 11th, and was striving to reunite its columns, which had been sent to Cassel and Wtirzburg on offensive operations." This supposed position was quite inexact, for on the morning of the 11th the principal army was concentrated in the neighbourhood of Blankenhayn, south of Weimar. We perceive, moreover, on reading Napoleon's correspondence, that, on that morning of October 13, he was embarrassed by the lack of precision in his information. He was incessantly demanding news of the enemy's movements, which he awaited impatiently. But it was difficult for the Marshals' reports to reach him before the morning of the 13th. The day of the 12th had been a very hard one for the corps of the first line. Davout's march had been from forty to forty-five kilometres, Augereau's thirty-seven, and Lannes, besides covering twenty-four kilometres, had had an encounter. The reports could not be made out until night-time, and to carry them to headquarters at Gera the officers of the Staff had to cover forty kilometres through an unknown country. This slowness in the reception of information and also the imprecision of the news arose through lack of cavalry exploration between the corps of the army of the first line and the enemy. If the three divisions of the cavalry reserve which was marching with the baggage had been sent out at the beginning to the left of the army, in the direction of Erfurt, it is certain that the Emperor would have been better informed. But he had his reasons for acting otherwise: the Prussian cavalry's reputation for superiority prompted him to direct his own prudently.

In this state of mind the Emperor, at 7 a.m., wrote Murat the following letter:

GERA, Oct. 13, 1806, 7 a.m.

You have received orders from the Staff to make no movement to-day, in order to give the troops a little rest. If the Prince of Württemberg came to Leipzig it would be a good opportunity to give him a licking. I know his position exactly; he has not more than 10,000 men[12] I have no news either from Jena or Naumburg; I shall doubtless receive some in an hour. Let your dragoons rest, so that, according to *the order that I shall give to-night*,[13] they will reach Jena to-morrow. My intention is to march straight on the enemy. Send a commissary of war to Leipzig with an order to prepare there 30,000 rations of bread and to send them to Naumburg. I shall leave here at 9 in the morning, in order to be at Jena at noon or one o'clock. If the enemy is at Erfurt, my plan is to direct my army on Weimar and attack it on the 16th.

We will take this letter as the point of departure in following the thread of the Emperor's ideas on the day of the 13th. At the same time that he wrote it he sent officers in search of news. "General Lemarois must proceed to Naumburg (45 kilometres) *at full speed*. There he will see Marshal Davout's position. At Naumburg he will obtain information regarding the enemy. He will see if the river Unstrut has been crossed, and where the enemy is. Afterwards, *at full speed*, he will bring me the information he has collected to Jena (30 kilometres) where I shall be at noon."[14] "Orderly officer Seherb must proceed *at full speed* to Jena. He will see what is happening. He will obtain information regarding the enemy and return with it to me. He will bring me news of Marshal Lannes and of *the enemy's movements*."[15]

At the same time Captain Scherb received a letter from the Emperor to Marshal Lannes. Napoleon informed Lannes of his arrival at Jena at one o'clock, and of his route via Roda, and ordered him to send to him at that point "information concerning the enemy's movements." He added: "Marshal Ney will be at Roda during the day, barely three leagues from you. If the enemy attacks you, do not fail to inform him immediately."

The enemy's movements—that is what he wanted to know.

In the Emperor's opinion the enemy was at Erfurt on the 11th, but what had it done since? The three hypotheses still remained: immobility, offensive, or retreat. It was necessary to dispel the fog of war which hid the truth before giving orders. Between eight and nine in the morning the expected information arrived: Davout's report of the 12th from Naumburg, the examinations of prisoners and deserters, and also Lannes' report of the 13th from Jena. The latter, doubtless sent early on the 13th, reported events of the 12th. "The army corps arrived yesterday before Jena. The enemy was there with 12,000 to 15,000 men. After having fired a few cannon shots at us, they withdrew in the direction of Weimar ...

"According to information given by inhabitants, the King was still at Erfurt the day before yesterday; I cannot say if he wishes to wage battle on us instead of retreating." Marshal Lannes added, in a postscriptum: "I learn at this very moment that the enemy has a camp of 30,000 men a league from here on the Weimar road: it is very possible they intend to wage battle."

This information produced the following effect on the Emperor, who did not, however, yet seem to have an absolutely clear idea as to what the enemy was doing. He wrote to Murat at 9 a.m.: "At last the veil is drawn aside, the enemy having begun its retreat to Magdeburg. Move as soon as possible with Bernadotte's corps in the direction of Dornburg." His idea, therefore, was that they were retreating, but a few lines farther on the Emperor was much less affirmative. "I believe that the enemy will try to attack Marshal Lannes at Jena, or that they will flee. If they attack Marshal Lannes, your position at Dornburg will enable you to assist him."

In view of an attack on Jena, Soffit, with his cavalry and one of his divisions, was called from Gera to Roda. The two other divisions remained available at Gera, midway (about forty-five kilometres) between Naumburg and Jena, ready to leave at 2 a.m., so as to reach one or the other point eleven hours afterwards. The Emperor was to proceed to the vanguard at Jena, where he would see things for himself, which is often the quickest way of coming to a decision and also the best one, on condition that you do not attach too much importance to the necessarily restricted situation under your eyes.

At 10 o'clock the Emperor thought fit to send out a new bulletin, the fourth of the campaign and the second that day.

> Events are happening with rapidity. The Prussian army is taken in the act, its storehouses are captured, and it is outflanked. It appears that it has started to march to Magdeburg, but the French army has gained three marches on it … the battle will take place *in a few days*, and the result will decide the fate of the war. Frenchmen should be without anxiety.

Napoleon had, as we see, the greatest confidence in victory, and rightly so, and yet at that very moment Lannes was threatened with a disaster. Hohenlohe had set off at noon with his 50,000 men to attack him when a counter-order made him return to his Capellendorf camp.[16]

At 10 o'clock the Emperor set off on horseback from Gera to Jena, but, instead of taking, as he had informed Lannes, the Roda road, which was extremely bad and obstructed with troops and baggage, he followed the northern road, via Kostritz, Weissenborn, and Klosterlaunitz, longer by some kilometres, but easier to follow for a numerous staff and also nearer to Naumburg, in which direction the Emperor was still watching. After an hour and a half's march he reached Kostritz, "which is a fairly large place on the Jena road and where another road branches off to Naumburg."[17] He stopped there for a short time and established "his bivouac." He discovered that Soult's two divisions left at Gera, would be better placed at Kostritz, where they would have three leagues less march to make the next day, whether in the Naumburg direction or in that of Jena. He therefore ordered that these two divisions should sleep that evening at Kostritz, "one bivouacking on the Jena road and the other on that of Naumburg."[18] He then, about noon, mounted on horseback and continued his journey. From half-past one in the afternoon the firing of musketry and cannon was heard in the direction of Jena. At three o'clock the Emperor, still galloping towards the sound, was a league and a half from Jena, when he received fresh information from Lannes. Perhaps at that very moment, too, his orderly officer Seherb overtook him and reported what he had seen—namely the offensive movement started by Hohenlohe at noon. The Emperor and his Staff dismounted, and Berthier received orders to dictate and send off the following four letters, dated from the bivouac at one and a half leagues from Jena at 3 in the afternoon:

I. To Marshal Lefebvre, in Command of the Foot Guards

It appears, Monsieur le Maréchal, that the enemy will attack the army this evening, or certainly to-morrow morning. Its outposts are firing at this very moment. The Emperor orders you to advance as soon as possible. Send on this information to Marshal Soult who follows you. *Let an aide-de-camp ride his horse to death if necessary.*

II. To Marshal Soult

The Emperor wishes to inform you, Monsieur le Maréchal, that the enemy is marching in force on Jena, and it is even believed that it intends to attack this evening. Hasten your march on Jena.

III. To Marshal Ney, at Moesdorf[19]

The enemy, with 40,000 men, is between Weimar and Jena ; push on with your whole army corps as far as you can to Jena,[20] in order to be there early to-morrow ... Direct all that in the rear, with your light cavalry, to the gates of Jena. Endeavour to be at Jena this evening in order to be present at the reconnaissance which the Emperor will make.

IV. To Marshal Davout, at Naumburg

The Emperor, Monsieur le Maréchal, learns, one league from Jena, that the enemy is face to face with Marshal Lannes with nearly 50,000 men. The Marshal even believes that he will be attacked this evening. If, this evening, you hear an attack at Jena you must manoeuvre on the enemy and outflank its left. If there is no attack this evening at Jena you will receive to-night the dispositions for to-morrow.

V. The Same Order to Marshal Bernadotte

Napoleon's attention, as we see, was fixed more and more on Jena. Of the three hypotheses examined in the morning, regarding the possible conduct of the hostile army, he especially kept in view that which anticipated an attack on Jena. He put off, however, deciding on his final dispositions until after his *personal reconnaissance*. No leader of an army has ever accorded more importance to this essential and so often omitted operation.

What the Emperor did not know, owing to the lack of a service for exploration and discovery in advance of his corps of the first line, was that, at that very hour, the King's army, which had left Weimar at noon, was retreating to Auerstädt, via the main road from Erfurt to Leipzig, under the protection of Hohenlohe's army, camped on the plateau of Capellendorf, and that he had only half of the Prussian army before him in the direction of Jena. These orders, having been given, the Emperor continued rapidly on his way, and in half an hour had covered the eight kilometres which separated him from the heights to the east of Jena. He came up with Marshal Lannes there at four o'clock, and thence observed the enemy for the remainder of the day.[21] "After having dismounted on the plateau," writes Savary,[22] "he, alone, approached the enemy's outposts until they fired a few gunshots at him. He returned to hasten the march of his columns, and himself led the generals to the positions he wished them to occupy during the night, but ordered them not to take them up until they could no longer be perceived from the enemy's lines. His bivouac was established on the edge of the plateau." The grenadiers of the 40th regiment (Suchet division) hastened to erect a straw shelter for him, and were honoured by being entrusted with the guard of his august person.[23]

The Emperor kept all the generals who were there to supper. Before retiring to rest he descended the mountain of Jena on foot to see that no ammunition wagon had remained *en route*. It was there that he found the whole of Marshal Lannes' artillery involved in a ravine, which, in the darkness, he had taken for a road, and which was so narrow that the axles of the gun-carriages touched the two sides of the rock. In that position neither advance nor retreat was possible, for there were two hundred vehicles one after the other in the defile. It was intended that this artillery should be used first, consequently that of the other corps was behind it.

"The Emperor became very angry, which was shown by his cold silence. He made frequent inquiries for the general in command of the artillery of the army,[24] whom he was astonished not to find there. But, without wasting time over reproaches, he himself acted as an artillery officer, assembled the gunners, ordered them to get their tools and to light torches, and, himself taking one of the latter, held it whilst the gunners, working under his directions, enlarged the ravine until the axles of the gun-carriages no longer touched the sides of the rock. I shall ever have before my eyes," continues Savory, "the expression on the faces of the gunners on seeing the Emperor stand there, torch in hand, whilst they redoubled their blows on the rock. All were exhausted with fatigue, and yet not one uttered a complaint, realizing the importance of the work they were doing, and not hesitating to express their surprise at the fact that it was necessary for the Emperor himself to set this example to his officers. The Emperor did not leave until the first carriage had passed."

On returning to his bivouac, he thought of Davout. At ten o'clock in the evening he sent him a fresh order, the tenor of which was as follows: "The Emperor has recognized A PRUSSIAN ARMY[25] which stretches a league away before and on the heights of Jena as far as Weimar. He proposes to attack it on the morrow. He orders Marshal Davout to proceed to Apolda in order to fall on the rear of that army. He leaves the Marshal the choice of his route, provided he takes part in the fight." The Chief of the Staff added; "If Marshal Bernadotte is with you, you can march together, but the Emperor hopes that he will be in the position which he pointed out to him at Dornburg." No other order was to be sent to Davout and Bernadotte before October 15, at 5 a.m.

Davout, nevertheless, acted with a vigour which we admire, but Bernadotte profited by this silence to remain inactive on October 14 during the two battles which were being waged on his right and left.

After sending this order to Davout, Napoleon took a little rest, then, at one o'clock in the morning, made a fresh reconnaissance of the enemy, accompanied by General Suchet, a general of division of Lannes' corps. On the occasion of this reconnaissance he went so far outside the line of the outposts that, on returning, an advanced guard, knowing that the Prussians were but a few yards away, mistook him for the enemy and fired. The Emperor had just time to throw himself to the ground to avoid the discharge of musketry.[26] After getting himself recognized, he returned to his bivouac, where we shall shortly return to him.

We might thus follow Napoleon during the days which preceded his other great victories: Austerlitz, Eckmuhl, and Wagram; and we should again note the same activity of mind and body, "the same care in the calculation of all the elements of the resolution he had to come to,"[27] and the same anxiety to inspire confidence and the sacred fire in his army. He visited his soldiers, he spoke to them, he addressed proclamations to them, he assembled his generals, and always, on the night preceding the battle, he himself made a reconnaissance of the enemy. To this last named duty he attached particular importance. By his own confession, he committed a grave piece of negligence in not making "that reconnaissance of the enemy" on the eve of Eylau. He listened that evening to Murat's boasting and allowed himself to be persuaded, without making sure for himself, that Bennigsen had continued his flight. "Several times," he said to Davout, the day after the battle, "ready to respond on that evening to a secret inspiration, I wished to advance on that rideau, but they persuaded me not to do so. That was a great mistake on my part. I placed my trust in Murat. He insisted that the enemy was not behind. I had but to mount that hill and I should have seen everything for myself. The battle of yesterday would then have only taken place to-day and would have been won. But, because bullets were raining down upon that hillock, they succeeded in dissuading me, and although, under such circumstances, a general should always be ready to risk his life, I played the Emperor—I allowed myself to be treated with care."[28]

In 1812, on the four nights which he spent at the bivouac before the Moskova, he was constantly seen on foot, but he was then already less able to support the great fatigue which he formerly imposed upon himself under similar circumstances. He contracted, during those nights, a cold which degenerated the day after the battle into a loss of voice which greatly annoyed him. He was then obliged to scribble his orders on little squares of paper.[29]

On the eve of the battle, Rapp, the aide-de-camp on duty, slept in the Emperor's tent. He relates that Napoleon slept very little that night. Rapp woke him up several times to hand him reports from the outposts, all of which indicated that the Russians expected an attack. At 3 a.m. Napoleon summoned a valet-de-chambre and ordered punch, which he divided with his aide-de-camp.

"He asked me,"relates Rapp, "if I had slept well. I replied that the nights were already fresh and that I had been often awakened. He said to me: 'We shall have to deal to-day with that famous Kutusow. You will doubtless remember that it was he who commanded at Braunau, at the time of the Austerlitz campaign. He remained three weeks in that fortified place without once leaving his room; not once did he mount on horseback to see the fortifications. General Bennigsen, although as old, is a much more vigorous fellow than he. I don't know why Alexander did not send that Hanoverian to replace Barclay.' He took a glass of punch, read a few reports, and added: 'Well, Rapp, do you think we shall do good business to-day?'—'Without a doubt, Sire; we have concentrated all our forces and we are certain to win.' Napoleon continued reading and went on: 'Fortune is an arrant courtezan; I have often said so and I am beginning to perceive it.'—'Your Majesty will recollect that you honoured me by saying at Smolensk that, the wine being poured out, it must be drunk. This is now the case more than ever. The army, moreover, is aware of its position, it knows that it will find provisions only at Moscow and that it has only thirty leagues to travel.'—'This poor army is very reduced,' replied the Emperor, 'but what remains is good, and my guard, moreover, is intact.'

"He sent for Prince Berthier and worked until 5.30 ... He mounted on horseback. The bugles sounded, the drums rolled; and as soon as the troops saw him there was a storm of cheering. 'This is the enthusiasm of Austerlitz,' cried the Emperor, who forthwith ordered the following proclamation to be read: 'Soldiers, here is the battle that you have so much desired! Henceforth victory depends upon you. It is necessary for us, it will give us abundance, good winter quarters, and a prompt return home. Bear yourself as at Austerlitz, Friedland, Witebsk, and Smolensk, so that the most distant posterity will speak of your conduct on this day, so that they will say of you: "He was at the great battle under the walls of Moscow."' The cheering was redoubled, the troops desired nothing better than to fight, and the battle soon began."[30]

We here once more recognize, in a general way, the manner of his best days: the redoubling of his activity on the eve of the battle, night work, and an anxiety to increase the soldiers' *moral* by promises of rest, abundance, and glory. However, he no longer showed the activity of Austerlitz, Jena, and Eckmuhl. The Emperor had grown older and had given way to his need for comfort; he no longer displayed splendid confidence in his star, or his former alertness of mind in striving towards a unique object–victory; he wasted a part of his time over idle things and gossip.

This degeneration was still more pronounced in 1813. A few days before Leipzig the Saxon Major Odeleben found him plunged in a sort of torpor. He was sad, anxious, and as though weighed down by fortune, awaiting news of Blucher's army, which had thwarted his plans, and so unhappy that he had no strength to occupy himself with anything.

There was no movement in his antechamber, which formerly "resembled the stomach of the horse of Troy," so great was the crowd there, ready to serve him. His usual collaborators[31] surrounded him with idle, pendant arms, whilst he, seated upon a sofa in front of a large table, sought to divert himself by tracing large letters on a sheet of white paper.

He was no longer the man of Austerlitz and Jena who, at the slightest hesitation, "struck fire with his four feet."—"Careless and fearing fatigue," writes Marmont, "used up, indifferent to everything, with no belief in truth unless it agreed with his passions, interests, or caprices, filled with a Satanic pride and a great disdain for man, his mind was still the same, the broadest, the deepest, and the most productive that ever was, but, without will-power and decision, fickle almost to the point of weakness."

It is not this Napoleon of 1813 that we shall take as a type of a General-in-Chief, but the one whom we have followed from Auma to Jena in the month of October 1806. Had a similar activity and a like determination to conquer but been shown, in the preparation for battle, by those in command of the French army on October 18, 1870, we should have been able to reply to the simple question as to which army would have been victorious.

NOTES

1   See the sketch map for the entry on campaign of the Grand Army in 1806, and Petri's
     map of Saxony, pp. 189, 192.
2   The Emperor to Marshal Lannes, Gera, October 13, 7 a.m.
3   The Emperor to Murat, Gera, October 13, 7 a.m.
4   The Emperor to Davout, Auma, October 12, 8.30 a.m. The Emperor to Murat, Gera,
     October 13, 9 a.m.
5   The Emperor to Murat, Gera, October 13, 1806, 7 a.m.
6   The Emperor to Marshal Lannes, Gera, October 13, 7 a.m.
7   Hohenlohe's *Letters on Strategy*, vol. i. p. 59.
8   The Chief of the Staff to the Grand Duke of Berg, Gera, October 13, 1806. The
     Emperor to Marshal Lannes, Gera, October 13, 7 a.m.
9   *Ibid.*
10   The Emperor to Murat, Gera, October 13, 7 a.m.
11   We once more see from this letter that night work was habitual with Napoleon. I lay
     stress on this fact because I see in it one of the causes for his superiority in war.
        Here is what Constant writes in his *Mémoires* (vol. ii. p. 286) on the subject: "The
     Emperor slept on a little iron bedstead whilst I slept where and as I could. Hardly had
     I gone to sleep than the Emperor called out to me: 'Constant!'—'Sire.'—'See who is on
     duty.' He wished to speak to the aide-de-camp. 'Sire, x— is there.'—'Tell him to come
     and speak with me.' I then left the tent to go and tell the officer, with whom I returned.
     On his entering, the Emperor said to him: Go to such or such a corps, commanded by
     such or such a Marshal; order him to send such or such a regiment to such or such a
     position; find out that of the enemy and then return to me with your report.' The aide-
     de-camp left and mounted on horseback to carry out his mission. I lay down to sleep
     again. The Emperor pretended to go to sleep, but after a few minutes I heard him shout
     again: 'Constant!'—'Sire.'—'Call the Prince of Neuchâtel.' I sent to summon the Prince
     who soon arrived, and whilst they were conversing I remained at the door of the tent.
     The Prince wrote a few orders and withdrew. These derangements took place several
     times during the night. Towards morning His Majesty went to sleep, and it was then
     that I too got a few moments rest.
        "When aides-de-camp brought news for the Emperor, I awakened him by gently
     shaking him. 'What is it?' said His Majesty, waking up suddenly. 'What time is it? Show
     him in.' The aide-de-camp made his report. If need be, His Majesty rose immediately
     and left the tent. He was not long over his toilette …
        "Sometimes the Emperor returned, worn out with fatigue. He took a light meal and
     lay down to rest, once more to recommence the interruptions in his sleep …
        "During the three or four days preceding a fight the Emperor passed most of his time
     stretched out on large maps, into which he thrust pins with heads of was of various
     colours."
12   As usual the Emperor underestimated the strength of his adversary. Prince Eugène of
     Württemberg's reserve (18 battalions, 20 squadrons) numbered about 15,000 men.
13   Except under exceptional circumstances, he did not give his orders until night-time,
     between midnight and 4 a.m., after the receipt of the "daily reports."
14   The Emperor to General Lemarois, Gera, October 13, 1806, 7 a.m.
15   The Emperor to Monsieur Scherb, Gera, October 13, 1806, 7 a.m.
16   Hohenlohe's *Letters on Strategy*, vol. i. p. 91.
17   The Chief of the Staff to Marshal Sault at the bivouac of Köstritz, October 13, 1806, 11.30 a.m.
18   The Chief of the Staff to Marshal Sault at the bivouac of Köstritz, October 13, 1806, 11.30 a.m.
19   Mœsdorf is six kilometres before Roda, on the road from Gera to Jena.

20 Ney was following the Roda road preceded by three divisions of the cavalry reserve; the
    Imperial Guard, followed by Scull's light cavalry and the Saint-Hilaire division of the
    same corps, was following the road via Saint-Gangloff, Hermsdorf, and Rödigast; the
    two other Soult divisions were following the same road as the Emperor, the northern
    road, via Weissenborn and Klosterlaunitz.

21 Report of Marshal Suchet.

22 *Mémoires du duc de Rovigo.*

23 Report of Marshal Suchet.

24   General of Division Songis, Commander of the army artillery. The artillery of the 5th
    corps (Lannes) was commanded by Brigadier-General Fouchér.

25 From this expression, "a Prussian army," we see that the Emperor did not believe he had
    the whole of the Prussian army before him. In reality he thought that he was face to face
    with the King of Prussia and the principal army.

26 *Mémoires de Ségur* and *Mémoires de Rovigo.*

27 *Mémoires du baron Fain*, pp. 247 and 248.

28 Ségur's *Histoire et Mémoires*, vol. ii. p. 155.

29 Méneval's *Mémoires*, vol. iii. p. 62.

30 Rapp's *Mémoires*, p. 211.

31 Bacler d'Albe, Fain, and d'Ideville

X[1]

Napoleon on the Battlefield: The Battle

Napoleon's ardent desire for the fight—He gave battle ever to the fullest extent—Final reconnaissance on the morning of the fight and order of engagement—Action on the soldier—The central point of observation—Sureness of his survey of the field of battle—His extraordinary talent for finding his way—The Emperor's action in the course of the battle; the bringing about of the issue—No formula for the Napoleonic battle—The management of a battle, the development of strategical manoeuvres—The Emperor on the battlefield of Jena—Reflections on the manner in which the battle of Jena was fought—Action of a General-inChief in the great battles of the future.

A T LAST THE DAY OF battle—that battle for which Napoleon had prepared with so much care and passion, and which he desired with so much ardour—arrived. That *ardent desire* for the fight was *a new and characteristic trait* of his genius, for how many generals-in-chief hesitate the moment they enter upon that terrible drama which is played at the cost of so many human lives, and on which there so often depends the fate of empires and nations? Napoleon himself said "that people formed a very inaccurate idea of the strength of mind necessary to enter upon, with full knowledge of its consequences, one of those great battles on which depended the fate of an army and a country and the possession of a throne. Consequently he observed that it was rare to find generals who were in a hurry to give battle. They carefully took up their positions, and thought out their combinations, but there began their indecision. Nothing was more difficult and more precious than to know how to make up your mind."[2]

On the other hand, "he was always ready and easy in his mind on days of action, days of chance which pleased him, and the very strong and violent situations which he sought—days on which the more danger there was, the more he felt that his ready genius was able to come to a decision with more rapidity than any of his adversaries."[3]

On that final struggle, which he sought, not only through his natural inclination for strong and violent situations, but also because it was the consecration of an intense personal labour, he entered to the fullest extent, with the passion and audacity—calculated—of a great gambler. Certain historians have condemned him for not having stopped the fight on the eve of Waterloo on the approach of the Prussians, and for not having made a hazardous retreat; but such prudence was at that time out of place, and, moreover, was quite contrary to Napoleon's principles. In his *Commentaires*,[4] he glorifies Conde for having, on the day of Nordlingen, after the defeat of his right and centre, continued the battle with his left, the only troops he still possessed. "Observers of ordinary intelligence will say that he ought to have used the wing which was still intact to effect his retreat and not to risk the remainder of his men, but with such principles a general is certain of missing every opportunity of success and to be constantly beaten ... The glory and honour of arms is the first duty that a general giving battle ought to consider, the salvation and preservation of the men are only secondary. But it is also through that audacity and stubbornness that the salvation and preservation of the men is effected, for even if the Prince de Conde had retreated with Turenne's corps (left wing) he would have lost almost everything before reaching the Rhine."

When Napoleon had given his orders for the assembling before the battle, outside the reach of an attack, of all his forces "without neglecting one of them, for a battalion sometimes decides a day,"[5] when he had given his troops, as far as possible, a good night's rest, he entered upon the day of the battle with serenity and confidence. On the very morning of the fight, at daybreak, he made a final reconnaissance of the enemy before giving his last orders. Preparatory dispositions for the entry into line of the corps were fixed on the previous evening, but the definite direction in which the columns were to be sent was not ordered until the very morning of battle, after a final reconnaissance. A propos of the battle of Minden, which was lost on August 1, 1759, by Marshal de Contades, Napoleon blamed the French general "for not having kept to the dispositions which he fixed on the previous evening in an order of the day of five or six pages, which is indeed the stamp of mediocrity. Once the army is ranged in battle, a general ought *at daybreak* to reconnoitre the enemy's position and its movements during the night, and on the data obtained form his plan, send out his orders, and direct his columns."[6] That was his method of procedure at Austerlitz. "The general dispositions for the day of December 2 were fixed on December 1 at 8.30 p.m.; they indicated to each corps its position in the line of battle and the hour at which it must be in place; exceptionally they gave even the evolution to be executed, which was 'a march forward by *échelons*, with the right wing in advance,'[7] and they concluded with this direction: 'At 7.30 Marshals must be with the Emperor at his bivouac, in order, according to the movements the enemy may have made during the night, to receive fresh orders.'"

The same method of operating was adopted at Jena, as we shall soon see—a rational and fruitful method which, if it had been followed in certain battles with which we are acquainted, such as those of Saint-Privat and Sedan, would have saved us from disaster.

His orders having been given in the main, Napoleon rode on horseback along the lines, seeking to influence the minds of his soldiers by some act or other calculated to excite their enthusiasm and animate their ardour. He was received, during his days of glory, by loud and prolonged cheers from the columns.[8] Then the first shots announced the beginning of the engagement and the Emperor took up his position at a central point whence he could see everything that happened—a point "easy of access for reports and whence orders could be sent out with rapidity. A portion of the Imperial Guard was before him and the remainder, as a last reserve, in the rear.[9] By the Emperor's side were the Chief of the Staff, the Master of the Horse, two aides-de-camps, and two orderly officers, a page, Roustan, an officer of the stables, and an officer-interpreter. Some distance away stood the remainder of the suite with the four squadrons who were on duty selected from each of the four regiments of the Imperial Guard, the chasseurs, the Polish light horse, dragoons, and mounted grenadiers.

"This point of observation having once been chosen, the Emperor hardly left it except at interval to go and see if anything unexpected had happened on the wings, to remedy by his presence any disorder that might have arisen, to encourage an attacking column, or to receive the news of a success and compliment the one to whom it was due ...

"When the Emperor advanced too near danger, he sent those who were with him away, and hardly allowed either Berthier or Caulincourt, Master of the Horse, to follow him. The page alone had the privilege of not being sent back, and he owed it to the telescope of which Napoleon might have need."[10]

From his point of observation he followed the battle with extraordinary sureness of vision.

"Napoleon had acquired," relates Odeleben, "the extraordinary talent of judging the position and state of things at decisive moments. He was never mistaken when he delivered judgment as to the distance or the drawing near of the enemy's fire. He noticed every movement and perceived the strength of the enemy and whether its movements were retrograde or to the flank much better and quicker than any of his generals. He had only to glance through his telescope[11] to sum up with extraordinary rapidity the position and forces of an entire army.

"He possessed, in addition, the extraordinary talent of being able to find his way rapidly ... He had in his mind's eye the whole of the localities and position of a district. He found out his direction once by the aid of the map in the open air, then, on advancing, he recognized everything according to the idea which he had first of all formed, just as if he were born in the district. But then, in truth, he no longer judged most of the movements except on a large scale and, without paying heed to unknown difficulties, ordered operations, which, executed to the letter by his generals, resulted in the sacrifice of many men."[12]

What action did the Emperor exercise in the course of the battle?

We are acquainted with the conversation he had at Dresden, a few days before Bautzen, with Marshal Gouvion-Saint-Cyr. When he informed Saint-Cyr of the dispositions which he intended to take in attacking the Prusso-Russian army, and which consisted in outflanking it with the army of Marshal Ney, whilst he himself attacked the front, Saint-Cyr expressed his astonishment to see him prefer a wing attack to his ordinary method of attacking the centre. But Gouvion-Saint-Cyr's words have so much weight that we must give them textually: "... Afterwards, the Emperor informed me of his plans for the attack, which were good; as are almost all those made by an experienced man; *for it is only in the carrying out of a thing that one generally encounters great difficulties, which often become complicated through lack of collaborators, through the manoeuvres and plans of the adversary, or sometimes through chance alone.* The means on which Napoleon appeared to me to count the most was the plan which he had made to outflank the enemy by means of his right at Bautzen. I pointed out to him that he seemed to me to be departing from his ordinary method, in as much as I thought that he preferred attacks on the centre to those on the wings, whilst the latter appeared to have been almost always preferred by Frederick II; that the former, though presenting first of all the greatest obstacles, offered afterwards, when they were entirely successful, infinitely greater results, since it was almost impossible for an enemy that was beaten and routed at its centre to avoid a complete rout and make a passable retreat. I added that that method of attack had always appeared to me to be the most in harmony with the nature of his genius and the need that he had of being on a day of battle the *unique spring of that great machine*; that it lent itself better than any other to the *union in his hand of all his means*. He replied that he did not admit any preference to an attack on the centre over that on the wings, that it was a principle with him to fall on the enemy by every possible means, that, the nearest corps being engaged, he left them to themselves without troubling himself much over their good or bad chances, only he took great care not to respond too readily to demands for help on the part of their leaders. He cited, as an instance, Lützen, where, he said, Ney had demanded the most prompt reinforcements, although he had still two divisions which had not entered into the action; and he assured me that, in the same engagement, another Marshal had also asked him for more men before having an enemy before him. He added that it was not until the end of the day, when he perceived that the enemy, fatigued, had called into play most of its means, that he got together what he had been able to keep in reserve in order to hurl on to the field of battle a strong force of infantry, cavalry, and artillery; and that, owing to the enemy *not having foreseen it*, he created what he called an event, and that by this means he had almost always obtained the victory. I admit that this system may, as experience has proved, offer great advantages, especially when it is put into practice by a sovereign general, as long as it is not perceived, judged, and combated by his adversary, as it may be."[13]

We see from this—for, under the circumstances, Napoleon had no interest in saying the contrary of the truth—that he had no preference for a fixed mode of attack. But he ever conformed to the superior principle of concentrating his forces and fire against the point he wished to force, for "the breach having been made, the equilibrium was upset, and the place was taken."

In a more general manner, we believe that we must not seek in Napoleonic tactics on the field of battle for any scheme, any system, or any narrow formula. Without entering into the details of facts, which may be interpreted in many different ways, we give, as a guarantee of this assertion, the very nature of Napoleon's genius and his oft-repeated personal declarations.

Every formula is the negation of art and irreconcilable with the inspired thoughts and breadth of mind of a great master of war. Moreover, he himself expressed himself on this subject in the following formal terms:

"The fate of a battle," he said to Las Cases, "is the result of a moment, of a thought: you approach with various combinations, you mingle, you fight for a certain time, the decisive moment comes, a moral spark is generated, and the smallest reserve accomplishes the end."[14]

He declared to Gourgaud that what was good under one circumstance was bad under another, and that the principles themselves ought only to be considered as axes to which a curve was drawing nearer.[15]

He has even enumerated, in his *Commentaires*, the various circumstances which influenced the variety of his dispositions:

1. The number of the troops, infantry, cavalry, and artillery composing the army;
2. The relation existing between the two armies and their moral faculties;
3. The object in view;
4. The nature of the battlefield;
5. The position occupied by the enemy and the character of the leader in command.

One cannot, he added, and one ought not to prescribe anything positive.

Of these various considerations, the one he regarded as the most important, in the choice of the point on which he was concentrating his attacks,
was the strategic object he had in view. Battles were not to be regarded as
independent and isolated pieces of work; they had never been anything else
but a part of very extensive combinations.[16]

"He ever assigned to his attack the object which promised him the most
success from a strategic point of view, but, whereas at the beginning, whilst
choosing his point of attack in accordance with strategic considerations, he
strove at the same time to obtain from the situation the tactical advantages it
might offer, he afterwards became more and more indifferent to this point of
view, and, finally, having freed himself from every tactical anxiety, he came to
make, on the plains of Russia, his attacks in a most brutal manner, without
troubling himself over the enormity of his losses."[17]

From the point of view of tactics, he seemed to trouble himself much less
over the nature of the battlefield and the difficulties of the ground than over
the movements or counter-movements of the enemy. In Napoleon's eyes, "a
battle was a dramatic action with a beginning, a middle, and an end. The
order of battle assumed by the armies and their first movements to get into
contact with each other were the exposition, the counter-movements made
by the army attacked formed the knot, which necessitated fresh plans and
brought about the final crisis, whence came the result or *dénouement*." That
is what he set forth in his *Commentaires*,[18] and he added, on the subject of the
Battle of Waterloo: "As soon as the attack of the centre of the French army
had been unmasked, the opposing general made countermovements either
with his wings or behind his line to make a diversion or come to the assistance of the point attacked. None of his movements could escape Napoleon's
experienced eye in the central position where he was placed, and he had in his
hand all his reserves, ready to place them where circumstances most urgently
required their presence."

If Napoleon's intervention showed itself most particularly in the hurling
forward of this mass of infantry, cavalry, and artillery, with which he created
in some of his battles a surprise, this intervention was not limited to this decisive act, it was applicable at any time.

He wished to see things for himself, "for a general who sees with the eyes
of others will never be in a position to command an army as it ought to
be commanded;"[19] he was present at the fight; from that time, how, with
his authoritative and absorbing temperament, could he respect, there more
than elsewhere, the initiative of his subordinates; how could he fail to be, as
Gouvion-Saint-Cyr told him, the mainspring of that great machine, the bat-

tle? There, indeed, as elsewhere, all intellectual activity was concentrated in himself, leaving to others but the role of executants.

"The most difficult thing," said Napoleon to Gourgaud,[20] "is to discover the enemy's plans and to detect the truth in all the reports one receives; the remainder only requires common sense, it is a bout at fisticuffs, and the more blows you get in, the better it is for you …" He also said: "To tell the truth, what has won me so many battles is that, on the eve of the fight, instead of giving an order to diverge, I converged all my forces on the point that I wished to force and massed them there. I overthrew that which was before me, for naturally it was a *weak point*."

We find in these few lines the principal characteristics of the Napoleonic battle:

1. To converge all the forces on the eve of the battle on the point he wished to force and to mass them there, this point, *chosen on the eve of the fight*, being a *weak point*;
2. To begin the fight, a bout at fisticuffs, and get in as many blows as possible. This then was taking the offensive in dead earnest along the whole front;
3. Finally, at the weak point and at the moment chosen by him, the General-in-Chief himself gives a formidable and decisive blow which overthrows his adversary.

If there is no formula, there was, in every Napoleonic battle, Napoleon's personality. But this personality was never the same. What a difference there was between the conqueror of Austerlitz and.Jena, "who fought with all his might," and the Emperor of 1812 and 1813 "who thought so much of his comfort, and who, during the battle, sometimes no longer left his bivouac fire and had the air of slighting everything."[21]

In order to learn a lesson from this study, we naturally choose to follow the Emperor of War during his brilliant days, and in order to understand his method of acting in a concrete case, we will go back to the place where we left him, his Landgrafenberg bivouac, on October 14, 1806, and follow him step by step on the battlefield of Jena.

After his reconnaissance of the enemy, which he made at 1 a.m. with General Suchet, the Emperor returned to his bivouac.

"The night presented a spectacle worthy of observation: that of two armies, one of which deployed its front over an extent of six leagues and lit up the atmosphere with its fires, the other, whose visible fires were concentrated on a small point, and, in both armies, activity and movement. The fires of the two armies were within easy range of cannon; the sentinels almost touched one another, and not a movement was made that could not be heard."[22] The whole of Marshal Lannes' corps was ranged on the edge of the plateau; the Imperial Foot Guards were stationed on the slopes, as it were attached to and suspended on the flank of that steep ascent;[23] Augereau was in the rear of Jena; Davout, Bernadotte, and Murat in the neighbourhood of Naumburg; the corps of Soult and Ney, the cuirassiers of Nansouty and d'Hautpoul, and Klein's dragoons were hastening to the Emperor's battle. From the town of Jena and neighbouring valleys outlets had been made permitting the more easy deployment of the troops which they had not been able to place on the plateau, for it was perhaps the first time that an army had had to pass through so small an opening.

At his bivouac the Emperor handed Berthier the dispositions for the battle, and his Chief of the Staff put them into the following order of the day:

Order of the Day
Dispositions for the Order of Battle

At The Bivouac Of Jena, October 14th, 1806.
Marshal Augereau will command the left, and will place his first division in column on the Weimar road up to the height by which General Gazan[24] mounted his artillery on to the plateau; he will hold the necessary forces on the plateau on the left on a level with the head of his column; he will have tirailleurs facing the whole line of the enemy at the various outlets from the mountains. When General Gazan has debauched forward, he (Augereau) will debouch on to the plateau with his whole army corps, and will then march, according to circumstances, to take the left of the army.

Marshal Lannes will have, at daybreak,[25] all his artillery between his spaces, and in the order of battle in which he passed the night.

The artillery of the Imperial Guard and the Guard will be behind the plateau, ranged in five lines, the first line, composed of chasseurs, crowning the plateau.

The village on our right[26] will be bombarded by the whole of General Suchet's[27] artillery, and immediately afterwards attacked and taken.

The Emperor will give the signal, and every one should be in readiness at daybreak.

Marshal Ney will be placed, at daybreak, at the extremity of the plateau in order to be able to mount and proceed to the right of Marshal Lannes the moment the village has been captured, and, in consequence, there is room for deployment. Marshal Soult will debouch by the road which has been reconnoitred on the right, and will keep himself continually in communication to sustain the right of the army.

The order of battle in general will be for MM. les Maréchaux to form themselves into two lines, without counting that of the light infantry; the distance of the two lines will be at most a hundred *toises*.[28]

The light cavalry of each army corps will be placed, in readiness for the use of each general, according to circumstances.

The heavy cavalry, as soon as it arrives, will be placed on the plateau and in reserve behind the Guard, ready to proceed wherever circumstances require it.

The important thing to-day is to deploy on to the plain; *the dispositions necessitated by the enemy's manoeuvres and forces will be fixed afterwards*, in order to drive it from the positions it occupies and which are necessary for the deployment.

By order of the Emperor,
Chief of the Staff,
MARSHAL ALEX. BERTHIER

Let us direct our attention for a moment to this order of the day, which is, in reality, what we now call a general order for operations. Its object was to range the army in order of battle. The vanguard—Lannes' corps—found in it instructions regarding the formation it was to assume, the general direction it was to follow, the hour of its departure, and the first object it was to attain.

Instructions, in a general order of operations, given several hours before the beginning of an action, to bombard a village and then to attack and capture it seem premature to us nowadays, for they presuppose that the enemy will continue to occupy the village in question. Nowadays, artillery only enters into play to overcome resistance made to the progress of its infantry.[29]

The other corps and the cavalry were instructed with precision as to the movements they had to make to debouch and unite themselves with the vanguard.

Finally, the order indicated at its close the object of the first day's operations, which was to deploy on to the plain.

From the point of view of the manner in which it is drawn up, the order is heavy in style, inaccurate, and diffuse. A certain looseness about it gives us the impression that it was written to dictation; one fails to recognize in it the Emperor's manner. Doubtless Berthier dictated it himself in accordance with the Emperor's indications.[30]

With the exception of the name of Weimar, there is not the name of a single place in it. "The plateau on the left," "the village on our right," "the height by which General Gazan mounted his artillery," etc., such are the expressions used to direct the troops. This method of procedure was rendered necessary owing to the scarcity of maps, with which even the Marshals themselves were not always provided. Preliminary reconnaissances made up for this deficiency. Neither was time mentioned, since watches also were lacking; they went by the "break of day," and things proceeded none the worse for that.

Let us return to the employment of the Emperor's time.

During the end of the night, he slept very little. About 4 o'clock in the morning he summoned Marshals Lannes and Soult to communicate his plans[31] to them and give his final orders. Lannes was to proceed by the plateau on Closwitz, whilst Soult was to debouch on to the plateau with the Saint-Hilaire division by the roads fixed upon on the previous day (Rau-Thal and Zwetzen road), to occupy the wood on the east, and thus to wind round the village of Closwitz by the left.

The plan of action, which followed naturally on the strategic manoeuvre, was to manoeuvre on the enemy's left in such a manner as to cut its line of retreat; a success on the left of the Prussian army would compromise the retreat of all the rest, and so much the more so as Davout and Bernadotte were expected on that side.

Lannes left the Emperor about 5 o'clock. Napoleon, alone with Soult, then said to him, "Shall we beat them?" "Yes, if they are there," replied the Marshal, "but I fear that they are no longer there."[32]

At that moment the first gunshots were heard, whereupon the Emperor joyfully cried: "There they are!—The action is beginning!" Then, his way lit up by soldiers carrying torches, he went to harangue the infantry, touching their honour against that Prussian cavalry which was so celebrated, he said, "that it was necessary to exterminate them in front of our squares, as we crushed the Russian infantry at Austerlitz."[33]

Until 8 o'clock, an extremely thick fog obscured the horizon and the tirailleurs, as it were, groped their way, guided merely by the flash and the noise of the gunshots which responded to their attack.

At 9 o'clock, the fog cleared away, and Suchet, dashing on Closwitz, took the village.

This *début* brought about a first intervention on the part of the Emperor. Owing to a change of direction to the right, which the 5th corps had had to make when marching on Closwitz, an opening occurred between this corps and the 7th, so Napoleon filled it with the Guard and a big battery of twenty-five guns, "the big central battery," formed with the artillery of the Guard and part of that of the Gazan (5th corps) and Desjardins (7th corps) divisions. He thus performed the work of a General-in-Chief by assuring connection between the various corps.

After the taking of Closwitz, Lannes took up a position on the Dornburg, between Closwitz and Lützeroda.

"It was nearly 10 o'clock, and one could already hear on the right the cannon of Marshal Soult who, having debouched in his turn on to the Landgrafenberg by the two roads of Rau-Thal and Zwetzen, was driving the Prussian left wing (General Holtzendorf's detachment) from the wood of Closwitz to the village of Rodigen. Finally, General Holtzendorf, separated from the Prussian line, withdrew to the heights of Stobra, and took no further part in the action."

These first successes at the centre and on the right of the French enabled them to gain the ground necessary for the deployment of their masses, and facilitated the debouchment of the troops of the left wing and the reserves.[34]

The first operation prescribed by the Emperor had been carried out. They had gained the ground necessary for their deployment on to the plain; they had now to take dispositions necessitated by the enemy's manoeuvres and forces. "The Emperor would have liked to have put off the struggle for two hours, in order to await, in the position which he had just taken after the morning attack, the troops which were to join him, and especially his cavalry, but French ardour prevailed."[35] Marshal Ney intervened with his customary impetuosity: he arrived on the field of battle at 10.30 with all his grenadiers and light infantry soldiers, the 25th light horse, and his cavalry brigade, impatient to take part in the fight, and, passing between the Gazan and Suchet divisions, made for the village of Vierzehn-Heiligen.

During this time the 7th corps, that of General Augereau, marched on to the plateau by the left and reached the neighbourhood of Cospeda.

About 11 o'clock, at the moment Marshal Ney arrived opposite Vierzehn-Heiligen, the Emperor, at the head of his Guard, had proceeded to the Dornburg where; with the plain stretched out under his eyes, he remained almost the whole day. Hardly had he arrived when the plateau was invaded by hundreds of horsemen driven at full speed by the Prussian cavalry; they were squadrons of the 10th chasseurs, whom Ney had sent to the attack of the enemy's artillery, and who had been charged in flank by Prittvitz's dragoons and Holtzendorf's cuirassiers. "Napoleon was momentarily surrounded by the routed chasseurs, and they only stopped on seeing his look and his gesture of discontent."[36]

Brought into such close contact with the fight, the Emperor had necessarily to intervene in its details. He summoned General Durosnel, Commander of Augereau's cavalry brigade, and ordered him to charge; and at the same time he himself hurled the 40th infantry regiment of the Suchet division on Vierzehn-Heiligen.

Shortly afterwards, whilst the violent and indecisive fight was in progress around blazing VierzehnHeiligen, he employed another of Augereau's infantry brigades to strengthen the attack on the village.

About 1 o'clock, Marshal Soult, continuing to approach on the left flank of the Prussians, came on a level with Vierzehn-Heiligen, which had been chosen on both sides as the principal point of attack; at the same time the Emperor was informed of the arrival on the field of battle of two divisions of the 6th corps and divisions of the cavalry reserve. The decisive moment therefore was clearly indicated. At that moment the Emperor had near him:

The six battalions of the 100th and 103rd regiments of the Gazan division;

Four battalions of the 60th and 88th regiments of the Vedel brigade;

The nine squadrons of the cavalry brigade of the 5th corps; and

The Imperial Foot Guard.

On an order from Napoleon, Marshal Lannes proceeded to the left flank of Vierzehn-Heiligen with the 100th and 103rd regiments of the line and six pieces of artillery of the Gazan division, commanded by General Fouchér, commander of the artillery of the 5th corps. "This manoeuvre astonished the enemy. They showed uncertainty, their fire slackened, whereas ours redoubled, and they lost ground. Lannes, seizing the opportunity, charged them with his two regiments *en masse, the whole army corps following this decisive impulsion.* The Prussian army was routed."[37] It was 2 o'clock.

However, the battle was not yet over. On the Prussian right wing the Saxons were still resisting on the Schnecke. Rachel, arriving late from Weimar, deployed on the height called the Sperlings-Berg, north-west of Vierzehn-Heiligen, and then advanced, flanked on his two wings by cavalry.

"Numerous squadrons, formidable in appearance, appeared on the horizon and appeared to be making ready to attack Marshal Lannes on the right flank. The Emperor, perceiving this cavalry, became anxious, and, pointing it out to his orderly officer, Ségur, sent him with an order to the Suchet division to form itself into squares against it. At the same time, he sent the Vedel brigade of the 5th corps to support the Desjardins division of the 7th, which was debouching from the wood of Isserstedt on to the heights of Gros-Romstedt. In the course of the action the Imperial Foot Guard saw with undisguised vexation everybody fighting and itself inactive. Several voices were heard to say: 'Forward!'—'What is that?' said the Emperor. 'It can only have been a beardless youth who can have wished to prejudge what I ought to do; let him wait and command in thirty ranged battles before pretending to give me advice.'"[38]

Meanwhile, pressed in front by Videl, attacked on the right flank by Desjardins, and on the left flank by Lannes and Soult, Riichel in turn abandoned the struggle.

"Look at them," said Lannes to Ségur, "they are all in flight towards Weimar! The road is strewn with their caissons. Hasten and inform the Emperor."

Ségur found Napoleon still on the Dornburg. It was about 3 o'clock. Whilst listening to the aide-de-camp's report, several Saxon bullets bounded almost between the Emperor's horse and that of Ségur. Interrupting him, he exclaimed: "It is useless to get ourselves killed at the end of a victory, let us dismount." He ordered Ségur to have the artillery of the Guard advanced to where they were, after which Ségur thought well to repeat Marshal Lannes' advice. "Good," he said, "go then and follow their retreat on Weimar, but before doing so, see on our left what has become of our Saxons and finish with them,"[39]—and to do that he sent on their flank the Marchand division (Ney corps). By this manoeuvre the Saxons, almost entirely cut off, were nearly all made prisoners. It was 4 o'clock.

The pursuit then commenced and was continued that evening beyond Weimar, which Murat entered at 6 o'clock. Ever a gallant knight, he hastened to present his respects to the Duchess of Saxe-Weimar, who kept him to dinner at her residence.

We have just seen the Emperor follow, from his position on the Dornburg, the movements of Lannes' corps, and intervene very actively, too actively, in the fight by giving direct orders to the brigades and the regiments themselves. It was the same in the case of Augereau's corps, which, debouching about 10 o'clock on to the left of the Jena plateau also fought within immediate reach of the Emperor. It was Napoleon himself who successively pointed out their objectives (the wood of Isserstedt and the small wood Vierzehn-Heiligen) to the regiments of Augereau's first division.[40] On the other hand, the corps further away, Soult, Bernadotte, and Davout, received no order from Napoleon in the course of the battle.

The battle having been won, the Emperor, after having, as usual, ridden over the battlefield to comfort the wounded, re-entered Jena. In the evening he received the university authorities. Ségur, returning from Weimar, handed in his report at midnight. The following is the narrative of his audience:

"The Emperor's quarters, as far as I can recollect, were in an inn;[41] his bed, in the corner of a fairly large room, was that of the place. The Emperor was not then surrounded with all those comforts which have since contributed to make war less fatiguing, and perhaps too easy for him. I entered alone, a light in my hand, and approached his bed. It was but a moment afterwards that the dim light of my torch awoke him from a deep sleep; for he could not bear any light at night, and to prevent him sleeping the dimmest light of the smallest lamp sufficed. His awakening was as calm as usual and like that, they say, of happy men; it was sudden, complete, without astonishment, as usual, and like the ordinary awakening of military men. The reading of the report[42] being over, I informed him of the capture of the Saxon corps, which I estimated at 6000 men. 'I saw them,' he replied, ' they were more, at least 8000!' Then when I added that at Weimar we had almost taken the Queen, his voice, in replying to me, became more animated. 'That would have been but justice. She indeed merited it, for she it is who was the cause of the war!' Then, with a thoughtful air, he continued: 'But in riding towards Weimar did you not hear in the distance, on your right, a loud cannonade?' On my replying in the negative and that it would have been difficult to distinguish the noise amidst that of our own battle, he added: 'That is singular, yet there must have been in that direction a considerable battle.'

"In fact, two hours later (about 2 a.m.) one of Davout's officers, Bourcke, again awakened him and informed him of the victory of Auersthdt, a victory so much apart from that of Jena, although simultaneous, that even eight to ten hours after the conclusion of the latter the Emperor was in ignorance of it, made inquiries about it, and had not even heard the noise."[43]

Bourcke's narrative did not fail to cause surprise to the Emperor, who thought that he had fought the principal Prussian army, and when Davout's aide-decamp told him the number of the intrepid Marshal's enemy, Napoleon replied: "Your Marshal, who generally sees nothing, has seen double to-day."

"One must not be astonished if, in his bulletin of the following day, he thought fit to confound this victory with his own. It was especially at Auerstädt, and face to face with only one of his lieutenants, that the three more numerous *élite* of the Prussian forces, with its most renowned generals, its princes, and its king himself, had just been annihilated, whereas at Jena the Emperor, as strong as the enemy, had only conquered two lieutenants, whom, moreover, he had surprised and separated. The glory was too disproportionate for him to display it to the eyes of nations—he who lived above all for glory. Later, when less hampered by politics, he was truer in his words and more just in his praise and gratitude."[44]

At 3 o'clock in the morning, the Emperor announced his victory to the Empress in the following short letter:

Jena, October 15th, 1806, 3 a.m.

MON AMIE,—I have made some fine manoeuvres against the Prussians. Yesterday I gained a great victory. They numbered 150,000 men. I have taken 20,000 prisoners, a hundred pieces of artillery and flags. I was face to face and near the King of Prussia. I missed capturing both him and the Queen. I have been in camp for two days. I am in excellent health.

Farewell, mon amie, keep well and love me.

If Hortense is at Mayence, give her a kiss, as well as Napoleon and the little one.

(Signed) NAPOLEON

As we see, Napoleon related the facts in his own way and to his greatest advantage.

At 4 o'clock in the morning, in spite of the fatigue of the preceding days, work was continued. Napoleon gave orders for the continuation of the pursuit which the cavalry had begun of its own accord at the end of the battle, a pursuit which was to annihilate the Prussian army and complete the victory.

If we now consider the Battle of Jena in the light of the three great principles which, according to Napoleon, ever made fortune favourable to him:

Concentration of forces;

Activity;

A firm determination to perish with glory,

we note that once again it was to their application that he owed the victory.

If we were only to consider the distance of the battlefield of Jena from
Davout's and Bernadotte's corps and a part of the cavalry reserve, we might
think that Napoleon did not observe the principle of the concentration of
forces. But the dispersion of October 14 was the result of unforeseen events.
When, on the night of October 11-12, following his strategic idea of taking
possession of his adversary's communications, Napoleon broke up his square
of 200,000 men, he did not expect a battle before the 16th, but as soon as
he saw on October 13 at 3.30 p.m. that it was imminent, his first thought
was to group all his forces in the region between Weimar and Jena. Without
losing a minute, he sent the most pressing appeal to all his marshals, and
that appeal, to which Davout responded with the resolution and vigour we
know, contained the germ of the victory of Auerstädt. The principle of the
concentration of forces was therefore ever present in his mind. Is there any
need to recall the Emperor's activity during the three days which preceded
the battle? We have seen him on horseback during the greater part of the
day, then at work in his study for half the night, and taking but four or five
hours sleep in the twenty-four. This activity resulted in a gain of time which
surprised the enemy, as evidenced by those words of the Duke of Brunswick
when he received the news of the arrival of the French at Naumburg, "But
they cannot fly!" This prodigious activity electrified our soldiers and at the
same time overthrew the enemy's plans, "threw it into the uncertainty and
trouble of the unforeseen, into the disorder of counter-orders and counter-
movements, in which the scheme as a whole was lost, in which time was
wasted, and in which nothing was done opportunely, whilst on the other
hand everything having been settled in advance, *number, time, attack,* and
every advantage was on our side."[45]

Number is concentration of forces; time is activity; finally attack, and especially attack under the conditions under which it was made, could be inspired
only by the firm determination to succeed or perish with glory, for the situation of the French army on the evening of the 13th and the morning of the
14th was exceedingly perilous.

The Emperor thought that he had to fight at Jena the greater part of the
Prussian army, 100,000 men, placed in an advantageous position; he attacked
this army with inferior forces, at least during the first part of the day, "arriving

precipitously and successively through a defile, in a ravine, whose outlet had to be forced in order to deploy, and to which they had to have their backs during the fight."[46]

Hohenlohe himself refused to believe that he could be attacked in that direction, and his arrangements had been made to reply to an attack on the south-west. The audacity of the attack contributed just as much as the boldness of the strategic manœuvre and the rapidity of the movements to surprise and disconcert the adversary.

It seems, therefore, that it is much more in the application of these three great guiding principles than in tactical combinations on the field of battle that we must look for the secret of victory. These tactical combinations, which, in short, were limited to a decisive attack on Vierzehn-Heiligen, combined with Soult's enveloping movement on the left wing of the Prussians, present nothing extraordinary, whereas the boldness of the idea, the audacity with which it was carried out, and the activity and moral courage shown by Napoleon were truly characteristic of a master of the art of war.

By an examination of the tactical role played by Napoleon in the battle of October 14, 1806, we see that he was completely absorbed, in the course of the fight, by the events which occurred between the Landgrafenberg and Capellendorf, he remained during almost the whole day on the Dornburg, between Lutzerode and Closwitz, almost on the line of combat, participating in the emotions of the struggle, giving orders to the regiments of the 5th and 7th corps directly, and also using his reserves to bring about a decision on that part of the field of battle. One may say that the only part of the battle that he saw was the village of Vierzehn-Heiligen in flames and the wood of Isserstedt, a very small corner of the whole of the picture.

During this time, ten kilometres from him, Bernadotte, with the 1st corps and half of the cavalry reserve, was remaining inactive on the plateau of Utenbach, and Davout at Hassenhausen, six leagues from Jena, was waging battle with his 25,000 men against 60,000 Prussians. Up to what point was Napoleon preoccupied by this important part of his forces? It is said that he was anxious about them the whole day. In any case he neither sought to obtain news of them nor to send them any order. This shows an absolute lack of connection. On the morning of the 14th at 6 o'clock, Davout, ever cautious, had sent Captain de Trobriand to the Emperor to inform him of the movement of the 3rd corps. Trobriand must have handed in his report to the Emperor between 8 and 9 in the morning on the Landgrafenberg; he was back to his Marshal about noon.

This is the only connection of which we have any trace; it was sufficient to call the attention of the head of the army to that distant part of the field of battle. But, too near the line of fire, Napoleon only took heed of the fight which was in progress under his eyes. We have noticed the same thing happen too often in history to be astonished at it in this case. If, therefore, we confound, as Napoleon did in his bulletin of October 15, the two actions of Jena and Hassenhausen in a single battle, we must admit that the superintendence of the whole of the battle escaped the Emperor because the whole of his attention was absorbed by the struggle which was taking place under his eyes.

In his fine book on the campaign in Prussia in 1806, in which we have found so many precious documents for this study, Major Foucart gives the following opinion:[47]

"It is not the battles of the future alone, which will be fought on immense battlefields, that the Commander-in-Chief will be unable to take in at a glance. The day of October 14 presented an example of a battle with a front of twenty kilometres. The art of a Commander-in-Chief consists in being with the mass of his forces where he can decide the battle by giving a decisive blow."

May we be permitted to say that on the morning of October 14, 1806, Napoleon in no way thought of a battle with a front of 20 kilometres; he only saw the battle before Jena, between Muhl-Thal and the ravine of Alten-Gonne, with a front of 5 kilometres. If he had thought of a battle with a front of 20 kilometres from Mühl-Thal to Hassenhausen it is very probable that he would have conducted it otherwise.

If we consider the battles for which we are preparing—battles which will be fought with a front of 100 kilometres—we have a right to ask ourselves if the art of a Commander-in-Chief will consist in being personally present during the whole day on that corner of the battlefield where he presumes that the decisive blow will be given.

The Commander-in-Chief must not cease to exercise in the course of the battle the superintendence indispensable to ensure a concordance of efforts and the affiux of superior forces to the decisive point. He must constantly set his subordinates right concerning the general situation, the development of the action, and his intentions. He must watch over the execution of his orders which are often counteracted by a thousand unforeseen circumstances, put right errors of direction, and quicken or slacken the movement of one or the other army. On their side the subordinates must keep the commander acquainted with their particular positions, the movements they have in view, and any serious or imminent events. These constant communications will alone establish unity in the command.

The position taken up by a General-in-Chief must be chosen in such a way that these communications are made as easy and as rapid as possible—that is to say, it should be a central position, at a junction of roads and railways, sufficiently far from the fighting line to enable one to view the whole of the battle and be at liberty to direct one's attention to this or that part of the immense front. It is from this point, where he remains the greater part of the time, that the General-in-Chief must direct the battle.

We do not wish to imply from this that he must remain fixed at this centre of information, whence, however, will always start, thanks to a well-organized staff, the directing wires of the battle. That would be renouncing designedly the utilization of a force of the first order, the presence of the Chief, who at such or such a moment, particularly at the beginning and the end of the battle, may be useful and even necessary in one or another district. In this order of ideas, it is most desirable that at the supreme moment the General-in-Chief should be at the decisive point to develop and direct the impulsion which must triumph over all resistance, but it will often happen, doubtless, that the event will occur independently of his action.

In short, his influence must make itself felt by means of a regulating action on his immediate subordinates, the commanders of the army, and not by a direct intervention in the vicissitudes of the fight, thus differing from what we have just seen Napoleon do at Jena.

NOTES

1   See the plan of the battle of Jena, p. 190.
2   *Mémorial de Sainte-Hélène.*
3   Ségur's *Histoire et Mémoires*, vol. i. p. 504.
4   *Commentaires de Napoléon; Guerre de Turenne*, vol. vi. p. 1645.
5   *Commentaires de Napoléon; Guerre de Frédéric; Campagne de 1759.*
6   *Ibid.*
7   *Correspondance militaire de Napoléon.*
8   Obeleben's *Campagne en Saxe en 1813*, p. 55.
9   *Mémoires du baron Fain*, pp. 248 and 249.
10 *Ibid.*
11 Napoleon, as we know, was slightly short-sighted.
12 Odoleben's *Campagne en Saxe en 1813*, p. 165.
13 Gouvion-Saint-Cyr's *Mémoires pour servir à l'Histoire onilitaire sous le Directoire, le Consulat et l'Empire*, vol. iv. p. 40 *et seq.*
14 Comte de Las Cases' *Mémorial de Sainte-Hélène.*
15 Gourgaud's *Journal de Sainte Hélène*, vol. ii. p. 20.
16 Comte de Las Cases' *Mémorial de Sainte-Hélène.*
17 Yorek de Wartenburg's *Napoléon, chef d'armée*, vol.ii. p. 377.
18 *Commentaires de Napoléon*, vol. v. p. 166.
19 O'Meara's *Napoleon in Exile*, vol. ii. p. 377.
20 Gourgaud's *Journal de Sainte Hélène*, vol. ii. p. 418 *et seq.*
21 Odeleben, pp. 313 and 314.

22 Fifth bulletin of the Grand Army. Campaign of 1806.

23 Ségur's *Histoire et Mémoires*, vol. iii. p. 18.

24 Of Lannes' corps.

25 About 5.30 a.m.

26 Closwitz.

27 To-day we should consider this order as premature.

28 A *toise*, an ancient long measure in France, contained 6.39 English feet.

29 As a matter of fact, the fog which rose about 5.30 and did not clear away until about 9, resulted in the attack on Closwitz being quite different to what the Emperor had ordered.

30 In a general way Berthier's style lacked elegance. One must admit, however, that on October 14, 1806, at 2 a.m., in a straw shelter and after several almost sleepless nights, he had some excuse for not writing in a polished manner.

31 Report of General Victor, Chief of the Staff of the 5th corps (Foucart's *Campagne de Prusse*, p. 625; Ségur's *Histoire et Mémoires*).

32 In reality, Soult was partly right: the principal Prussian army was no longer there.

33 Ségur's *Histoire et Mémoires*.

34 According to the narrative of Mathieu Dumas, *Précis des Évenéments militaires*, vol. xvi.

35 Fifth bulletin of the Grand Army, Jena, October 15.

36 Ségur's *Histoire et Mémoires*, vol. iii. p. 23.

37 Report of General Victor, Chief of the Staff of the 5th corps (Foucart, 1806, p. 625).

38 Fifth bulletin, Jena, October 15, 1806.

39 Ségur's *Histoire et Mémoires*.

40 Reports of the 16th light horse, 14th, 44th, and 105th regiments of the line (Foucart, 1806, p. 657 *et seq.*).

41 In reality, the Emperor slept on October 14 at the Castle of Jena (letter from Commissary Daru to the Chief of the Staff, Berlin, October 25, 1806. Foucart's *Campagne de Prusse*, vol. ii. p. 66).

42 Murat's report brought by Ségur from Weimar.

43 Ségur's *Histoire et Mémoires*.

44 *Ibid.*

45 Ségur's *Histoire et Mémoires*, vol. iii. p. 30 *et seq.*

46 *Ibid.*

47 Foucart's *Campagne de Prusse* (1806), (Prenzlow-Lübeck), p. 7.

General Conclusions

WE HAVE JUST FOLLOWED, AS closely as possible, Napoleon during the first part of the campaign of 1806. His genius was then at its highest development. In the intimacy of his study, we have been present at the birth and evolution of his thought and the establishment of his orders, we have seen him, whilst exercising his command, superintending and controlling the execution, distributing rewards magnificently, repressing errors generally with indulgence, and thus giving his whole army an irresistible impulsion. Finally, under our attentive gaze, he has prepared, waged, and won a great battle. During this time, we have striven to share, in the closed chapters of history, his daily existence, noting, from time to time, our personal observations. Now that our period of instruction with the Imperial Staff is over, what is our impression?

Of all that brilliant, ardent, and agitated military court we remember only the physiognomy and the manner of existence of a single man—Napoleon. He is so entirely distinct from those surrounding him that he seems to belong to a higher order of humanity. In the army he is the motor centre of all action, and suffices for that formidable task by the strength of his will, the breadth and penetration of his mind, and by a physical and intellectual labour as it were incessant.

Such a method of command, practised by a man of thirty-seven, of prodigious activity, of an iron constitution, and of unparalleled intelligence and character, gave for a time the results with which we are acquainted. This centralization of command has without any doubt great advantages: it assures originality and strength of thought, vigour, and concordance of effort, secrecy and rapidity of operations, and takes the adversary by surprise—all elements of victory.

It presents, on the other hand, the very serious inconvenience of suppressing all initiative and all activity of thought in the ease of subordinates, of sacrificing consequently the future, and of only being applicable by a man of genius and during a short space of time, for it involves an excessive tension of all natural forces. Napoleon himself was able to stand it only during a part of his career. It was a *tour de force* which cannot be given as an example.

With this Napoleonic method of command, we will compare that in which the decision of the General-inChief is the result of what I shall call "a staff conference." This was the method of the Germans in 1870.

Here, according to Verdy du Vernois, then lieutenant-colonel and *chef de section*,[1] is how things were done at the German headquarters in 1870.

"Every morning we met at General von Moltke's to study the situation and the steps which it demanded. At this conference there were present the quartermaster-general, the three lieutenant-colonels, the commissary-general of the army, the chief of the *bureau des opérations*, von Moltke's chief aide-decamp, and often the director of the Telegraph—eight persons, without counting Moltke. At the conclusion of this meeting General von Moltke submitted his proposals, as well as the means of carrying them out, to King William."

As King William was only, in a way, in nominal command of the armies, the superior superintendence of operations was exercised in reality, under the presidency of General von Moltke, by that assembly of nine officers of very different ranks and ages. We will examine the application of their method of procedure in a concrete case, one in which a grave decision was to be made, and, recollecting what Napoleon did at Auma on the night of October 11-12, 1806, we will note the difference in the two methods of command and accord our preference to one or the other.

It was on the night of August 6-7, 1870. The German headquarters were at Mayence, the King was in residence at the Grand Ducal Castle, and the Staff was in an hotel situated on the banks of the Rhine. We will leave Verdy du Vernois to speak.

"On the evening of the 6th various information came concerning the Spicheren fight without our being able to form a clear idea of the importance and consequences of the encounter. Of this we were sure, that the troops of the first and second armies had taken part in it, and that the superintendence of the fight had passed from one hand to another. We were anxious the whole night of August 6-7. I had just retired to rest about midnight[2] when there came a knock at my door, and after it had been opened, some one said to me: 'Verdy, are you there?' I recognized the voice to be that of Prince Antoine Radziwill, His Majesty's aide-de-camp. After having entered, he told me that the King had sent him to me[3] because of a telegram which he had just received and which was not very comprehensible. I hastily lit a candle and, still in bed, I began to read the dispatch, which began thus, 'two eagles, etc. ...' It appeared from it that the army of the Prince Royal had waged a battle and had been victorious, but, to begin with, the dispatch did not make clear where the action had taken place. However, as we knew all the army's movements up to that time there was perhaps a chance of finding the spot. I therefore jumped out of bed and sat down at a table on which *maps were spread out.*[4]

"Our conversation awakened Brandenstein who was sleeping in an adjoining room. 'What is it? What is the matter?' he said. 'Come here a little,' I replied. He appeared in the same costume as myself and we sat down at the table, just as we were on leaving our beds, and each with a candle in his hand.

"The first idea which struck us and which later was found to be correct was that we had before us only the second half of a telegram, the first half of which, for some unknown reason, had not reached the King.

"In any case, the news was so important that it was necessary to *discuss* whether measures had not to be taken. Whereupon we awakened Bronsart, Cler (von Moltke's first aide-de-camp), and I believe, also Blume, and proceeded together to Quartermaster-General Podbielski's.

"After having communicated the dispatch to him, he took us to General von Moltke, whom we awakened. I shall never forget the expression on the General's face when, without his wig and lit up by the moon, he raised himself on his bed and looked at us as though he would say, 'What are all these people doing here?'

"After having conversed awhile, we concluded that the battle had taken place in the neighbourhood of Woerth, and that not only we ought to inform the other armies of it, but that we ought to give fresh directive instructions to the corps of the second line which had not yet been assigned to one or the other army.

"We also ordered the first and second armies not to approach the Saaxe, their concentration not being sufficient.

"On the other hand *we did not wish*[5] to prevent them following the principal hostile army they had before them if it was in retreat, which we counted on learning during the day."

Compare the scene at Mayence on the night of August 6-7, 1870, with that of Napoleon working in his study at Auma on the night of October 11-12, 1806, and the difference in the two methods of command will strike you forcibly.

On the one hand, the decision come to is the result of the will of a single man who, in the twinkling of an eye, discovers everything for himself, seizes an opportunity, precipitates movements, and exploits time to its maximum. On the other, we have an intermediate, rational, and methodical solution, the result of an exchange of views between officers of a staff who hold the same doctrine, and who, as Blume has written, were "all friends, each carrying out his duty with zeal and without either envy or jealousy."

Between these two methods it is permissible for each of us to make his choice. As far as I am concerned, whilst being a zealous partisan of a division of work, of the development of initiative, of a wide diffusion in the army of intellectual life, and whilst considering that it is indispensable to modify, in that way, everything that was tyrannical and absolute in the Napoleonic method, I firmly believe that nothing can replace the personal work of a leader, that incessant intellectual work is the safeguard of the authority and prestige of a commander-in-chief and of the originality and force of his conceptions. By the very fact that he exists, and that his action is felt, he increases everybody's force of impulsion and "sacred fire" tenfold, and, by his firmness and rapidity, he gives a characteristic turn to the execution of his orders. A command thus exercised, if addressed to an army exalted by ideas of duty, patriotism, and sacrifice, will obtain from it that intense effort which is an almost certain pledge of victory. Consequently, I would quote, in conclusion, those words of Machiavelli:[6]

"Let one alone command in war, for several minds weaken an army."

This maxim is to-day truer than ever, for, with our rapid means of communication and information, a leader of armies must more than ever utilize the maximum of his time, profit immediately by the errors of his adversary, and seize his opportunity.

NOTES

1   Verdy du Vernois's *Souvenirs personnels: Au grand quartier général en 1870*, translated by Soubise.
2   Once more we note that midnight is the hour for the arrival at chief headquarters of important news, a fact which justified Napoleon's method of work.
3   Verdy was chief of the information department; Lieutenant-Colonel Bronsart von Schellendorf head of the *section des opérations*; and LieutenantColonel von Brandenstein head of the transport department. Major Blume was head of the *bureau des opérations*.
4   Note the parallel. At Napoleon's headquarters the map, drawn up by Bacler d'Albe, was spread out in the Emperor's study or bedroom.
5   The resultant of a number of opinions was, as we see, substituted for the will of a chief, which generally ended in an intermediate solution. The orders were indeed given in the name of the leader who assumed the responsibility for them, but everybody knew that he was not their author, and that he had adopted—without enthusiasm—a collective creation. From a moral point of view this effacement of the leader has a tremendously debilitating influence.
6   Machiavelli's *Discourse on the first decade of Titus Livius*.

Appendix I

Biographical Notice Concerning Bacler D'albe

Baron Bacler, known as Bader d'Albe (Louis Albert Guislain), son of Philippe Albert Hector and Anne Cécile Delattre, born October 21, 1761, at Saint-Pol (Pas de Calais), married on March 31, 1808, to Mlle. Marie Marthe Alexandrine Godin.

Positions

Volunteer with the 2nd battalion of the Ariège, May 1, 1793;
Captain of cannoneers in the 56th demi-brigade, October 20, 1793;
Assistant to the adjutant-majors of the park of campaign artillery of the Army of Italy, September 3, 1796;
Chief of geographical engineers employed at the Depot of War, December 22, 1799;
Major-Geographical Engineer, September 23, 1801;
Chief of the Emperor's topographical office, September 23, 1804;
Colonel, June 21, 1807;
Adjutant-Major, July 5, 1807;
Brigadier-General, October 24, 1813;
Director of the Depot of War, March 2, 1814;
Unattached, July 10, 1815;
Unattached, April 1, 1820;
Died at Sevres (Seine et Oise), September 12, 1824.

Campaigns

1793, Army of the Alps and Siege of Toulon.—1794, 1795, 1796, 1797, 1798, and 1799, Army of Italy.—1804, Army of the Coasts of the Ocean.—1806, 1807, 1808, Grand Army.—1808, Spain.—1809, Army of Germany.—1812, Russia.—1813, Saxony.—1814, France.

Wounds

Wounded in the neck, on the right and left hand at the Sieges of Lyons and
Toulon in 1793.

Decorations

Officer of the Legion of Honour, April 10, 1813;
Knight of Saint Louis, July 19, 1814.

Titles

Baron of the Empire (Letters patent, December 9, 1809, to February 2, 1810).

Dotation

Annual income of 10,000 francs from property reserved in Westphalia by a
decree of March 17, 1808.

Biographical Particulars

At the time of the birth of Bader d'Albe at Saint-Pol (Pas de Calais) on
October 21, 1761, his father was quartermaster treasurer of the Toul artillery
regiment, now the 4th artillery regiment. In 1772 Bacler d'Albe's father had
retired and held the position of postmaster at Amiens.

He gave his son a certain amount of education, notably with regard to
mathematics and drawing.

At the age of fifteen young Bacler was head post-office clerk at Amiens.
His father being often ill he frequently replaced him as postmaster, and had,
therefore, the prospect of easily making his way in his father's career. But at
fifteen, in 1781, he was seized with an irresistible taste for art. He threw up his
position as post-office clerk and set out for Italy. Captivated by mountain-
landscapes, he stopped in the region of the Alps and remained there seven
years. He surveyed Haut-Faucigny for his own satisfaction. On the breaking
out of the Revolution he embraced the new ideas and enlisted on May 1, 1793,
as a volunteer in the 2nd battalion of the Allege. On October 20, 1793, he
organized at his own expense a company of gunners in connection with his
battalion, and was appointed its captain. He took part in that capacity at the
sieges of Lyons and Toulon in 1793. At the siege of Toulon General Laharpe

entrusted him with the defence of the camp called Invincibles, of the artillery of which he was in command. He made the acquaintance of Bonaparte.

On Germinal 13, Year II, General Bonaparte employed him to survey the whole of the coast from Nice to Savona, and in conjunction with Captain Muiron to decide on the position of the batteries along the whole of that line. He was afterwards employed in military reconnaissances along the whole of the eastern Riviera and at the outposts.

On Ventose 23, Year IV, Bader was appointed assistant captain on the artillery staff, chief of the topographical bureau, and was specially charged with the instruction of artillery lieutenants in the planning of fortifications and the drawing up of plans. Finally on Messidor 2, Year IV, he was appointed chief of the topographical bureau with the Army of Italy, and General Bonaparte, to whom he was personally attached during the war. He went through the campaigns of 1797, 1798, and 1799, with the Army of Italy. He then became geographical engineer at the Depot of War, and held the position until September 23, 1804, when he was appointed chief of the Emperor's topographical office. He was with the Emperor on the campaigns of 1806, 1807, 1808, in Spain, 1809, 1812, 1813, and 1814.

Placed on the retired list by the government of Louis XVIII, deprived of his dotation, and put on half-pay, Bacler d'Albe spent the final years of his life in straitened circumstances.

The Russian campaign, in the course of which he lost all his equipages and twenty horses, burdened him with a debt of 60,000 francs. After the fall of the Empire, in order to pay off his debts and support his family, he had to publish his collection of lithographs of the suburbs of Paris, and paint china for the Sèvres manufactory.

Bacler d'Albe had at least two sons. The elder, Joseph Bader, was, like his father, a remarkable topographer. Aidede-camp to Duroc and Soult, captain at twenty-three, and a major at twenty-six, he was implicated after the Restoration in a Bonapartist plot. Obliged to flee from France he entered the service of Chili as an officer of engineers. He died the same year as his father in 1824.

Another son had as a descendant M. Bacler d'Albe (Maurice Wilhelm Emilien Martin), now (1912) honorary general treasurer, to whom we are indebted for these biographical details.

Bacler d'Albe's artistic work is considerable: he left more than 500 works, pictures, water-colours, engravings, and lithographs; but unfortunately we have neither notes nor memoirs from his pen, a fact which is very regrettable, for Bader d'Albe, who had lived so long at the Imperial Staff, on intimate terms with Napoleon, and who was a personal friend of Duroc, at whose death he was present, was acquainted with a thousand anecdotes which he related admirably. Bacler d'Albe's memoirs would certainly have given precious details concerning life at Imperial headquarters, Napoleon's work, and the part he took in it. But it is clearly evident from this short notice that, although Bacler d'Albe was an eminent topographer, he was a poor tactician, and in no way qualified to collaborate with the Emperor intellectually. His collaboration, though undoubtedly precious, was essentially material in its character

Appendix II

Notes on the Maps

To enable the reader to follow the operations of the campaign of 1806 until October 14, and the operations at the battle of Jena, there have been added to this work:

1. A sketch of the operations of October 8-14, 1806;
2. The reproduction of a map of the suburbs of Jena, published at Weimar in 1800;[1] and
3. A part of the "new general geographical map of the Electorate of Saxony," drawn up from 1759 to 1763 by Petri, a Prussian lieutenant-colonel of engineers, to the scale of $\frac{1}{171,000}$ th

Petri's map was the only detailed map of Saxony at Napoleon's disposal in the course of his campaigns.

The following letter from Berthier to Marshal Soult clearly shows that Petri's map was indeed the one used by Napoleon and his Marshals during the campaign of 1806.

The Chief of the Staff to Marshal Soult

> AT THE BIVOUAC OF KÖSTRITZ,
> October 13th, 1806, 11.30 a.m.

"The Emperor, Monsieur le Maréchal, orders that your two divisions should sleep this evening at the village of Köstritz, which is a fairly large place on the Jena road, and where there is another road branching off to Nurmburg …

"The village of Köstritz is three leagues from Gera, *via* Langenberg …

"I would point out to you that this village is marked on the map of Saxony, but that the name is not given; it is situated three leagues from Gera on the road to Jena which the Emperor is following."

If we refer to Petri's map we shall find that on the road from Gera to Naumburg, via Langenberg and Crossen, ten kilometres from Gera and on a level with Weissenbrunn, a locality is indicated the name of which is not given but which is evidently K7stritz, as we can easily verify by looking at the present map, to the scale of $\frac{1}{100,000}$ th, of the German Empire.

The road from Kostritz to Jena is not marked on the map, but it existed in 1806, passing by Weissenbrunn and Klösterlausnitz.

It is interesting to the reader to have render his eyes a specimen of the map which Napoleon used when giving his orders, a map on which the conformation of the ground is barely indicated and on which only the principal roads are marked. We thus see that Napoleon could only give general instructions to his army corps as to the direction in which they were to march. It also shows us the importance at that time of reconnaissances, and explains Napoleon's constant anxiety to obtain information by every means in his power regarding peculiarities of the ground.

NOTE

1   This map of the suburbs of Jena is in the archives of the historical section of the Ministry of War, and bears upon it the positions of the troops at the beginning of the battle and the movements of the Sachet division (Lannes' corps), the Desjardins division (Augereau's corps), and Imperial Guard. In all probability this copy was, in 1806, in the hands of some general or officer of the staff, if not in those of the Emperor himself.

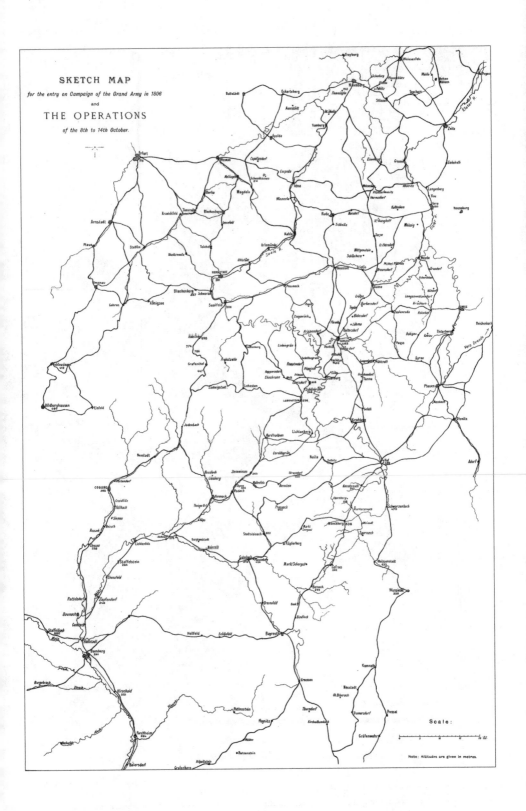

SKETCH MAP

for the entry on Campaign of the Grand Army in 1806

and

THE OPERATIONS

of the 8th to 14th October.

Scale:

Note: Altitudes are given in metres.

PLAN
von der
STADT JENA
nebst der umliegenden Ge-
gend, aus eigenen Messun-
gen und andern Zeichnungen
zusammen getragen
von F.L. Güssefeld
1800

TOPOGRAPHISCHE CHARTE
der umliegenden
GEGEND von JENA
Nach eigenen Messungen und andern
Originf. Zeichnungen neu entworfen
von
F. L. Güssefeld
Weimar
im Verlage des Industrie Comptoirs
1800

Maaßstab von dreyviertel einer geographischen Meile von

Eine Stunde, 25 auf einen Grad oder 1182,i Rheinfuß 9&9, 4 Weimar. Ruthen groß